THE ESSEX HUNDRED

London's

METROPOLITAN ESSEX

Events and Personalities, from Essex in London, which shaped the nation's history.

Andrew Summers &
John Debenham

www.essex100.com

Published by Summersbook (UK) Ltd
Essex Hundred Publications
Rutland House
90 – 92 Baxter Avenue
Southend-on-Sea
Essex SS2 6HZ
www.essex100.com

First published April 2013
reprinted August 2013 with changes
Written by Andrew Summers and John Debenham
© Copyright Andrew Summers and John Debenham
April 2013

British library cataloguing in Publication Data:
A catalogue record for this book is available from
The British Library.

ISBN 9780955229558

Typeset by Hutchinson Creative

Printed by 4edge Publishing
7a Eldon Way
Eldon Way Industrial Estate
Hockley Essex SS5 4AD

Contents

Acknowledgements

In bringing this book to publication we have benefited greatly from the help of curators, archivists, editors, librarians and many others throughout the county. Without them the book would not have been possible and we are indebted to them.

Establishing the detail of some of the events we relate has been a lengthy and complex process. Researching some items has, for both of us, meant stepping back into our childhood and early years to recall events we lived through and places we knew; at times finding that memory is not always as reliable as we think. In some cases, we have had to rely on anecdotal evidence and personal recollections. We have taken every care to check our facts however we are aware that we are fallible. For any errors found in our text we humbly apologise. For example on page 42, we describe the seizure of Thomas of Woodstock in Stratford. The source of this interpretation was taken from *Chronique de La Traison Et Mort de Richart Deux.* There are many other works on Richard II, none of which mention this sequence of events. Should any reader be able to provide additional information to enlighten us on this, or any other chapters in the book, your comments would be most welcome and we offer our thanks in advance.

Special thanks are due to Adele Fewings, for her enthusiastic administration and management of our website and to our wives, Greg Debenham and Glenis Summers, for their patience and continuing support.

We would also like to give special thanks for their invaluable help to John Blake and Bill George of the Barking and District Historical Society and to Val Bryant of the Local Studies and Archives in Redbridge. We also thank Elli Constantatou of Visit Essex at Essex County Council for helping us out with our understanding of Greek. Derek Adams was kind enough to allow us to reproduce his award winning poem, Odysseus in London, which can be seen on page 120.

The substance of our piece on *Evacuation* (page 144) was provided by the late Eric Fewings, a long term Dagenham resident who endured the London blitz. He was supposed to have been evacuated but chose, along with his brother, to remain with his family and not leave the capital. Sadly Eric did not live to see this book come to fruition.

List of Maps and Illustrations

Eton Manor's the Wilderness and Clubhouse around 1950
Author collection
See pages 128 and 129

The Authors

ANDREW SUMMERS

 Born within the sound of Bow Bells, Andrew has lived for the last 20 years in Hadleigh and been married to Glenis for 46 years. Andrew has bought books, sold books, and created an export market selling English language books in Europe. He has also printed books. With a change of tack he has moved on to write and publish books too!

JOHN DEBENHAM

 Born in Romford John has always lived in Essex. On retirement from engineering he took a BA History degree at the University of East London, followed by an MA in Intellectual History at Queen Mary, London University where he studied 'Civilisation and Barbarism'. He has an innate curiosity over what makes us what we are, which is satisfied by research, in particular the history of Essex, and writing about it. John is a member of Southend Poetry Society. He writes poetry and short stories with longer works in 'perpetual progress'.

London's Metropolitan Essex
An Introduction

London's Metropolitan Essex is the latest volume in the Essex Hundred Series and follows on from the *Essex Hundred, Essex Hundred Histories* and *ON THIS DAY in Essex. Metropolitan Essex* concentrates on the part of today's London that, until 1965, was in Essex, one of England's oldest counties.

Essex was founded as the Eastern Kingdom of the Saxons. Its name derives from the Old English 'Eastseaxe'. This Kingdom may also have included parts of modern Hertfordshire and Middlesex. It had natural borders, the River Stour to the north, the North Sea to the east, the Thames to the south and the River Lea to the west. These borders were well established when England became a united kingdom under the rule of King Alfred over 1000 years ago. They remained more or less intact until the creation of the Greater London Council in 1965.

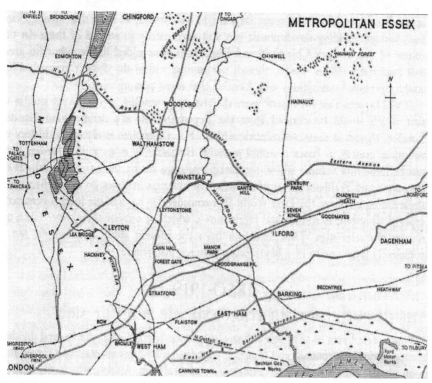

Metropolitan Essex circa 1920

10

Until 1888, London was governed by a patchwork of authorities who were often in conflict with each other about whose job it was to provide and pay for local services. These included police and education, and especially the essentials of water, gas, electricity and sewage disposal. The whole system was overhauled with the formation of the London County Council (LCC) which became a London wide administrative body.

In 1899 there were 28 Metropolitan boroughs operating within the London County Council area, although the LCC's administrative reach had, as yet, to extend into Essex. In 1907, Walthamstow Urban District Council was asked by one of it members to look into the possibility of joining London, as they were dissatisfied with the services given by Essex County Council. East Ham Council members had also expressed similar opinions and in 1908 the *Stratford Express* declared in an editorial *'That West Ham will shortly be united to London, is as certain as the sun will set tonight and rise again tomorrow'.*

Over the next 60 years the London County Council became more assertive in trying to extend central control. Royal Commissions on the running of London came and went yet the status quo was grudgingly maintained. However, some London services, like the Metropolitan police, had already extended their influence into Essex as far as Dagenham as early as 1840.

As London continued to expand, the original natural border of the River Lea was no longer relevant as the same economic and social conditions prevailed on both sides of the river. There was an increasing need for a sophisticated infrastructure including roads, public transport and health services to name but a few. Add to this the severe damage wrought on the city during the Second World War and it became increasingly essential that Metropolitan (built up) London needed a central governing body that could co-ordinate central services efficiently.

On 1st April 1965 the new Greater London Council was created with 33 local authorities under it. At a stroke the Essex boroughs of East Ham, West Ham, Barking, Chingford, Dagenham, Hornchurch, Ilford, Leyton, Romford, Walthamstow and Woodford and Wanstead, all of which had played major roles in the County's history, were dissolved. The areas lost from Essex were absorbed into London and five new Greater London Boroughs were created; Barking and Dagenham, Havering, Newham, Redbridge and Waltham Forest. It is these that are the nucleus of our book.

The boundary changes were no doubt necessary and the Greater London Council was created without any noticeable popular dissent. This has not always been the case when Essex borders have been tampered with.

In 1888 William Fuller-Maitland, the wealthy and influential owner of Stansted Hall, led a revolt by Essex villagers against a bureaucratic proposal to change the county boundary and move five Essex villages into Hertfordshire. The Poor Law Act, 1834, had led to the creation of institutions such as the Bishops Stortford Union, which took care of the poor over a wide area. Ever conscious of the need to reduce costs, the board of guardians sought to expand their scope into Essex villages.

In collusion with this suggestion the boundary commissioners, bureaucrats to the core who loved straight lines on maps, saw an excuse to straighten out a kink in the boundary line. This would mean that Elsenham, Farnham, Manewdon, Stansted and Ugley, would become Hertfordshire villages. The plan met with fierce opposition and cries of, 'We have been Essex Men since Alfred the Great,' were heard from the villagers. These individual village outcries, organised into a co-ordinated protest by Joseph Green, a storekeeper, were strengthened by the considerable political weight of Fuller-Maitland. Under this storm of well organised protest the authorities were obliged to back down and the plan was abandoned.

No cries of, 'We have been Essex Men since Alfred the great.' were heard protesting in 1965 when the Greater London Council was formed. However, despite the fact that the five Metropolitan Essex boroughs have been part of London for almost two generations, much of Dagenham, Romford, Redbridge and Waltham Forest are still referred to by commentators today as being in Essex.

In *Metropolitan Essex,* as in our other *Essex Hundred* titles, we have done our best to record some of the memorable events, people and places that have played a role in the development of the county of Essex. We do confess to having a slight advantage, perhaps, as both of us were born in the Essex that is now in London.

Andrew Summers
John Debenham

The Hundred

Prior to 1965 the five new Greater London Boroughs of Barking and Dagenham, Havering, Newham, Redbridge and Waltham Forest, the area we have termed *Metropolitan Essex*, were enclosed in the Essex Hundreds of Waltham, Becontree, Ongar and Chafford.

What is the *Hundred* and where did the name come from? It is fair to say that there is no definitive consensus among historians. The use of the term hundred and its subdivision the *hide*, as measurements of land, dates back to Saxon times.

In many parts of England in Saxon times the 'Free Peasant' formed the basis of society and the primitive unit of land, known as a 'hide', was an area supporting one household of a peasant's extended family, his livestock, and any live-in help. The actual land area of a hide would depend on the size of the household, the quality and productivity of the land and the standard of living associated with the social standing of the peasant required.

The hundred was a natural progression to a larger administrative area consisting of 100 hides. King Edgar (959 – 975) is recorded as regarding the hundred as an established institution. The *Hundred Court* was formed as the administrative and judicial basis of society in England south of the River Humber. In time it came to be a subdivision of a county or shire and had its own court with the power to settle local disputes.

After the Battle of Hastings in 1066 and the Norman invasion, William the Conqueror, determined to organise England, formalised the hundred as a fiscal unit. By 1086 Norman England was stable enough for William to be able to send out Royal Commissioners to overhaul the system of hundreds. This resulted in the *Domesday Book*, the first national asset register which was used to settle property disputes, usually in favour of the ruling Normans. More importantly this register was, for William, a basis for the efficient collection of taxes. From this it could be said that the Normans were the first to introduce taxation on an organised basis.

Norman times were turbulent times and areas of a hundred were often subject to land grabs by rival barons or the church, sometimes with the approval of the King and sometime without. It was not unknown for a Norman baron to lay claim to a neighbouring parcel of land and then occupy it by force or the threat of force. Once the land was acquired, possession became perhaps nine tenths of the law and, of course, title deeds could be, and frequently were, then altered to fit in with the new facts.

(continued page 16)

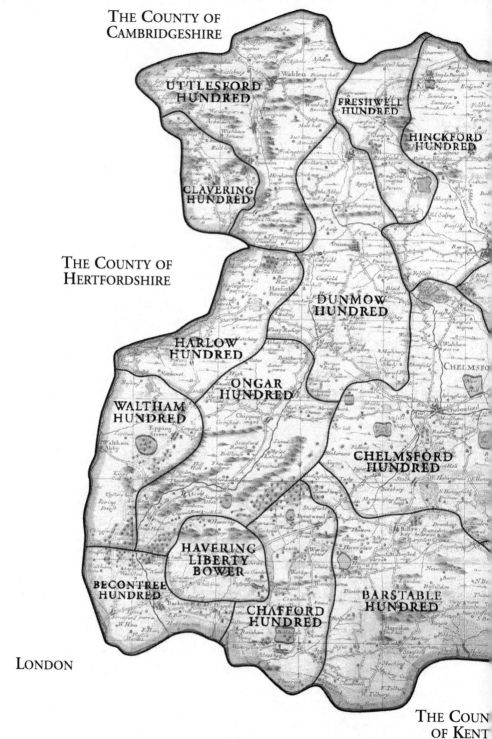

THE COUNTY OF
CAMBRIDGESHIRE

UTTLESFORD
HUNDRED

FRESHWELL
HUNDRED

HINCKFORD
HUNDRED

CLAVERING
HUNDRED

THE COUNTY OF
HERTFORDSHIRE

DUNMOW
HUNDRED

HARLOW
HUNDRED

ONGAR
HUNDRED

WALTHAM
HUNDRED

CHELMSFORD
HUNDRED

CHELMSFO

HAVERING
LIBERTY
BOWER

BECONTREE
HUNDRED

BARSTABLE
HUNDRED

CHAFFORD
HUNDRED

LONDON

THE COUN
OF KENT

THE HUNDREDS OF ESSEX

THE COUNTY OF
SUFFOLK

LEXDEN HUNDRED

TENDRING HUNDRED

ITHAM NDRED

WINSTRED HUNDRED

THURSTABLE HUNDRED

THE NORTH SEA

DENGY HUNDRED

ROCHFORD HUNDRED

THE RIVER THAMES

(continued from page 13)

Studies of old manorial records reveal an almost continual tussle of land ownership in and around the Harlow and Waltham hundreds for nearly 200 years. Another good example of Baronial maneuverings resulted in the existence of 'Detached Woolwich' - see page 30.

To add to any confusion over the hundred, there were also half-hundreds and even double hundreds. These areas were literally larger or smaller units in land area or population size or a mixture of both. Thankfully the double hundred has not survived from the middle ages.

The *Hundred Court* as the basis of social organization, lasted right up until the 1867 County Courts Act which supplanted it with the County Court. The hundred served well as an administrative unit until it was replaced by the modern urban borough and district councils from the early twentieth century onwards. When the Essex Police was formed in 1840 the police forces were organised along the divisions of the hundreds which continued until 1900.

On the previous pages we show a map of the Hundreds of Essex. It was engraved by Ogilby and Morgan and published in 1678. Although that was the position then, as with all government administration there has been a certain amount of tinkering with boundaries over the years.

There is also a view that the hundred in Saxon England was just a translation from the Roman (Latin) 'Centurion'. The Centurion was the officer supposedly commanding one hundred men known as the Centuria. This notion would not seem to fit the facts since the Centuria most frequently consisted of only eighty men and sometimes as few as sixty. Another plausible view might be that the term hundred could have been the land area that, in times of trouble, was required to raise a force of a hundred men bearing arms. Alternatively, areas of land termed hundreds may have incorporated several villages or settlements controlled simply by councils of 100 men.

The English word hundred has Germanic origins. However it is possible that England having accepted the word into the language may then have exported the term hundred, as a land area, back to Scandinavia and northern Germany where the hundred was also used as an administrative land area. In Sweden it was known as the Härad, in Denmark the Herred and in Germany as the Harde. On the other hand it may be that the *Hundred* arrived in England from Germany via Scandinavia sometime during the Viking or Saxon incursions but this must remain conjecture.

16

Dates and Time

Like much historical research the 'facts' as such are open to interpretation and sometimes the conclusions reached are no more than informed speculation. Journeying back in time for research purposes becomes increasingly difficult the further back you go. Where possible the best source is usually the official documents that relate to the event in question. Yet over the centuries many such documents have been lost or destroyed, either deliberately or by accident. Sometimes 'facts' have been created by chroniclers long after the event took place; as is case with Boadicea that we have outlined on pages 20-23. Contemporary chroniclers often have different interpretations of what happened depending on who was their paymaster. Subsequently 'facts' have been reinterpreted, then copied (sometimes incorrectly), and repeated down the ages. The cut and paste of today is nothing new. Furthermore there is no way to check it!

Further confusion, particularly over dates, was added with the passing of the *British Calendar Act of 1751*. This introduced the Gregorian calendar which was adopted in Britain a year later and is still in use today. Before that the Julian calendar (established by the Roman Emperor Julius Caesar) was in operation. The new calendar lopped eleven days off September 1752. People going to bed on the 2nd September woke up the next day to find it was the 14th September! The Gregorian calendar was introduced as the existing Julian calendar was slightly too long, which caused the Easter celebration to drift slowly forward. The new system brought the calendar back into synchronization with the seasons and for it to remain accurate new rules were adopted for leap years.

Although the Gregorian calendar was adopted in Great Britain in 1752, it had already been introduced in much of mainland Europe by Pope Gregory (where the name came from) 170 years earlier. It is possible that the new calendar had been used in parts of England during the reign of Queen Elizabeth I who, although strongly Protestant, was unable or unwilling to fully suppress the strong Roman Catholic sentiment in the country.

Although historical research in the 19th and 20th century is generally easier to undertake there are still pitfalls. Buildings and monuments may have been open (known as the soft opening) well before their 'official' opening which may have been months, or even years, later. Also official accounts of events may have been commissioned long after the actual event took place.

The fixing of time is even more curious. Time was not standardised on the British mainland until the Victorian era.

On 1st June 1880, the Statutes (Definition of Time) Bill was read for the first time in the House of Commons and received the Royal Assent on 2nd August 1880. Prior to that, time was different in different parts of the country. Owning a watch or timepiece was an expensive luxury item. Although clocks and watches of the day were reasonably accurate it was sunrise and sunset that were used as the basis of local time.

The result of this was that the time on clocks in the west of the country could be 20 minutes behind that showing in London. Even in Essex, there was a few minutes difference in the time recorded in Harwich and that in Stratford. In 1852 London time became known as Greenwich Mean Time (GMT).

In general, variations in local times didn't matter but this changed with the arrival of the railways and then the electric telegraph. Standardising time became a critical factor. Today it is difficult to imagine different times applying all over the country as it would create chaos with radio and television programming together with everything else.

The pioneers of standardising time in the UK were the railway companies who created what was known as, 'railway time'. It was essential to have standardised time for timetables and a smooth running operation. It was also vital for safety. The railway companies in their efforts to impose 'railway time' frequently faced strong opposition from local groups. These groups refused point blank to adjust their public clocks to bring them in line with 'railway time'. One particularly vociferous opponent of 'railway time' was the Dean of Exeter Cathedral, Thomas Lowe, who refused to be dictated to by the railway companies and change the time on his beloved cathedral clock.

Nevertheless the new 'railway time' became the default time. For many years, however, provincial towns had either two clocks or clocks with two minute hands showing both local and 'Railway or London time'. Railway punctuality is a hot topic today but we have to thank the railways for being in the vanguard to get a standard time introduced in the first place.

DATE	EVENT
43 AD	*Romans Invade England*
61	*Boudicca's rebels sack Colchester, London and St Albans*
122	*Building of Hadrian's wall begins in Northumbria*
407	*End of Roman occupation of Britain*
487	*Birth of St. David, Patron Saint of Wales*
604	*King Aethelbert of Kent founds Cathedral church of St Paul in London*
628	*Mohammad captures Mecca*
871	*Alfred the Great becomes first King of England*
1066	*Battle of Hastings, William the Conqueror becomes King of England*
1070	*Hereward the Wake leads Saxon Revolt*
1096	*The first Crusade is launched*
1215	*King John signs Magna Carta at Runnymede*
1216	*King John dies; his nine year old son becomes King Henry III*
1219	*Newgate Prison founded in London*
1348	*The Black Death (Bubonic Plague) first arrives in England*
1377	*Death of Edward III, ten year old grandson becomes King Richard II*
1381	*Peasants revolt ends at Smithfield*
1397	*Thomas of Woodstock, Duke of Gloucester murdered in Calais*
1399	*Richard II deposed, Henry Bolingbroke crowned King Henry IV*
1431	*Joan of Arc burned at the stake in Rouen*
1440	*Eton College founded by King Henry VI for poor scholars*
1445	*Birth of Sandro Botticelli in Florence*
1450	*Jack Cade's rebels beat Henry VI at Battle of Sevenoaks.*
1474	*William Caxton prints the first book in English*
1485	*Richard III dies at Bosworth Field Henry VII is first of Tudor dynasty*
1500	*First Caesarean birth in Switzerland*
1508	*Michelangelo begins painting the ceiling of the Sistine Chapel*
1527	*Pope refuses Henry VIII a divorce from Catherine of Aragon*
1536	*William Tyndale burnt at the stake*
1536	*Dissolution of Monasteries begins*
1552	*St Andrews Golf Club founded*
1556	*Walter Raleigh introduces Tobacco to England*
1564	*Birth of William Shakespeare*
1576	*Martin Frobisher explores Canada and 'The North West Passage'*
1588	*Spanish Armada defeated*
1593	*London theatres closed for a year due to The Plague*

Thomas Thornycroft's sculpture of Boadicea at Westminster erected in 1902, nearly 2000 years after the revolt.

Queen Boadicea, or Boudicca, is one of Britain's greatest heroines. A statue of her stands on the Embankment, by Westminster Bridge, opposite the Houses of Parliament. She is remembered for her challenge to the dominance of the Romans nearly 2000 years ago. Boadicea is her Latin name although another variation is Buduica. Her Celtic name is Boudicca and she was given the name Θρίαμβος by the Greek born Roman historian Dio Cassius. Θρίαμβος roughly translates to triumph in English.

Much of what we know of Boadicea is legend. We do not know when she was born, who her parents were or even exactly where she came from. It is recorded that in AD 59 or AD 60, following the death of her husband, King Prasutagus of the Iceni tribe of East Anglia, Roman rule became increasingly repressive. They broke their promises about Boadicea's inheritance, publically whipped her and humiliated her family. Boadicea retaliated by leading an avenging army that stormed and destroyed Roman Colchester (Camulodunum) and killed all its inhabitants. Her forces then swept westward across Essex to burn and sack an undefended London (Londinium) as the Roman garrison had fled. Shortly afterwards Boadicea went on to mete out the same fate to Roman St Albans (Verulamium). Archaeological evidence is conclusive in finding that Colchester, London and St Albans were methodically destroyed about 2000 years ago and all the buildings and contents were incinerated. Digging almost anywhere in Colchester, and to a lesser extent in the City of London and St Albans, will reveal layers of red soot known as 'Boadicea's Destruction Horizon'. In all three urban locations Roman artefacts have been recovered that show evidence of severe scorching.

Following Boadicea's triumphs her army moved northwards. However, by this time they were over confident and undisciplined and fell into a carefully laid trap set by the Roman Commander Suetonius Paulinus. The Britons were annihilated and the revolt quashed. To avoid capture, Queen Boadicea is believed to have killed herself by taking poison. One popular myth suggests she is buried under platforms 8 or 9 at Kings Cross Station. Where Boadicea's forces made their final assault has led to much speculation. Staffordshire, Cambridge, Worcester and the East and West Midlands have been suggested along with Surrey and even Kings Cross itself. To date no mass graves, supposedly containing the remains of up to 80,000 bodies, or weapons caches have been unearthed that could confirm where this decisive encounter took place.

It should be noted that all the recordings of Boadicea's revolt have come from two sources. Both are Roman and both written years after the revolt. There are no 'British' records of the insurrection, only those based on the Roman ones. The first source comes from the Roman historian Publius (or Gaius) Tacitus in his books *Agricola* and then *the Annals of Ancient Rome*.

Tacitus was perhaps four or five when the revolt broke out. *Agricola* was published some 40 years afterwards and it is a semi-biographical account of Julius Agricola, a Roman Officer at the time of the uprising.

The other main source, published nearly 150 years later, was the Greek Roman Historian Dio Cassius who wrote *Romaika*, a history of Rome. His works were written in Greek. Thus all the 'facts' on Queen Boadicea have come from the 'other' side and were written in Latin or Greek. Over the centuries these works have been reinterpreted, translated and retranslated several times, regularly copied, frequently inaccurately, and with large parts missing. Most of the original manuscripts have disappeared. It was literally a case of the 'victors writing the history' after the event. Yet even in this case Roman official historians had to take great care as to what they wrote as penalties would be severe if their words did not tally with the views of their masters. Nevertheless, and maybe quite bravely, the injustices suffered by Boadicea at the hands of the Romans are documented in some detail by Tacitus. However, this was more than made up for in the graphically reported atrocities committed by Boadicea's forces when they sacked Colchester and London.

Much of the romance and myth that surrounds Queen Boadicea was created by the Victorians well over 1,800 years after the revolt took place. The statue of Boadicea on her chariot at Westminster is good example of this. It is the work of Thomas Thornycroft who began sculpting it in 1856. Thornycroft died in 1885 but the statue survived. It was cast in bronze 17 years later and erected in 1902.

Boadicea's attack on Colchester is well documented as is the assault on London. What is questionable is the size of Boadicea's army and exactly how it travelled from Colchester to London. Tacitus in his *Agricola* writes of Boadicea's Army initially numbering 100,000 which doubled in size by the time they had arrived in London. As there is no suggestion that the Britons used any ships, the rebel army would have had to travel overland from Colchester perhaps following roughly the route of the present A12. This would have been a huge logistical exercise. In AD 60, Essex had virtually no roads on which such a large force could easily march. There is no detail of the quality of the 'Roman Road' from London to Colchester so Boadicea's advance would have meant squeezing huge numbers of people along narrow tracks. Every single river and stream, no matter how small, would have presented a major obstacle. In Chelmsford there was once a Roman wooden bridge across the River Cam but whether it was useable or even there during the revolt is unknown. As Boadicea's army approached London the problems would have multiplied.

The area that is Romford and Ilford today was then densely forested. The River Roding and then the River Lea would have been exceedingly difficult to cross, not only for people but also for fighting chariots, baggage wagons and pack animals. In Roman times these rivers were not the tightly embanked waterways we know today. They grew and shrank over wide flood plains with the tides or seasons. Either side of the rivers were marshes that covered much of present day Stratford, Walthamstow and Barking and stretched all the way to the banks of the River Thames.

It is worth remembering that the first Bow Bridge across the River Lea wasn't built until 1100 years after Boadicea's revolt. It is unknown too how this vast army, together with all their animals, camped out on marshland and were sheltered and fed whilst Boadicea's generals devised a way to cross the rivers and then built the necessary bridging. Roman records give no clue as to how long it took Boadicea's army to trek from Colchester to London. For the reasons outlined above it must have taken some time. It is conceivable with such numbers, despite the distance (just over 60 miles), that the vanguard of Boadicea's Army could have arrived on the edge of London whilst the rearguard was still departing from Colchester.

According to Tacitus, Boadicea's decision to attack London was made in the heat of the moment after the destruction of Colchester, so by its very nature no advanced planning had been made for the journey overland. Thus it is surprising that the Romans abandoned London to its fate as it must have taken quite some time for Boadicea's army to reorganise and get to London. The Roman accounts of the size of Boadicea's Army need to be examined. They may well be exaggerated. Rebel army figures of 100,000 and up to 230,000 along with 80,000 dead during the final battle are quoted. If this were the case it would seem virtually the whole population of the British Isles would have been in Boadicea's Army.

There are no reliable estimates for the size of the English population before 1813 when the first census was undertaken. The best guess in the late Tudor era was a population of just over four million, based on the numbers of baptisms, burials and marriages recorded. Analysis of the *Domesday Book* (compiled around 1068) suggests less than two million. As Boadicea's revolt took place 1000 years before the *Domesday Book* was completed, it is quite likely the 'English' population would have been far smaller. Since the rebel forces were drawn mainly from the East Anglian, Iceni and Trinovantes tribes, the Roman accounts of the numbers in Boadicea's army seem at best grossly exaggerated, at worst quite implausible.

Boadicea's story, as a celebrated Celtic queen, wife, and mother is destined to remain a historical mystery unless *Metropolitan Essex* gives up some secrets hidden beneath Stratford or Walthamstow that will reveal all.

Wrong Turning

Records from the *Anglo-Saxon Chronicles* describe that in 895, a substantial force of Danish (Viking) raiders abandoned their encampment on Mersea Island off the Essex coast in the Blackwater Estuary. They took to their long ships and sailed south towards to the Thames Estuary. Their objective was to overrun and destroy London and with it the authority of Alfred, the Anglo - Saxon King. Also, London was a very wealthy city holding out the prospect of much booty for the invaders. The Danish force consisted of around 3000 warriors and a fleet of at least 100 vessels of all shapes and sizes. Whilst the number of fighters were relatively small, (four or five modern day battalions), in Anglo-Saxon England such a force was a real threat.

The Danish fleet left Mersea early in 895 which was an odd choice considering that the short days and inclement weather were hardly the best conditions for seafaring. After pausing at Shoebury to regroup and obtain supplies and fresh water, the fleet turned west into the River Thames and headed towards London.

They passed the ruins of the camp at Benfleet, which three years earlier had been one of their principal raiding bases until it was destroyed by the Saxons in a surprise attack.

Progress up the Thames was difficult and slow. Whilst the Viking long ships were flexible and manoeuvrable, they were weighed down with fighting men, weapons and armour.

The 1949 replica Viking Ship 'Hugin' at Pegwell Bay in Kent. The elaborately carved menacing figure on the prow is probably due more to Victorian imagination that historical reality.

24

Since the encampment at Mersea had been abandoned they also carried huge amounts of supplies, animals, plunder from previous raids, women, children and assorted camp followers. Although most of the ships were under sail, a great deal of physical effort was still needed to make headway, especially against the outgoing tide. Many of the vessels in the fleet had seen a lot of action. Some were the battered survivors from other Danish fleets, that had already suffered defeat at the hands of King Alfred or had retreated from forays into France. Others had been patched up and were barely seaworthy.

At Tilbury lookouts reported their progress. As they travelled further upstream a more intense watch was kept by King Alfred's pickets. In London Alfred, now fully aware of the threat, hastily put plans in place to counter the incursion. Realising that he didn't have enough men to fight the Danes head on, he cautiously moved his forces down river, whilst making allowance for a speedy retreat should it became necessary.

Finally the vanguard of the Danish fleet reached Bow Creek, opposite the present day O2 Arena, and then for some inexplicable reason turned north into the River Lea where they proceeded to head up stream. The rest of the Danish fleet obediently followed.

The landscape of the River Lea was very different 1000 years ago to what it is today. There was no industry, no housing, very little settlement and almost no organised agriculture. Whilst most of the land bordering the lower Lea and Thames was unattractive marsh, the middle and upper reaches of the Lea were lush and enclosed by dense forest.

The Danes pressed on regardless and followed the course of the River Lea through the middle of the area that is today's Olympic Park at Stratford, on past Stoke Newington, Tottenham, Walthamstow, Enfield and Waltham Abbey. At Ware, in Hertfordshire, 20 miles distant from the River Thames, it was impossible for the Danish ships to navigate any further. Ware itself was a border town between Anglo-Saxon Wessex and the Viking controlled, *Danelaw*. *Danelaw* was simply a historical name given to the part of England in which the laws of the Danes (or Vikings) held sway. The River Lea was part of the frontier which may have explained why the Danish captain chose that route. The Danes remained at their base in Ware for six months unmolested.

Sensing an opportunity Alfred, with an army of Londoners, followed the Danes up the River Lea. Throwing his customary caution to the winds he attacked the Vikings in their newly fortified compound. It was a disaster. His forces were defeated and four of his leading commanders killed.

Alfred retreated to Waltham Abbey. He deployed his remaining forces to protect the gathering of the summer harvest which, should it have fallen into the hands of the Danes, would have had dire consequences for Londoners.

Using tactics once employed by the Danes, Alfred set to work diverting the course of the River Lea. He also built a series of fortifications on either side of the bank at strategic points. The Danes were trapped. They had sailed into a bottleneck and then Alfred had sealed it with a cork. An 18th century historian, William Robinson, speculated that the 'works' carried out by Alfred on the Lea to block the Dane's escape were built across the River Lea in Tottenham.

Tottenham Lock today. Did King Alfred trap the Vikings in the River Lea here 1000 years ago?

The outcome of these actions resulted in a stalemate. The Danish forces were not strong enough to attack London overland. Alfred, in a similar plight, did not have the resources to penetrate their stronghold. It developed into a waiting game. With the onset of winter the Danish fighting men decamped. As they were unable to use their ships, they simply abandoned them and marched west across the country to the River Severn.

Their women, children and the sick were left behind in Ware along with much of their plunder. At the River Severn the Danes intention was to link up with their fellow compatriots who were based there and form a stronger force which could perhaps attack Alfred from the south west.

After the Danish departure a jubilant Anglo-Saxon army of Londoners marched into the Danish camp and seized whatever of value remained. Some of the Danish ships were seaworthy. Others could be repaired with little work.

The salvageable boats were towed back to London in triumph by Alfred's jubilant army. The rest were burnt. There are no records as to the fate of the Danish women and children..

There had been almost 30 years of continuous warfare. This was followed by nearly a hundred years where the Danes posed little threat and there was relative peace. However, in 991 the Vikings were back with a vengeance and, under the command of Olaf Tryggvason, they crushed the Anglo-Saxon forces at the Battle of Maldon on the Essex coast. Twenty-five years later in 1016, another legendary Viking, Canute or Cnut, routed the English at the battle of Ashingdon to become the King of England. It was left to a French Norman, William the Conqueror, to finally overthrow the remnants of Viking and Saxon rule in England which was achieved at the Battle of Hastings in 1066.

A peaceful border. House boats on the River Lea

Returning to Alfred the Great, as he became known, he is best remembered for the enduring legend of his burning the cakes when he was on the run from Viking forces in Somerset. He died on 26th October 899. One of his abiding legacies must be that, following his efforts, the River Lea became established as the western border of Essex and it remained so until 1965.

Not a lot of People Know that!

Beside the present church building,
An inscription, on a stone lying flat,
Reads: 'HAROLD KING OF ENGLAND 1066'
Now - 'Not a lot of people know that!'

Waltham Abbey lies just outside Metropolitan Essex in modern day Essex. Previously the Abbey was the epicentre of the old Waltham Hundred which stretched from Harlow south along the east bank of the River Lea and took in much of Chingford, Walthamstow and Woodford.

The earliest recorded history of Waltham Abbey goes back to King Canute, the undisputed victor of the Battle of Ashingdon in Essex in 1016. Eighteen years later, towards the end of Canute's reign, far away from Essex, legend has it a blacksmith in the village of Montacute in Somerset discovered a large black flint cross. The cross was removed from the hill where it was discovered and placed in a wagon on the orders of Tovi, the then Lord of Montacute, who was also a close advisor to the King. However, the beasts (12 red oxen and 12 white cows) pulling the wagon refused to move.

There was much discussion as to what to do next. Tovi addressed the crowd gathered around and called for suggestions. Someone shouted, 'Take it to Canterbury', another called 'Winchester' but the wagon stood rooted to the ground. Tovi then remarked out loud he was going back to Waltham in Essex, where he owned a hunting lodge on the banks of the River Lea. Suddenly the wagon started to move and appeared to push the animals forward. The animals, accompanied by a great throng of people from Montacute escorting the cross, pulled the wagon non-stop until it reached Essex. Tovi saw it as a sign and decided to build a place of worship on the spot – where Waltham Abbey now stands.

To honour the cross Tovi selected fine jewels to decorate it. However, on attempting to fix them with nails to the right arm of the cross it was said that blood suddenly gushed out. Tovi was stunned by this happening. The jewels were immediately removed and placed in a small bag close by and the blood was kept in a silver goblet. So the legend grew that just by touching the cross a miracle might happen and Waltham and its cross (now known as the Holy Rood) became a centre of pilgrimage and celebration.

In 1060 Harold Godwinson, Earl of Wessex and later to be the last Saxon King of England, consecrated a new, larger church on the site after apparently being cured of a paralysis through praying there. Harold became King in January 1066 following the death of Edward the Confessor. Edward was alleged to have said to Harold on his deathbed, "I commend my wife and my entire kingdom to your care".

Duke William of Normandy however disputed the succession. He asserted that Edward had told him virtually the same thing. King Harold, although supported by most of the English nobility, soon had other problems to worry about. In September 1066 he had to fight off a large Viking force from Norway led by his brother Tostig, Earl of Northumbria, who also claimed the throne.

Tostig's forces were successfully repelled at the battle of Stamford Bridge in present day Yorkshire but then a more potent threat materialised with the landing of William and his Normans in Sussex. Harold hurried south. He stopped at Waltham to prostrate himself before the cross. Whilst he lay there on the ground the figure on the cross is said to have looked away. This was seen as an ill-omen, however the King was not told. In view of this the Abbey insisted on sending two of their most trusted brethren, Osegod and Ailric, to accompany Harold to Hastings.

William, Duke of Normandy's claim to the English throne was settled in the time honoured manner. In the battle that ensued Harold was despatched by that famous arrow in the eye and William was victorious.

Osegod and Ailric saw the King struck down. When the battle was over they began a painstaking search to find the body. This was very difficult as many of the dead had been stripped and mutilated. Harold's mistress Edith Swan-Neck was then summoned to Hastings to assist with identification. She recognised certain marks known only to her on one of the bodies as belonging to Harold.

Immediately the monks asked the victorious William's permission to remove the body to Waltham Abbey for burial. Initially William refused but eventually relented. Harold's remains were then collected and carried back to Waltham Abbey. Here Harold was buried with great honour and to this day a memorial stone marks his grave in the Abbey Gardens.

Waltham Abbey became rich from the pilgrims flocking to the Shrine of the Holy Rood. It remained wealthy until the time of Henry VIII. In 1540, after Henry's break with Rome, the Abbey fell victim to his dissolution of all the powerful and wealthy religious foundations. The Abbey was dissolved and many of the buildings demolished. As for the stone cross, it disappeared at that time and has never been seen since.

Detached Woolwich

Woolwich, on the south bank of the River Thames, is linked to North Woolwich by a ferry and foot tunnel. It is thought that Woolwich was so named as it was 'a port from which wool was shipped'. Located in the original Essex Hundred of Becontree, North Woolwich is a tract of land measuring about 500 acres, bordered by East Ham, Barking and of course the river.

However, although North Woolwich was geographically in Essex on the north bank of the River Thames, it was administratively part of Kent. It was described as 'Woolwich in the parts of Essex' and later 'detached Woolwich'. This strange anomaly originated after the Norman Conquest and remained in place until 1965 when North Woolwich was incorporated into the London Borough of Newham, following the reorganisation of local government in London.

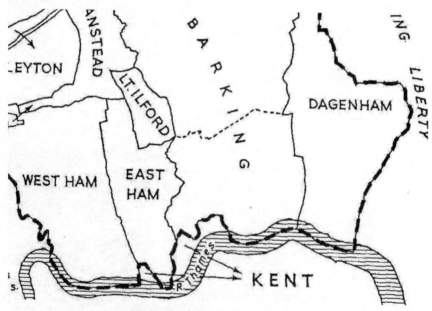

Detached Woolwich (In Essex) but part of Kent

In 1086, Hamon Dapifer was the Sheriff of Kent appointed by William the Conqueror. He held lands in many parts of Kent and several manors in Essex. At Woolwich, Hamon was not only County Sheriff but also Lord of the Manor. He was known to be unscrupulous and high handed.

It was also not unknown for Norman Sheriffs to encroach upon the lands of their neighbours and tamper with boundaries if they felt they could get away with it. So it is highly probable that the acquisition of Woolwich that was 'North of the Thames' was the result of sharp practice, and quite possibly force, by Hamon Dapifer. What made 'North Woolwich' especially attractive was the prospect of collecting all the taxes and tolls from the cross-river traffic on both sides of the river.

Originally 'Woolwich in the parts of Essex' was one continuous parcel of land between Ham Creek and the River Roding. However, by 1850, following changes to parish boundaries, a finger of East Ham had been extended south to the River Thames effectively cutting the Kent administered area in two. 'Woolwich in the parts of Essex' now became known as Detached Woolwich No. 1 and Detached Woolwich No. 2.

The term 'North Woolwich' first came to be used in 1847 following the construction of the railway line that terminated by the (north) Woolwich ferry landing pier. Gradually the name North Woolwich spread from the area surrounding the station to encapsulate all of 'Woolwich in the parts of Essex'. 'Detached Woolwich' soon fell out of use and the area simply became known as North Woolwich. The Station closed in 1979 and for a while it became 'The Old Station Museum' dedicated to the impact on the area of the 'Great Eastern' and 'London and North Eastern' railways.

North Woolwich is now served by the King George V station of the Docklands Light Railway which, with its extension under the Thames to Woolwich Arsenal station, despite administrative separation, provides a physical attachment to Woolwich. Further strengthening the area's ties with Kent is the giant London *Crossrail* project that is presently under construction, see page 182.

Stratford Langthorne Abbey
or West Ham Abbey

Long before it became part of the London Borough of Newham, Stratford was the site of one of the largest Cistercian abbeys in England; Stratford Langthorne Abbey, or the Abbey of St Mary's. It occupied some 1500 acres adjacent to what is now the Stratford Olympic Park, and extended to the Blackwall Tunnel northern approach road in the west and as far as the River Thames at North Woolwich. It was also known as West Ham Abbey as it was in the Parish of West Ham. Founded in 1135, on eleven acres of land given by William de Montfitchet, Baron of Stansted, the Abbey expanded rapidly and came to own more than twenty manors spread across Essex.

The Abbey could be said to have been the industrial heart of the community. It was self sufficient and in addition created wealth from the many trades and industries it sponsored. Apart from the religious house of the Abbey itself, the accommodation for Lay Brothers and the hospitality rooms the Abbey provided, there were buildings to house bakeries, a brewery, a tannery and weavers. With its many ancillary buildings the Abbey may, at times, have resembled an industrious village rather than just a religious house.

One of the monks' most prosperous activities was milling. The Abbey owned mills on the 'Bow Back Rivers' – the lower reaches of the River Lea. Most of the mills were tidal such as those at Three Mills (see page 186), which still exist today. The mills ground wheat for local bakers who in turn supplied the city of London with bread. The trade was so successful that at one time the Guild of Bakers tried to gain the power to impose a toll on loaves entering the City.

Such was the status of the Abbey that for a period in 1267 it became King Henry III's court following the Crown's defeat of Simon De Montfort at the battle of Evesham. De Montfort, who was married to the King's sister, had led a Barons rebellion against Henry's mismanagement of the country in a time of great famine and failed expensive foreign wars.

The ensuing negotiations at the Abbey were virtually a re-run of the Magna Carta discussions that King John held with his Barons nearly fifty years earlier. (see next chapter Magna Carta). This time Henry, with the help of Papal legates, made peace with the rebellious Barons and was restored to full power.

Due to its proximity to the City of London the Abbey came to be a popular retreat for the nobility. It was later visited by many monarchs, Richard II and Edward IV among them. Local tax records were held there probably causing it to be ransacked by rebels during the Peasant's Revolt.

The Abbey prospered and by the sixteenth century a small river port had developed at Stratford to assist the many trades carried on there and supply the mills. Then came Henry VIII's fight with the Pope and the dissolution of the monasteries.

In 1538 the Abbey was dissolved. The lands were given to Sir Peter Mewtas and Johanna his wife 'for their true and faithful service' and the monks were allowed to relocate to a mansion they owned in Plaistow. The Abbey mills continued until at least 1613. After this the traditional mills ceased operation due to reduced water levels in the non-navigable channels of the Lea caused by the construction of the 'New River'.

With the monks gone the Abbey was left to go to ruin and the much of building stone was taken by local landowners. By the eighteenth century nothing remained, even the foundations were dug up. In the 1840s the

North Woolwich railway was built and by the early twentieth century the site had disappeared beneath railway sidings, a sewage works and factory buildings.

Today, though almost nothing remains of the Abbey, its crest can be seen over the doorway to the Old Court House, in Tramway Avenue, Stratford. Also both a stone window and a carving of skulls from the Abbey, dating from about 1180, survive in All Saints West Ham Parish Church, Church Street, Stratford.

Archaeological investigations carried out on land cleared for the Jubilee Line extension identified the Abbey's Cistercian cemetery and more recently, in early 2008, continuing excavation identified the former gatehouse, north east of the Abbey Church. This defines the eastern edge of the precinct. This area has been awarded 'Scheduled Ancient Monument' status, giving it protection from further development.

Artists Karen Guthrie and Nina Pope of *Somewhere* (artist collective) designed a major community garden in 'Bakers Row'. The name no doubt a legacy from the early tradition of bread making linked to the abbey's millers. Today the garden is run by 'Friends of Abbey Gardens' on behalf of Newham Council and is open to visitors from dawn till dusk.

Magna Carta

On June 15th 1215, at Runnymede, King John made his seal on the Magna Carta (or Charter), the most significant constitutional act in the history of the British Isles. The charter lies at the root of the British constitution. It was the beginning of all the freedoms that the British people were to gain over the next eight hundred years. It included the clause, *'That laws should be good and fair and that no freeman be imprisoned or punished without going through a proper legal system'.* The document's overriding principle was that the monarch was not above the law. The King could only act in accordance with the legal principles that had been enacted by representatives of the people.

King John preparing to sign the Magna Carta watched by Robert Fitzwalter

The Magna Carta signing was undertaken very reluctantly by King John and only came about following extreme pressure from a group of powerful English Barons, who along with many others, were completely dissatisfied with the way the country was run. The Barons had threatened to take up arms against the King unless he agreed to reforms set out in the charter.

There were 25 rebel Barons charged with ensuring that the King respected the charter. Their leader was Robert Fitzwalter, Lord of Dunmow. This group included four more powerful Essex figures; Richard de Montfitchet, Sheriff of Essex Geoffrey de Mandeville of Pleshey, William de Lanvallei, the Governor of Colchester Castle, and Robert de Vere of Castle Hedingham.

Although Robert Fitzwalter's seat was in Dunmow, a small town close to present day Stansted Airport, he was also the Constable of Baynard's Castle, in London, and owned Benington Castle near Stevenage in Hertfordshire. His estates included great swathes of land, much of it wood and forest throughout *Metropolitan Essex* in the Waltham and Ongar Hundreds.

Three years before the Magna Carta, Fitzwalter had been implicated in a plot against the King. As a result he was exiled and fled to France. In his absence King John destroyed Baynards Castle.

However within a year the King declared an amnesty and all charges against Fitzwalter were dropped and he was even given licence to rebuild Baynards Castle.

On his return Fitzwalter continued to take the lead in the Barons' revolt against the king. Declared "marshal of the army of God and Holy Church" he headed an imposing force of nobles. King John realised he was completely outmanoeuvred and had no choice but to agree to their demands. Fitzwalter now became head of the group of 25 barons appointed to enforce the promises made in the Magna Carta.

For his part, King John had no intention of honouring the charter. Almost immediately he claimed that he had signed under duress. Before the year was out he had mustered an army of loyal forces and mercenaries to march upon the rebel Barons.

Pope Innocent III supported the King and excommunicated all who had effected the signing of the Magna Carta. In the church's view the Barons' actions were a direct assault upon the divine right of a King to rule. In August 1215, a papal bull was issued annulling the charter.

The Barons cause was not helped though by Robert Fitzwalter's aggressive attitude that alienated his supporters and somewhat incompetent leadership. Fitzwalter insisted on seeking help from King Phillip of France. The help in the form of several thousand soldiers was promised but failed to materialise when it was needed due to poor communication and bad planning.

King John's men sensed an advantage and moved quickly. They seized Fitzwalter's estates, including his seat in Dunmow, before moving on to demolish his castle at Benington. The Royal forces went on to destroy Montfitchet Castle, take Pleshey, capture de Vere's Castle at Hedingham and force the capitulation of Colchester. All the while the promised French reinforcements for the rebels still failed to arrive.

Yet within a year everything had changed. Louis, the son of Phillip of France, returned with an army to support the Barons. King John was defeated. He fled northwards and died of dysentery in Newark after reportedly losing the Crown Jewels whilst crossing the Wash in Norfolk.

As we have seen in the last chapter the new King, Henry III, made peace with the rebels and twice issued a revised Magna Carta. The 'rebel' Barons, including Robert Fitzwater, were returned to favour and regained their lands. Despite exile and his many mistakes Robert Fitzwalter is remembered as a champion of English liberty. He died peacefully in 1235. There have been many changes since King John signed the Magna Carta. Despite this its guiding principles survive to this day.

Frankpledge in the Waltham Hundred

During the final years of the reign of Henry III, in 1270, Waltham Abbey was in continuous dispute with two other powerful organisations, the Dean and Chapter of St Paul's and the Knights Templars. The Abbey, The Dean and the Templars acted like, and had many parallels with, modern corporations. Headed by a Chief Executive Officer (CEO) with a board of directors, they employed lobbyists to persuade the King, or even the Pope, to their way of thinking. All three had commercial interests in the Waltham Hundred. Frequent leasing or renting of land from each other often resulted in disputes, sometimes over boundaries or grazing rights. They were particularly vigilant over failure of one of the other bodies to fulfil its 'civic' responsibilities or pay its fair share of tax.

One of the most serious disputes was between Waltham Abbey and the Knights Templars. The newly appointed acting 'CEO' of Waltham Abbey, Prior Geoffrey, acting on evidence from his subordinates, ordered the seizure of cattle belonging to the Templars who were in leasehold possession of the manor of Chingford. The Templars were accused of failing to perform the services due to the Hundred. These included paying their tax dues and attending the renewal of the *frankpledge*. The *frankpledge* was a system in force in England under which nearly all households within the Hundred were bound together by a mutual responsibility to keep the peace. This was pledged by a form of financial surety which could be traced back to the time of King Canute It was confirmed at the equivalent of an annual general meeting.

The *frankpledge* obliged any of its members accused of a crime to attend court for a trial. If the man did not appear, the entire community could be fined for his offence. Once again the Normans refined the existing system, just as they had done with the Hundreds by creating the *Domesday Book,* as a basis for taxation. With the *frankpledge* the Normans had another means of snuffing out any of the sporadic rebellions that occurred by imposing draconian collective fines on a community where disorder occurred. It is remarkable that these internal Waltham Hundred disputes were nearly all resolved peaceably through courts of law, not by force. The losing party generally accepted the outcome. The Abbey's seizure of cattle from the Templars was upheld in the Hundred Court. The animals were returned only when the Templars had fulfilled their obligations. Oddly, whilst supposedly bitter rivals, the Dean and Chapter of St Paul's and the Abbey would come together against the Knights Templars. At other times St Paul's would join the Templars against Waltham Abbey or alternatively the Templars and the Abbey would take on St Paul's! *Frankpledge* today is commonly known as bail.

36

Lucky Escape
Serfs ye are, and serfs ye shall remain
King Richard II 23rd June 1381

For two weeks, in June 1381, England was convulsed by widespread riot and rebellion. London bore the worst of the torment. On Thursday 13th June, thousands of men who had walked from the corners of Essex and Kent, angry at the imposition of harsh new 'poll' taxes, streamed into the City of London.

Forty eight hours later, many of London's most prestigious buildings such as the Savoy Palace and the Inns and Courts of Temple Bar, along with stately homes and offices in Westminster and Knightsbridge had been ransacked and burnt to the ground. The City of London's Newgate and Fleet prisons were stormed and the prisoners liberated. At the church of St Martins in the Vintry, 40 'foreigners', mainly Flemish or Dutch, were dragged out on to the street and decapitated.

On the eastern edge of the City of London, the Tower of London harboured two men fearing the rebels' arrival. They were Sir Robert Hales, the Lord High Treasurer (akin to today's Chancellor of the Exchequer), and Simon Sudbury, who had a dual role as the Archbishop of Canterbury and the Lord Chancellor of England (akin to the Home Secretary). The Tower was supposedly a well defended impregnable fortress.

However, on the morning of Friday 14th June 500 rebels, who were camped around the Tower, persuaded the guards to let them in. The rebels walked unchallenged across the drawbridge and began a systematic search for those, who in their view were the 'traitors'. Hales, nicknamed 'Hobbe the Robber' and Archbishop Sudbury were soon found, as were John Legge the architect of the invidious poll tax, and the somewhat unfortunate William Appleton. Appleton's only crime was being the personal physician of John of Gaunt the 'most hated man in England'. All four men were hustled out to Tower Green and summarily beheaded. On the searchers' lists were also the names of Judge Robert Belknap, John Bampton, an Essex JP, and Sir John Gilsburgh, the Speaker of the House of Commons. Luckily for them, they were all elsewhere.

Whilst these events at the Tower were unfolding, the fourteen-year old King Richard II was at Mile End, just west of the River Lea, addressing a rebel crowd estimated at 100,000. The King offered to suspend the poll tax and grant new charters of rights to all serfs and peasants. He left Mile End around midday to travel to his temporary residence, the 'Royal Wardrobe', that used to stand near Mansion House. He set his clerks to work drawing up new charters to fulfil all the promises he had just made.

That evening the King and his entourage nervously settled down for the night. Around them London seethed and burned. An unprecedented orgy of destruction had continued throughout the afternoon, evening and into the morning of Saturday 15th June. The rebels had first entered the City of London full of peaceful intentions. Their only objective had been to bring to justice the 'wrongdoers'. Yet, as the day progressed, opportunists and criminals joined the fray along with hundreds of newly released prisoners eager to settle old scores.

King Richard rose on Saturday to find the capital smouldering. Most residents had either fled or barricaded themselves in their homes. Following the Mile End meeting the King had agreed to speak to the rebels once more but this time at Smithfield. Addressing this meeting in the tone of a benevolent King to his subjects, he asked them why they had not gone home since he had granted everything they had requested.

Exactly what happened next is disputed by different chroniclers. After hearing the King words, the rebel's leader, Wat Tyler, stepped, or rode, forward to speak with the King. One account has it that he was 'the worse for drink' and was shouting a string of new demands. On hearing this William Walworth, the Mayor of London, accused him of being arrogant. During the altercation Walworth stabbed Tyler who immediately afterwards was fatally run through by the King's squire John Standwick. Another account reports that the crowd saw Wat Tyler alone and speaking with the King. On reaching to hold the reins of the king's horse, William Walworth remonstrated with him. Tyler was surrounded and unbeknown to the crowd killed in the way described above. At this point the young King rode forward to face the rebels shouting *You shall have no captain but me*. Promising them fair treatment in exchange for their loyalty he told them that Tyler had been knighted and if they marched to St John's Fields close by Tyler would meet them there. The crowd obeyed but at St John's Fields with no leader confusion reigned. King Richard, reneging on his promises, had won time to assemble his forces. For the rebels, some no doubt still believing that the King meant what he said, the revolt was effectively over. They dispersed back across Bow Bridge over the River Lea to their homes in Essex, some, maybe, clutching papers with promises bearing the King's name. They were to find, in a very short time, that these promises meant nothing and that the King would have vengeance.

The revolt had been sparked two weeks earlier in Brentwood. On 31st May, John Bampton, an Essex JP and the Estate Steward of Barking Abbey, was sent to Brentwood accompanied by Sir John Gilsburgh MP, the Speaker of the House of Commons. Escorted by two sergeants at arms, their purpose was to enquire into the steep drop in tax receipts from the Barstable Hundred.

John Bampton was notoriously corrupt. During his career he had acquired several properties in Essex by dubious means. Sir John Gilsburgh owned many properties in Essex including a large estate and Manor House at Wennington, close to Aveley. He was also an unashamed champion of the war with France and had campaigned energetically in Parliament for additional funds to billet the English army in Brittany during the winter.

In Brentwood the men from the villages of Fobbing, Corringham and Stanford-le-Hope, who had been summoned to the enquiry, were in no mood to listen to Bampton. Their spokesman, Tomas Baker, stated in no uncertain terms that not a penny more would be paid in tax. On hearing this Bampton ordered his sergeants to arrest Baker. This action incensed the 100 strong angry 'peasants' who promptly set about beating the sergeants and then stoning the whole entourage. Bampton, the hapless Gilsburgh and their men, in fear of their lives, were sent fleeing back to London.

The incident brought to a head numerous grievances, particularly the unfair taxes being levied to finance the hugely unpopular war with France and the iniquitous feudal system's labour charters that tied peasants and serfs to their masters. The 'Black Death' had decimated the population in recent years. As a consequence labour was in short supply and many peasants and smaller tenanted land holders challenged the system. However the mob's worst venom was reserved for the corrupt judiciary who nearly always settled disputes to their own advantage.

Three days after Bampton had been sent ignominiously packing, Sir Robert Belknap, the Chief Justice of the Common Pleas, was sent to Brentwood. He was given strict orders to seek out and punish the rioters. However, the Essex men were well prepared. During the intervening three days messengers had galloped all over Essex and what is now East London, calling for resistance at Brentwood.

Belknap arrived on 2nd June to find perhaps 2000 armed men waiting. The judge was seized before he had a chance to utter a word and forced to swear on the Bible that he would never again hold such a session. All his official documents were snatched and burned. The judge was then stripped of his fine robes and unceremoniously ejected from Brentwood. Belknap had been very lucky; his clerks, together with three sequestered local jurors, were beaten to death then decapitated to appease the angry mob.

From this point there was no going back, the event was a catalyst. Almost immediately much of Essex and Kent exploded into open rebellion. Judges and officials and their properties, were attacked. Court papers and tax records were destroyed in bonfires.

To begin with assaults on officials' homes followed a similar pattern. Gilsburgh's house in Wennington was a good example and a prime target. Rebels arrived at Gilsburgh's Manor House from Essex, Kent and Surrey. Firstly all of the household staff were 'persuaded' to leave, although some of the staff willingly joined the rebel cause. This was followed a rigorous search of the property for any 'traitors' with Sir John high on the list. The other main objective of the rebels was to find the manorial records and then ceremoniously burn them.

The rebels considered themselves honourable men and not thieves. They were simply seeking justice and freedom from the tyranny of a system stacked against them. Almost identical incidents occurred in Havering-atte-Bower, Barking and at Stratford Abbey as thousands of rebels made their way across *Metropolitan Essex* towards Mile End, destroying whatever official records they could get their hands on.

At Waltham Abbey, according to the *Calendar of Close Rolls*, one of their number, identified as Robert Ansty, was later charged with "making insurrection and assembling other evildoers to destroy the Abbey and burn its charters".

A week after the death of Wat Tyler at Smithfield, and once the City of London was considered secure, the King led a sizeable army to Waltham. There he issued a statement saying that the charters given in Mile End granting the rebels' demands were no longer valid. Since he had been forced to sign them under duress they were meaningless. When a group of peasants complained, Richard replied "Serfs ye are, and serfs ye shall remain".

Within the space of a month the great revolt was over. Royal vengeance was swift. A large group of rebel diehards camped out at Billericay, were crushed by loyal forces led by Thomas of Woodstock, the King's uncle.

Over 145 rebel leaders were identified including Jack Straw and Thomas Baker. No mercy was shown and after a short trial they were executed.

Both John Bampton and Sir John Gilsburgh resurfaced to take prominent roles as new champions of justice. The Crown gave both men licences to "recover what so ever they pleased". As far as it is known both lived to old age and died of natural causes.

The Church of St. Mary and St. Peter in Wennington is over 800 years old and dates back to the time of Edward the Confessor before the Norman conquest when the parish belonged to Westminster Abbey. The Church was spared the wrath of the peasants during the Great Revolt, unlike Sir John Gilsburgh's mansion which was ransacked and is now a storage yard.

Dark Deeds at Stratford

In the 1377, on the death of his father Edward the Black Prince, Richard II, at the tender age of 10, became King of England. Until his majority he ruled with the help, and at times the hindrance, of guardians; his uncles the Dukes of Lancaster, York and Gloucester. Richard had quite firm ideas as to how he should rule but felt continually frustrated by the continuing interference of his uncles, particularly Gloucester. In 1397 the King was 30 years of age and his frustration had turned into nervous jitters. Rumours abounded of a plot to oust him allegedly inspired by his uncle, Thomas of Woodstock the Duke of Gloucester. Richard's reaction sparked one of the most infamous events in English history which would usher in the Lancastrian dynasty.

Richard was staying at his palace in the Liberty of Havering-Atte-Bower, near Romford and now in the London Borough of Havering. Here, on 12th July 1397, the King ordered the arrest of two of the imagined principal conspirators, Richard FitzAlan, the Earl of Arundel, and Thomas Beauchamp, the 60 year old Duke of Warwick. They were immediately condemned as traitors and their lands confiscated. Richard FitzAlan was incarcerated in the Tower of London. Two months later he was put on trial, condemned and executed on the same day. Thomas Beauchamp was more fortunate - his life was spared but he and his wife were exiled to the Isle of Man.

The worst of the King's malice however was saved for his uncle the Duke of Gloucester. Once he had confirmation that the other plotters were in custody the King left the Royal Palace and travelled east into Essex to arrive unannounced at his uncle's castle at Pleshey, west of Chelmsford, around five in the afternoon. It is recorded as having been a very hot day. The Duke, though not in good health, greeted the King in the customary fashion and later that evening Richard is said to have dined with his uncle.

During dinner Richard persuaded Gloucester that he was required to attend an urgent state council meeting in London. The following morning the King, the Duke and Thomas de Mowbray, the Earl Marshal of England, together with a small retinue of squires, yeomen and bodyguards, left Pleshey for London. The King and the Duke rode side by side and by all accounts chatted convivially. En-route the party probably stopped for refreshments and a change of horses at Havering-Atte-Bower.

In the afternoon the party continued their journey to London with the aim of getting there before night fall. It is assumed that they would have followed the old Roman road, more or less the route of the present day A12.

At Stratford Langthorne Abbey, close to the site of the present Olympic Stadium, the party paused, whereupon King Richard suddenly announced he would ride ahead to ensure that safe passage across the River Lea could be obtained. Although it was late evening, being July it was still light. The King departed leaving Gloucester bemused.

A short distance behind was the Earl Marshal of England. As the King disappeared into the distance the Earl Marshall rode up and overtaking the Duke, cried "I arrest you in the King's name". Gloucester was stunned. The King was too far away to hear his frantic calls. Resistance was useless; as well as being in poor health, the Earl Marshall's men far outnumbered Gloucester's personal entourage.

Thomas of Woodstock. Murdered on the Kings Orders?

It was now late evening. With his prisoner secure Thomas de Mowbray, under the cover of darkness, conveyed the Duke three miles down the River Roding to Creekmouth where a barge was ready to transport Gloucester to Calais.

King Richard subsequently declared Gloucester a traitor guilty of plotting against him. The Duke should have been tried at the same time as the Earl of Arundel. When requests for his return were sent to Calais the reply came back that he had died in prison.

The Duke's nephew, Henry Bolingbroke, vowed to revenge his uncle and asserted his claim to be King; he and Richard both had the same grandfather in Edward III. Henry's forces prevailed and Richard was captured and imprisoned in Pontefract Castle where he died; probably murdered on the new King's orders in 1400. How the Duke of Gloucester had died in Calais was never established with any certainty. An inquisition set up by Parliament after the accession of King Henry IV found, "...that he had been fraudulently and wickedly smothered, by the King's orders at Calais". Henry decreed that all of Gloucester's possessions, including Pleshey that had been confiscated by Richard, were restored to his widow Eleanor.

The capture and murder of the Duke of Gloucester is immortalised by William Shakespeare in his play, *Richard the Second,* where he uses it as the trigger for Henry to depose Richard and seize the crown. Alas Shakespeare does not mention the 'Dark Deed' of Gloucester's abduction taking place in Stratford.

Tyndale's Friend of North Ockendon

Up until the sixteenth century the general public's only knowledge of the bible, the foundation of their religious lives, would have come from whatever the clergy told them; unless they were very fortunate and read Latin. William Tyndale, a priest himself, thought the people should be able to read the word of God for themselves and wanted to translate the bible into the vernacular.

This was strictly forbidden in Henry VIII's England. Church leaders such as Cardinal Wolsey, and later Thomas More, vigorously enforced the law. Tyndale began translating the New Testament but was forced to flee England for Germany where he eventually completed it. By 1526, copies were being read in England, though Bishop Tunstall of London publicly burnt all the copies he could find. With both English and Papal authorities hounding him from place to place, in 1534 Tyndale fled to Thomas Poyntz's 'English House' in Antwerp where he could continue his work translating and publishing the complete English Bible in relative safety.

Thomas Poyntz, a merchant from North Ockendon, owned one of the many 'English' houses located close to the Grote Markt in the centre of Antwerp. Poyntz was sympathetic to Tyndale's work and did his best to make him welcome and secure in his house.

At this time, there was considerable trade between England and Antwerp. Bibles printed in English could be shipped relatively easily, hidden in bales of cloth or barrels. It was a highly risky business, as the east coast ports of England were watched continuously. Anyone caught with English bibles could be charged with heresy which carried the death penalty so Poyntz had to be very careful. Shipments were made at the dead of night and often landed in and around Purfleet or Dagenham. The contraband then had to be dispersed overland which was also extremely dangerous.

Seen as a heretic by the church, and not only in England, William Tyndale had many enemies. One of these was John Stokesley, who in 1530 succeeded Tunstall as Bishop of London. He blackmailed the aristocratic, but financially destitute Henry Phillips into acting as his agent. Phillips travelled to Antwerp posing as a student. With his smooth talking ways he managed to ingratiate himself in with the English merchant classes in Antwerp and discover the whereabouts of Tyndale. Taking advantage of Thomas Poyntz's absence on a business trip, Phillips succeeded in luring Tyndale out of the house. Thinking he was joining Phillips for lunch, he was ambushed in one of the many dark alleys that criss-cross the area. Tyndale was bound, gagged and put in a cart and removed to Vilvoorde Castle, just outside Brussels.

Hearing the news on his return, Thomas Poyntz strenuously tried to get Tyndale released. He even attempted, unsuccessfully, to make a deal with the guards at Vilvoorde Castle. Poyntz petitioned Thomas Cromwell and Henry VIII for Tyndale's release but all efforts failed. In 1536, after being incarcerated for year and a half in Vilvoorde's Prisoner's Tower, William Tyndale was taken to the Market Square, tied to a stake and strangled. His body was then burnt.

Thomas Poyntz was also branded as a heretic for his part in sheltering Tyndale and was placed under house arrest in Antwerp. He may well have received the same fate as Tyndale but through his many friends he managed to evade his captors and escape to England.

On his return to Essex Thomas' life was in ruins. As a known heretic he was under surveillance by Henry's spies and his continued involvement in the spreading of the new bible meant life was very difficult. This, despite the fact that John Poyntz, his elder brother, was a member of the household of Queen Catherine of Aragon, and had been at 'The Field of the Cloth of Gold' with Henry VIII. It could be that his brother was also concerned for his family and wanted to keep his distance from a known heretic.

Thomas may have felt vindicated when, two years after the death of Tyndale, Henry VIII decreed that Miles Coverdale's English Bible, based largely on Tyndale's translation, must be used in every parish church in the country. Vindicated maybe, but the damage was done and his fortunes did not improve. In 1547 his brother John died but his will left all his estate to his wife Anne and only on her death would it pass to Thomas and his sons. The only immediate benefit to Thomas was a length of black cloth for a gown and hood! It was not until Anne's death in 1558 that Thomas succeeded to the Manor of North Ockendon. By that time he was so poor that he could not afford to live there. He died in 1562 and is buried in St Dunstan's in the West, in Fleet Street, London.

North Ockendon's Church of St Mary Magdelene lies next to the site of the old Manor House. In its 'Poyntz Chapel', dedicated in the will of John Poyntz to 'Our Lady', the family are remembered. Thomas' son, Sir Gabriel Poyntz, twice Lord Lieutenant of Essex under Elizabeth I, restored the family fortunes. He commissioned the tomb effigies of himself and his wife and also a series of wall tablets commemorating his ancestors, including Thomas, which survive today. The church also boasts 'The Poyntz Singers' who are the present day church choir.

The Rise and Fall of Barking Abbey

All that remains of Barking Abbey today is the Curfew Tower or Fire Bell Gate (pictured opposite) which stands alongside the surviving St Margaret's Parish Church. The footprint of the Abbey has been preserved as an open space and stretches from old Barking Town Hall to the Abbey retail park on the banks of the River Roding. Since 1975 it has been a conservation area.

At its peak Barking Abbey was one of the biggest land owners in the south of England. It had extensive property holdings throughout Essex including large estates around Colchester, Harlow, Benfleet, Stansted and Brentwood. It was the third wealthiest nunnery in the country and enjoyed a huge annual net income.

Dorothy Barley was the Abbess in place when Henry VIII broke with Rome and dissolved England's monasteries and abbeys. During the dissolution some monasteries in England were seized by the King's, sometimes unscrupulous, agents. The occupants were summarily evicted, the Abbey buildings looted, demolished and all records burnt.

This was not the case at Barking since Abbess Barley was very well connected. She was a friend of Sir William Petre, the lawyer charged by Henry VIII with accepting the abbey on his behalf. She was godmother to Petre's daughter and his sister was one of her nuns. Petre received the deed of surrender of the abbey, its church and all its possessions from Dorothy Barley on 14th November 1539. In return she received a generous pension and was ensured that her nuns would be treated well.

Throughout its life Barking Abbey had enjoyed a close association with royalty. It was founded about the year A.D.666 by Erkenwald for his sister Ethelburga. Fifty or so years later The Venerable Bede wrote, in his *Ecclesiastical History of the English People,* of the Saxon King Sebbi authorizing the first construction of the Abbey. Two hundred years later Barking Abbey was destroyed by marauding Vikings. It was rebuilt by Edward the Elder, the son of Alfred the Great, after he had driven the Danes out of western Essex. William the Conqueror is known to have set up court at the Abbey in the New Year of 1067 while work began on the Tower of London. Over the next 300 years the Abbey was enlarged and extended to become one of the most impressive buildings in England.

A year after Dorothy Barley departed, demolition of the abbey buildings began in earnest and carried on for 18 months. The road to Creekmouth was repaired with abbey stone and much of the remainder was shipped down the Thames for building the King's new house at Dartford.

For the next 400 years part of the abbey site was used as a quarry and some of the land was farmed. However, with the industrial revolution and the steady expansion of London, new factories, warehouses, offices and, later, retail outlets and housing sprang up along the banks of the River Roding encroaching onto the former abbey lands. It is quite possible that if the conservation order had not been made in 1975 the remaining site would have disappeared too.

The Curfew Tower at Barking Abbey rebuilt in 1460

Waiting

As the sun rose on the morning of 19th May 1536, Anne Boleyn, the second wife of King Henry VIII, was secured in the Tower of London awaiting her fate. She had been found guilty of high treason and adultery. The usual punishment for such a crime was to be burnt alive but, as Queen, Anne could be burned or beheaded at the King's pleasure. The King had decided on beheading and the executioner of Calais had been chosen to perform the task. This executioner used a sword rather than an axe and was known for his surgical skill in removing heads with absolute precision. Executions were normally carried out at dawn, but for some inexplicable reason, there had been a delay.

Six miles east of the Tower, Henry VIII waited in the grounds of Pympe's Hall in Chingford, subdued but nevertheless a little agitated. He had not slept well the night before. Henry looked at the dovecote where pigeons were cooing occasionally and wondered if the birds knew of his Royal presence. Were they were aware of what was planned at the Tower of London? Everything seemed unnaturally still. Unusually, the dogs were quiet too. Two dozen hounds had been brought over the previous day from the Royal Kennels in West Ham. Instead of excitedly running around or straining on their leashes, they lay morosely on the ground. Henry slowly walked back and forth and looked out towards the capital that lay to the south-west. There was a good view. The Tower of London and the spire of St Paul's Cathedral rose prominently from the jumble of buildings that clustered around them. Fields, some ploughed

up, gently dropped down to the River Lea, although the water course was obscured by trees. A laden-down farm cart struggled up the incline. It stopped abruptly and two figures jumped off and scampered away in the direction of Hawk Hill. The King stared at them and wondered what mischief was afoot as the pair disappeared from view into the undergrowth.

Although dressed well, Henry felt a chill. This should have been a good day for sport. It was a clear day. The sun was out and not troubled by the white clouds scudding from west to east. Rain seemed unlikely.

For the first time in months Henry's leg ached. The cause was a wound he received in a jousting accident a year earlier. At first the flesh seemed to heal but there remained a wide scar that was soft and easily broken.

As Henry walked, his retinue of gentlemen and servants held back. Even the bodyguards kept their distance. When the Master of the Hounds made an inconsequential remark in earshot of Henry he received such a thunderous look that he thought his life was in mortal danger.

Just after midday Sir William Kingston, the Constable of the Tower of London, came to fetch Anne Boleyn. The Queen walked from her lodgings directly to the scaffold, accompanied by the four female attendants who had been billeted with her since her arrest.

On the scaffold Anne gave a short speech which included the words "I pray God save the King and send him long to reign over you". Anne removed her headdress and knelt before the executioner. Crowded around Tower Green were nearly 2000 spectators including the leading members of Henry VIII's court, Thomas Cromwell, the Chief Minister, Charles Brandon, the Duke of Suffolk, Henry Fitzroy, the Duke of Richmond and Thomas Audley, the Lord Chancellor. The executioner swung his sword and with one blow Anne's head was cleanly severed. Canons fired.

The boom of the gunfire echoed east and along the Lea valley where it was clearly heard at Pympe's Hall. Henry breathed a sigh of relief. The deed had been done. "It is time for sport" he cried. The hounds were roused and a great procession made its way into the forest for the hunt to begin. Within 24 hours of Anne Boleyn's execution, Jane Seymour and King Henry VIII were formally betrothed. Henry's third marriage took place ten days later.

Whether Henry's musings as he stood waiting on that fateful day were exactly as described above is of course unknown but the outcome is beyond dispute.

The modern name of Pimp Hall derives from the time when Reynold Pympe was Lord of the Manor in 1500. The original estate consisted of over 250 acres of farmland, fields, hedgerows and woods that encompassed much of present day Chingford. The site was acquired in 1934 by Chingford Urban District Council and in 1939 the hall, which was then a derelict farm house, was demolished. The local authority divided the area into allotments, a nursery and retained a small park. Much of the original Pimp Hall estate was developed as housing. Today Pimp Hall Park covers just six acres and incorporates a nature reserve, fronted by a recycling centre, and is located between the railway line to Chingford and Friday Hill. The dovecote that now stands in the park was in fact built after Henry's time and is a grade II listed building. Hawk Hill to the North West is now known as Pole Hill.

The Great Standing

In 1543 Henry VIII commissioned a 'Great Standing' to be built in Waltham Forest. Two hundred years later the forest became commonly known as Epping Forest.

The standing overlooked a hunting field, or clearing and was constructed on three floors to afford a grandstand view of hunting for chosen Royal guests and visiting dignitaries, in fact much as the 'corporate box' at major venues is used today. Guests could watch deer being hunted and maybe the occasional wild boar; they could even join in as there were gaps in the walls, designed to allow arrows to be shot through. How often King Henry VIII used the building is not known. He had always been a keen hunter yet when the standing was completed he was 51 years old, obese, lame and within four years was dead.

It was later, during Elizabeth's reign, that the structure became known as Queen Elizabeth's Hunting Lodge. Elizabeth was responsible for repairs and alterations carried out in 1589. There is also a legend that the Queen, to make a point, once rode her white horse up the steps of the grandstand. The lodge seems to have fallen out of use for hunting following the death of Elizabeth in 1603.

In 1895, the building was opened to the public as a museum

The Great Standing in 1543

of natural history and archaeology. Today it is a grade two listed building still overlooking the original hunting field. It is an outstanding example of the Tudor carpenter's craft. The three storey timber framed structure is unique and the only known standing to have more than two floors.

William Morris, the artist, who lived in nearby Walthamstow, discovered the lodge and was inspired by the romanticism of its medieval tapestries and ornate ceilings. Today the lodge, only a ten minute walk from Chingford station, retains many of its original features. It has many exhibits including the 'Willingale Axe', said to have been used by Thomas Willingale on 11th November 1860 to affirm his ancient lopping rights that were granted by Queen Elizabeth. (see the Lopper of Loughton page 110)

The Stratford 'Martyrs'

On 27th June 1556, eleven men and two women were burnt at the stake at Stratford Green. All were Protestants. In 1556 Stratford Green, where the University of East London now stands, was called Gallows Green. It was a large grassed area that stretched for just over half a mile from the present St. John's Church along what is today the Romford Road to Water Lane.

The burnings were carried out on the orders of the staunchly Roman Catholic Queen Mary, the daughter of Henry VIII and his first wife Catherine of Aragon. Known as 'Bloody Mary', on account of her persecution of Protestants, the Queen sanctioned nearly 300 executions during her reign.

Just over 300 years later, in 1878, a 65 foot high memorial commemorating the deaths was erected in St John's Churchyard. Designed by the architect J. T. Newman, it was financed by public subscription. Such is the hustle and bustle of today's traffic along Stratford Broadway past the church that many passers-by remain unaware of the memorial despite its imposing size.

The thirteen martyrs came mostly from Essex. Many of them were undoubtedly zealous anti-Roman Catholic Protestants but for some their only offence was in speaking out against what they saw as religious intolerance.

In memory of Henry Adlington, Thomas Bowyer, Lyon Cawch, John Derifall, Agnes George, William Hallywell, Edmond Hurst, Ralph Jackson, Lawrence Parnam, Elizabeth Pepper, John Routh, George Searle and Henry Wye.

All had been questioned and convicted by Bishop Edmund Bonner, Queen Mary's chief enforcer. At Stratford the martyrs were divided into two groups. The men were tied up, but the women were allowed to walk freely in the flames.

One women was pregnant. They all died bravely, embracing the stake. Many of the streets in the locality are named after the martyrs.

Guess who's coming to Lunch?

Her Majesty Queen Elizabeth I departed from Greenwich early on the morning of Friday 11th July 1578 to begin an eleven week progress - essentially a state tour of the realm. Leaving Greenwich by barge, the Queen crossed the Thames to continue up the River Lea to Stratford. Here she disembarked to visit the house of the Mewtas family in West Ham, the centrepiece of the former Stratford Langthorne Abbey (see page 32). The Abbey was 'acquired' by Sir Peter Mewtas, one of Henry VIII's loyal servants, at the dissolution.

Queen Elizabeth's arrival was planned like clockwork. The Mewtas family were entertaining the Queen to lunch. This in itself was no small affair. The Queen's immediate retinue consisted of nearly 60 persons including court officials, close bodyguards and ladies in waiting. Then there were the Yeoman of the Guard numbering some 130. Also, on leaving the royal barge, the Queen was joined by the Sheriff of Essex and local dignitaries from West Ham, East Ham, Plaistow and Stratford.

The host of the dinner was Hercules Mewtas the son of Sir Peter. It was not unusual for the hosts of Royal hospitality to bear all the costs incurred. However, on this occasion, as the stay was short and the timetable tight, most of the food and drink was provided by the Royal Household. The Queen's Gentleman usher Symon Bowyer had arrived earlier to organise the dining area and another official, Charles Smyth, had already prepared the 'Office of the Robes', so that the Queen could dress for the meal, and afterwards change back into to her travelling clothes if she so wished.

On these occasions hosts felt obliged, for the sake of their reputations, to make substantial financial contributions to the event as well as putting up with the considerable upheaval such a visit would cause to their homes. However, the Mewtas family were rich and the honour of the Queen choosing their household for a lunch stop would have raised the family status immeasurably.

It is not recorded what was on the menu but within two hours the Queen and all her retinue were on their way to the Royal Palace at Havering some ten miles to the north-east. Following the Queen's departure, it took two days for Symon Bowyer to remove all the special flags, banners, furnishings, dining ware and kitchen equipment the Royal household had brought to West Ham. It even took a whole day for Charles Smyth to pack up and remove the 'Office of the Robes'.

Hercules Mewtas died shortly after the Queen's visit. He was buried in West Ham Church where it was recorded that 'here his mother, brother and kindred lie'. The Mewtas mansion stood close to the church but it was demolished in the seventeenth century.

So Was Shakespeare an Essex Boy?

Less than 800 yards from the River Lea at the western end of Lea Bridge Road, at its northwest junction with Kenninghall Road and Upper Clapton Road, stands the 'BSiX', Brooke House Sixth Form College. Previously it was Brook House Comprehensive School which opened in 1960. It was one of the first comprehensive schools in the country, although it only catered for boys. Amongst its alumni are the television personality and business man Lord Sugar, the former Queens Park Rangers and England footballer Rodney Marsh and the current Editor of the Essex Hundred series of books Andrew Summers.

Prior to the school being built, the original Brooke House was one of Hackney's largest houses. The first construction dates back to 1476 when it was owned by the Dean of St Paul's. Over the years the house changed hands many times. In 1535 it was owned by Henry VIII and became a Royal residence. The house was enormous with an inner court yard, a huge brick built hall, a gate house and a chapel. Within the grounds were stables and several outbuildings. In July 1536, the house witnessed the reconciliation of Henry to his eldest daughter Mary, when she agreed to take the Oath of Supremacy recognizing the King as head of the Church of England. Following the King's death in 1547, the house and estates was given as a reward for loyal service to Sir William Herbert, one of the gentlemen of the Privy Chamber.

Herbert was quick to cash in on his reward and promptly sold the estate. Much later, in 1597, by which time the house had been renamed King's Place, the property was sold to Elizabeth Trentham, Countess of Oxford and a maid of honour to Queen Elizabeth. The Countess was the wife of Edward de Vere, the 17th Earl of Oxford.

Edward de Vere had largely retired from court life after his move to King's Place. There he probably devoted himself to his literary and theatrical activities. During this period his own company of players, the Earl of Oxford's Men, were still active and he also owned the lease of a small playhouse at the Boar's Head Inn at Aldgate.

De Vere died in 1604 and was buried at St Augustine's Church, Hackney, now lying within the grounds of St John's Church just off the current Lower Clapton Road.

Nineteen years after Edward de Vere's death, Shakespeare's First Folio was registered at the London Stationer's Company. It was priced at £1.00 and 750 copies were printed. Over 100 of the first editions survive today. The publication of 34 plays in this compendium attributed to Shakespeare unleashed a mystery that still has not been resolved.

St Augustine's Church Hackney. Was the True Bard buried here?

William Shakespeare came from Stratford-upon-Avon. Today this bald statement, largely unquestioned, is supported by a huge industry of theatre, tourism and Shakespeare memorabilia based there. To suggest that the revered author of 154 sonnets, 34 plays and two epic poems, in fact came from Essex would seem silly. During Shakespeare's lifetime, actors, fellow writers, such as Ben Johnson, and theatre owners, like John Heminge and Henry Condell, acknowledged Shakespeare's talents. Yet for more than 300 years sizeable groups of people have been casting doubt on Shakespeare as the author and posing alternative names as the TRUE BARD.

Candidates nominated at various times as the true author of Shakespeare's works have included, among others, the philosopher and lawyer Sir Francis Bacon, the playwright Christopher Marlow, the Earl of Derby, William Stanley, the Earl of Rutland, Roger Manners and Sir Henry Neville.

In 1920 an English School master, J. Thomas Looney, painstakingly researched the question and published *Shakespeare Identified*. In this book he suggested that Edward de Vere, the 17th Earl of Oxford, whose family seat was at Hedingham Castle, Essex, was the most likely creator of much of the work attributed to William Shakespeare. This claim has been made many times over the years since de Vere is known to have been a poet of some merit. He was also well educated, widely travelled and spoke several languages. He had played host to Queen Elizabeth at Castle Hedingham and was well known at court.

Shakespeare, on the other hand, was from humble stock and very few hard facts of his life were recorded. He was baptised in Stratford-upon-Avon on April 26, 1564 and was presumed to have been born three days earlier.

He may have attended Stratford Grammar school; however no records survive to show this. He married Anne Hathaway in 1582, or was it Anna Whately? There are entries in the Episcopal Register at Worcester for licences granted for both. Was it a clerical error or was it a late change to a shotgun wedding, since it is known that Hathaway was pregnant when they married?

Sometime after 1590, a William Shakespeare performed with the Lord Chamberlain's Men and other theatre troupes in London, possibly in front of Queen Elizabeth I. In 1597, William Shakspeare (there are many different spellings of his name) bought a large house in Stratford-on-Avon, where, in 1616, he died aged 52. He left no manuscripts, drafts or even letters and the only evidence of his handwriting are six different signatures, including the one on his will. Much of the rest of his life is guesswork and speculation. He seems never to have left England and, apart from London to Stratford-on-Avon, travelled very little. Claimants of de Vere as the true author, such as 'The Shakespeare Oxford Society', cite the lack of evidence supporting Shakespeare. They also ask how he could have known the details of court procedures and intrigues for the historical plays. Where did his knowledge of Italy, Denmark and Scotland, knowledge crucial to some of his plots, come from?

So who did write the Shakespeare plays we all know today? It is known that Edward de Vere was a writer and there are some parallels in his life with storylines

Wax model of Edward de Vere at Hedingham Castle

in Shakespeare's plays, particularly Romeo and Juliet. Edward de Vere had travelled all over England and Europe, particularly Italy. He had consorted with foreign ambassadors and the like. As a boy he had been a royal ward of Richard Cecil (Lord Burley), chief advisor to Queen Elizabeth I. De Vere's brother-in-law was well acquainted with Denmark so he would have known the details of the Danish court that were required to write Hamlet, Prince of Denmark.

So the question is, if de Vere indeed wrote the works attributed to Shakespeare, why did he publish them under a pseudonym?

One answer may be that in Elizabethan times it was not done for aristocrats to write plays. It was considered beneath them - if you were rich you employed people to do that.

More importantly, publicly reinterpreting history was highly dangerous if the content upset the Queen or her confidants. Elizabeth I had also recognized the power of the theatre for propaganda purposes which she used to consolidate her position and champion England.

In 1586 she awarded de Vere an annuity of £1,000; a huge sum of money for the day. Was this to allow de Vere to withdraw from court life to his London family home at Kings Place and spend his time writing, producing the works that bear the name William Shakespeare?

It seems many people think so, and in their eyes the Essex claim that Hedingham, in the middle of Essex, or Kings Place (Brooke House) on the fringe of Metropolitan Essex was where many of 'Shakespeare's plays were created. Whilst this case is no means proven it is at least as plausible as any of the many other theories put forward.

In 1621 Kings Place became known as Brooke House when Baron Brooke of the Greville family, of Beauchamps Court, inherited it. Whether the Greville Family ever discovered any of the original 'Shakespeare' manuscripts in their new house is open to speculation. However, it is believed that Elizabeth Trentham, de Vere's wife, was hostile to Edward's writings. She considered it demeaning so she could have quite possibly destroyed all the manuscripts on his death.

Brooke House was later used as a private mental asylum which continued until 1940. In October 1940 the house was severely damaged by bombing. Hackney Borough Council acquired it in 1944 and in 1954 the house was demolished. A careful archaeological investigation was undertaken which revealed the historical significance of the house.

The de Vere/ Shakespeare mystery was given a boost by the release of the Hollywood film *Anonymous* in October 2011. It was directed by Roland Emmerich, and starred Rhys Ifans, Vanessa Redgrave and Joely Richardson. The prologue and epilogue were provided by the notable Shakespearean actor Derek Jacobi. *Anonymous* pulled no punches in asserting that de Vere was the author of much of the work of Shakespeare – but that's Hollywood!

Castle Hedingham. Edward de Vere's birth place and Ancestral Home

DATE	EVENT
1603	Death of Queen Elizabeth I
1604	William Shakespeare writes Othello
1618	Sir Walter Raleigh is executed
1620	Pilgrim Fathers leave Plymouth for the 'New World'
1621	James I dies, Charles I is crowned King
1635	The speed of the Hackney carriage is set in London at 3mph
1642	Beginning of English Civil War
1644	Abel Tasman maps north coast of Australia (New Holland)
1649	Charles I found guilty of treason by Parliament and executed
1653	Oliver Cromwell becomes Lord Protector
1659	Richard Cromwell resigns
1660	Parliament restores monarchy; Charles II returns from exile
1666	Great fire of London
1672	Battle of Southwold Bay: 3rd Anglo-Dutch Naval War
1680	Penny Post is introduced in London
1682	Elias Ashmole founds Britain's first museum; the Ashmolean, Oxford
1685	Judge Jeffreys (The Hanging Judge) begins the 'Bloody Assizes'
1694	Bank of England is founded by Scotsman William Paterson
1698	London Stock Exchange is founded
1702	First English newspaper 'The Daily Courant' is published
1705	Construction of Blenheim Palace begins
1715	Jacobite revolt put down
1721	Robert Walpole becomes the first prime minister of Britain
1725	Black Watch founded in Scotland
1739	The 'War of Jenkins Ear' with Spain begins
1769	James Watt patents his steam engine
1770	Birth of Poet William Wordsworth
1755	Samuel Johnson publishes 'Dictionary of the English Language'
1775	American Revolution begins
1776	The American Declaration of Independence
1781	First Building Society founded in Birmingham.
1784	Benjamin Franklin invents bifocal spectacles
1793	Louis XVI of France executed
1797	Nore and Spithead Royal Naval mutinies
1798	Irish Rebellion defeated at Vinegar Hill

Remember, Remember the Fifth of November

In 1604 King James I authorized the First Westminster Company, under the directorship of Lancelot Andrewes, to begin a new translation of the Bible into English. It was finished in 1611; just 85 years after Tyndale's translation appeared (see page 44). The King James' Bible quickly became, and remains the standard for English speaking Protestants and has had a profound influence on English literature.

Lancelot Andrewes was born in 1555 in All Hallows, Barking. Although All Hallows was near the Tower it was part of Barking Abbey. The Abbey estate had been in the custody of the Petre family since Henry VIII's dissolution of the monasteries fifteen years earlier. Much of the Abbey and its outbuildings were still in the process of being torn down. Later Andrewes lived at Chichester Hall (now the Chichester Hotel) in the village of Rawreth in Essex. At the age of sixteen he entered Pembroke Hall, Cambridge. After graduating, with a master's degree, his reputation as a scholar grew rapidly.

Later he became Master of Pembroke College. After taking holy orders in 1580, he went on to serve as a chaplain to Queen Elizabeth I. In 1601 he was appointed Dean of Westminster where he was influential in the development of Westminster School.

Andrewes served at the coronation of James I who admired his intellectual capabilities. As one of the foremost scholars of the day it is no surprise that he was the first choice to lead the King James Bible project. His rise in status continued and in 1605 he was consecrated as Bishop of Chichester and subsequently made Bishop of Ely and of Winchester.

As well as the King James Bible, Andrewes may have another popular claim to fame. In 1605 the 'Gunpowder Plot' of Guy Fawkes and his accomplices, to blow up the Houses of Parliament and assassinate King James, was foiled. On the anniversary of this event, the 5th of November 1606, Andrewes was asked to prepare a sermon celebrating the King's, and Parliament's delivery. The sermon, now known as *'The Gunpowder Plot Sermon'*, became an annual event. In it Andrewes called for a lasting celebration of the King's deliverance. The sermon was the inspiration for, and foundation of, the celebrations of Guy Fawkes Day on November 5th which have continued to this day. It may even have inspired the rhyme still heard today:

Remember, remember the fifth of November
Gunpowder treason and plot
I see no reason why gunpowder, treason
Should ever be forgot.

The Plotters of Barking?

Following the receipt of an anonymous letter addressed to William Parker, Lord Monteagle, a search was made of the basement of the House of Lords on the evening of 4th November 1605. During the search 36 barrels of gun powder were discovered; enough to destroy the House completely, killing all those within. Hiding in the basement, desperately looking to make his escape, was one Guy Fawkes who was immediately arrested.

'The Gunpowder Plot' was a failed assassination attempt against King James I by a group of English Catholics led by Robert Catesby. The plan was to blow up the House of Lords the following day during the State Opening of Parliament on 5th November. The plot might well have succeeded since Monteagle had received the letter two weeks earlier warning, or at least suggesting, that he should find an excuse not to attend the State opening. Although the letter was immediately handed over to parliamentary authorities no searches were carried out until the night before the opening.

Ten miles to the east of the Houses of Parliament in Barking, just north of the present A13, close to the Lodge Avenue flyover, lies Eastbury Manor House. It was there, legend has it, that the Gunpowder Plot was supposedly hatched. At the time Eastbury was owned by Anne Steward, widow of Clement Sisley the original builder. The house was rented to Lewis Tresham, and his wife and his Spanish catholic mother-in-law lived there. Lewis was the brother of Francis Tresham and cousin of Robert Catesby the plotters' leader. He was also the brother-in-law of Lord Monteagle, the man who had received the tip off.

Further evidence linking the Gunpowder conspiracy to Barking is that on 9th November 1605, just days after Guy Fawkes was arrested, a Barking fisherman named Richard Franklin was questioned by magistrate Sir Nicholas Coote at nearby Valence House in Dagenham.

Franklin alleged that his master, Henry Parish, had hired a boat to Guy Fawkes (who was using the alias Johnson) in which he and other plotters had travelled in disguise from Barking back and forth along the River Thames to France. Franklin also claimed that Guy Fawkes had made arrangements for the boat to be made ready for his escape once the deed had been done.

There seems to be some truth in the questioning of the Barking fisherman but how much of the actual Gunpowder plotting was done at Eastbury Manor House is open to speculation.

The legend was boosted just over 100 years later by the author Daniel Defoe. He wrote in his 1727 book *A Tour Throughout the Whole Island of Great Britain:-*

"A little beyond the town, on the road to Dagenham, stood a great house, antient, and now almost fallen down, where tradition says the Gunpowder Treason Plot was at first contriv'd, and that all the first consultations about it were held there."

Seventy years later the story persisted when another author Daniel Lysons, wrote in his book *'Environs of London'*:-

"There is a tradition relating to this house, either, as some say, that the conspirators who concerted the Gunpowder Plot held their meetings there, or as others, that it was the residence of Lord Monteagle, when he received the letter which led to the discovery."

Eastbury Manor House was built around 1573 during the reign of Elizabeth I. It was a farm in 1913 and at the outbreak of World War One the House was requisitioned by the Army. For a time it was used as a factory for making observation balloons. After the war the House was purchased by the National Trust who leased it to Barking council. During World War Two it was a post for Air Raid Precaution (ARP) wardens and later it was home to a day nursery. The House was given Grade 1 listed status in 1954. With the help of the Heritage Lottery Fund, it has undergone extensive renovation and today the house is open to the public.

As to the gunpowder plotting actually taking place in Barking, the mystery remains. What is certain though is that the 13 conspirators were apprehended and either killed during their arrest or hung, drawn and quartered after trial and conviction.

Eastbury House. Was the Gunpowder Plot hatched here?

61

Into Essex

On April 3rd 1722, a 62 year old Daniel Defoe began his epic journey around Britain. He travelled eastwards from the City of London along the Mile End Road, the Bow Road and then crossed Bow Bridge, which he stated was where the county of Essex began. Defoe was described by many 'as the father of British journalism' and possibly 'travelwriting' too. He recorded his travels in a three volume book, *Tour Through the Whole Island of Great Britain,* published between 1724 and 1727. It was innovative partly because the author had actually visited the places he described.

Bow Bridge spanned the River Lea between Bow Church and Stratford, dividing Essex and Middlesex. The first bridge at Bow was built of stone around 1110 and was allegedly constructed at the behest of Queen Matilda (or Maud), the wife of Henry I. It was said to have been the first arched stone bridge in southern England. A replacement bridge was built in 1838 at the cost of £11,000.

Bow Bridge around 1832

After several repairs and rebuilds Bow Bridge, by then carrying the A11, was replaced in 1967 by a four lane flyover that crosses both the River Lea and the Blackwall Tunnel Northern Approach Road.

Daniel Defoe travelled on into *Metropolitan Essex.* He commented on the plotting at Eastbury Manor House (see page 60). Later Defoe made note of Dagenham's 'famous breach that had caused 5000 acres of land to be flooded for near ten years' (see page 66).

Defoe is best remembered for penning *Robinson Crusoe*. He was 59 when the book was released and it was a literary sensation. Less well known perhaps is his political and business career, much of which is surrounded by mystery and intrigue.

Daniel Foe was born in 1660, the son of a Stoke Newington butcher. He was later to change his name to the grander sounding Defoe. The years surrounding Daniel's birth and formative years were turbulent. After the death of Oliver Cromwell, Charles II had been restored to the throne. Religious intolerance stalked the land and plots to overthrow the monarchy were rife. A succession of Anglo – Dutch Wars broke out and London was hit by the great plague followed by the great fire.

From an early age Daniel Defoe had an entrepreneurial flair combined with an ability to borrow money to fund his schemes. In 1678, still under the age of 20, he speculatively bought a long lease on a parcel of land in Tilbury. In London he diversified, establishing a hosiery business and involving himself in shipping and importing.

Despite Defoe's flair, his business sense left much to be desired. His enterprises suffered ill fortune, or simple mismanagement, and numerous creditors pursued him. His personal life was equally complicated and costly as he maintained houses for three 'wives' and was responsible for at least nine children. In October 1692, he was jailed for bankruptcy with debts of £17,000. However Defoe managed to bounce back. On release from prison he took up a prestigious post with the commissioners of the glass duty and also became a trustee of the royal lottery - both government jobs. On his land at Tilbury he set up a brick factory in Chadwell St Mary with contracts to supply tiles for a number of prestigious projects.

Daniel Defoe lived in grand style. He had a large house close to Tilbury Fort plus a carriage, footmen and a pleasure boat, but his writing continually distracted him from concentrating on his business. In 1703 he was arrested and pilloried for writing a satirical pamphlet that upset Queen Anne. This and his lack of attention to business resulted in his brick factory becoming bankrupt.

With the act of Union between England and Scotland looming, Defoe was given a new challenge by a highly placed but secretive Government official - that of secretive intelligence gathering. It has been suggested this was one of the reasons why the *Tour Through the Whole Island of Great Britain* was undertaken.

Nevertheless, although Daniel Defoe was credited with publishing over 560 books and pamphlets, at the age of 71 he died alone, in debt and on the run from his creditors.

Stand and Deliver

"Stand and Deliver," these words of dread
Dick Turpin is reputed to have said.

Somehow a myth grew up that has led to Dick Turpin being honoured in the names of dozens of pubs and eateries up and down the country. Further plaudits came through film, television, books and comics depicting him as a latter day Robin Hood who took from the rich and gave to the poor. The Dick Turpin character has also been embraced by some 'Heritage' sites where factual credence to the entirely fictional horse 'Black Bess' is given. Even more bizarrely he is acknowledged in dozens of journals and websites connected with the meat and sausage trade!

However the real Dick Turpin, born in Hempstead, north Essex in 1705, was totally devoid of glamour. He was hanged as a common criminal at Knavesmire, York at the age of 34.

Dick Turpin began employment as an apprentice butcher (hence the meat trade connection above) after which, it is said, he set up as a butcher in Thaxted and later at Buckhurst Hill. Accused of involvement with poachers and stolen deer from nearby Waltham Forest, Turpin's career as a butcher was short lived. So he turned to a life of crime, graduating from deer and cattle rustling to smuggling, burglary, highway robbery and eventually murder.

Around 1732, Turpin teamed up with Samuel Gregory in what was to become known as the Gregory, or Essex, Gang. Over a two year period a series of horrific robberies were committed in Essex, Kent and London. The gang had no compunction about torturing or beating their victims or violating any women found on the premises whilst the robbery was in progress. They seem to have been based in East London, alternately staying in cheap lodging houses where few questions were asked or hiding out in Epping Forest

On 19th December 1734, the Essex gang struck in Barking. Turpin and five other men raided the home of Ambrose Skinner, a 73-year-old farmer. Skinner reported that six masked armed men broke into his house and threatened to kill him if he resisted. Understandably the farmer thought resistance was useless. A three and half hour ordeal followed where the gang dragged the hapless Mr Skinner from room to room ransacking each one in turn. They eventually left with an estimated £300.

A year later another brutal attack was reported in *Read's Weekly Journal* of 8th February 1735. The home of an elderly widow in Loughton was attacked.

This time the gang threatened to lay her over the fire unless she confessed to where her valuables were kept. During the robbery the thieves drank the place dry and even loitered to cook themselves a meal.

Large rewards were offered for the capture of the gang and one by one the outlaws were apprehended. Turpin, though, managed to remain at large but with a considerable price on his head. He went to ground, surfacing again in 1737 to team up with another villain known as Matthew (or Tom) King. However, the net was closing in and King was cornered in Whitechapel. Turpin rode to the rescue but all he achieved was to shoot his accomplice in the melee. On his death bed Tom King confessed all.

Meanwhile Dick Turpin fled north and assumed the name Palmer, his mother's maiden name. In spite of this his luck ran out. 'John Palmer' was arrested on an unrelated matter and put in York jail. Letters he penned to relatives identified the prisoner in the cell as the real Dick Turpin.

Convicted on two indictments, Dick Turpin was sentenced to death. On 7th April, 1739, he was put on an open cart and taken through the streets of York watched by gawping crowds. He met his end on the scaffold at York racecourse at Knavesmire

Nearly 100 years later a romanticised myth of Turpin was created in the novel *Rookwood* by Harrison Ainsworth. Turpin's horse 'Black Bess' was a creation based on Daniel Defoe's account of real life criminal 'William 'Swift Nick' Nevison' who, after committing a robbery rode non-stop from London to York to try and establish an alibi.

In 2009 York Castle Museum, in conjunction with North Yorkshire Police, created a 'WANTED' E-Fit picture of the man behind the mask using modern technology. Newspaper reports of the time were used as a source for creating the image. Turpin was described as: "5ft 9ins high, of a brown complexion, very much marked with the small pox, his cheek bones broad, his face slimmer towards the bottom, his visage short, pretty upright, and broad about the shoulders". The result was an unflattering pox-ridden face unlike the romantic, handsome, dashing figure frequently portrayed. Dr Katherine Prior, a researcher at the museum, said: "The results are not pretty".

The new image forms part of York Castle Museum's new interpretation of Turpin's cell and other parts of its 18th century jail.

WANTED

Richard Turpin
E-Fit by North Yorkshire Police

Breached

The course of the River Thames runs westwards in a series of curves between Essex and Kent towards London from the North Sea. It is tidal all the way. At Erith the river bends sharply north towards Essex where it narrows at Rainham, then Dagenham. As a result, the water pressure increases with the incoming tide and it scours the north (Essex) bank of the river. Over the years the water has regularly spilt over the river bank to flood the low lying area beyond.

Dagenham, Rainham and Barking have suffered several major floods over the years. They began to be recorded in detail by the scribes at Barking Abbey. Records describe several major inundations not only in the Abbey grounds itself but further downstream at Dagenham, which until the dissolution was mainly owned by the monastery.

Since Norman times large embankments had been built up along the river to protect the land behind from flooding. However, upkeep of the flood barriers was time-consuming and labour intensive. Following the third flood in a decade in the 1370s, much of the marshland was abandoned for nearly 200 years. In 1621 the whole of Dagenham and Hornchurch was swamped This resulted in the famous Dutch engineer, Cornelius Vermuyden, being invited to carry out repairs. His barrier lasted for 80 years. However, the overall responsibility for protecting Dagenham from flooding lay with the tenants who farmed the land. Landlords were very reluctant to assist and as a result the upkeep of the river defenses was haphazard. In the event of a flood many tenants would simply be put out of business.

In 1707 an incoming tidal surge destroyed the sluices fitted by Vermuyden and covered an area of land greater than that occupied by the Ford Motor Company today. It remained underwater for the best part of fifteen years. Changes in the tidal flow due to this new breach caused the build up of a huge mud bank that stretched nearly half way across the Thames, which in turn threatened to block the river to London for shipping access. For several years little or nothing was done. Each tide widened it, making the prospect of repair increasingly difficult and more costly.

Two attempts to reclaim the flooded land were made by the landowners. Both involved the dumping huge quantities of loose chalk and stones into the breach but both attempts were unsuccessful. The Commissioners of Sewers then contracted George Jackson and later John Ward to repair the breach. The work was completed in 1713 however the repairs were swept away in another storm four months later in February 1714.

Meanwhile the mud bank was becoming an increasingly dangerous obstacle to ships. In the summer of 1714, seven years after the original damage, an Act of Parliament was passed to make repairs at public expense. The contract went out to tender.

Two tenders were received, one from William Boswell for £16,300 and another from Captain John Perry for £25,000. Although Boswell's tender was accepted his works only made the breach wider. So in November 1715, the trustees exercised their right to cancel his contract without payment and Boswell's work was abandoned.

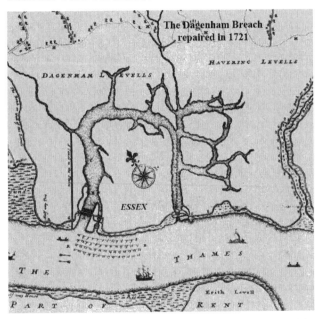

In June 1716, the trustees signed a new tighter contract with Captain Perry. Work began immediately and six years, and several setbacks, later Perry reported that he had completed all his work on the breach and adjoining sea walls and was in the process of clearing away the mud bank. Although the original quote had been £25,000, over the years the cost of the works had risen to £40,000.

John Perry chronicled his enterprise in great detail. He was especially critical of his predecessor's crude attempts to fill the breach. William Boswell, in defence, attributed his failure to the threats of sabotage, intimidation and bribery on the part of John Ward one of the original contractors. After a series of legal actions Boswell recovered £1,200 from Captain Perry for materials.

With the sea wall repaired, a large lake was left behind which became known as The Dagenham Breach. It soon became a popular fishing destination. In more recent times with industrial development the lake has been mostly filled in by the Ford Motor Company, although a remnant of the Breach remains beside one of the company's wind turbines.

The Fairlop Oak

Two hundred years ago Hainault forest covered much of present day Ilford, Barkingside and Chigwell. It was also the home of the original Fairlop Oak. One of the largest trees ever seen in Britain, it is thought to have been given that name by Queen Anne on a visit in 1704. It grew on a spot occupied by the present day boathouse at Fairlop Water. This enormous oak tree stood alone in a vast clearing and was the setting for the Fairlop Fair, which began in earnest in 1725. It became an annual event, taking place during the first week in July and ran almost continuously until 1900. Its founder was the jovially eccentric Daniel Day.

Daniel Day

Daniel Day had earned his fortune in marine engineering. He lived by the river Thames at Wapping. He also owned some cottages near Fairlop and made it his business to collect the rents there annually, usually on the first Friday in July. He decided to make this day a special occasion for his friends, his employees and his tenants. Bacon and beans were ordered from a local hostelry and a grand 'beanfeast' was held under the great canopy of the Fairlop Oak.

Within a few years others joined in and gradually the gathering turned into a gigantic fair. There would be puppeteers, circus acrobats and exotic animals on hand to provide entertainment. A market sprang up too, selling sweets, toys and nick-knacks. To begin with the fair was described "as most respected and well regulated". In 1736 however the first prosecutions were recorded of stallholders for indulging in gaming and illegal liquor sales.

Day would always attend the fair but was nervous of travelling by road as he had been involved in a serious accident. Accordingly he got his workers to put wheels on a masted boat which was decked out with rigging, flags and bunting. He would travel in style by river as far as possible and then by road for the beanfeast. On land the boat, nicknamed the *Fairlop Frigate*, was hauled by a team of six horses and preceded by a marching band.

By the 1750s, 100,000 people came to the fair from all over London. The large unregulated crowds began to cause all sorts of problems caused by numerous pickpockets, conmen and the usual opportunist thieves.

In 1765 the local constabulary reported that, "a great number of people meet in riotous and tumultuous manner selling ale and spirituous liquors and keeping tippling booths and gaming tables to the great encouragement of vice and immorality".

Daniel Day died in 1767 aged 84 and was buried in a coffin fashioned from a branch that had fallen from the Fairlop Oak. He was buried in St. Margaret's Church yard, Barking. He had originally asked to be buried under the Fairlop Oak but his request was denied.

Unfortunately the Fairlop Oak suffered numerous acts of vandalism and gradually the tree died. In 1820 it was blown down by a gale and the Fairlop Oak was no more. The fair however continued to grow, vying with the Derby on Epsom Downs as a semi-official holiday.

In 1839 over 200,000 attended the fair. It was one of the biggest carnivals in London and the roads to the area were jammed. However, not everyone approved. The Lord's Day Observance society frowned upon the proceedings as did the Religious Tract Society, a Christian book publisher, who counted 108 drinking booths and 72 gaming tables.

Over the years several Fairlop Frigates were built. One built in 1812 was discovered

The New Fairlop Oak at Fulwell Cross

in a Romford back garden in 1951; the hull was rotten, the wheels missing and the rigging and mast all gone. Although the fair ended in 1900, it was brought to life again in July 1989, when the Redbridge Community play used 40 performers to re-enact the spectacle at Fairlop Hall in Barkingside.

Today at Fullwell Cross, in the London Borough of Redbridge, there is a public house named New Fairlop Oak. In the same year as the frigate was found in Romford another oak tree was planted in the centre of the large roundabout facing the pub which is still there today.

Gunpowder's Lot

In 1787 the Essex Gunpowder Mills at Waltham Abbey, which straddled the River Lea on the County's border with Hertfordshire, were acquired by the Crown from John Walton for £10,000. Thus the Royal Gunpowder Mills came into being. In effect the factory was nationalised. Prior to that date all gunpowder was manufactured by private companies. The army and the navy were of the opinion that much of the gunpowder available was substandard. Shortages were frequent too as stocks had run out when they were most needed during the Dutch wars and the American Revolutionary conflict.

It is surprising to learn that many of the private gunpowder makers had no particular loyalty to the nation as their main interest was turning in a profit. Following the disaster of the American War and with conflict again looming with the French, the British Government decided to take control of most of the private factories.

Following the acquisition, the mills were turned into 'centres of excellence'. This was achieved under the watchful eye of Sir William Congreve, the Deputy Comptroller of the Royal Laboratory at Woolwich Arsenal. New standards were set and rigorous quality control enforced. Manufacturing processes were upgraded to ensure continuous supply and substantial resources were allocated to research and development.

The benchmarks of quality and cost established by the Royal Gunpowder Mills were then imposed on the few remaining gunpowder makers in the private sector.

For over 200 years the mills remained under Government control with many innovations such as gun cotton, cordite, and the plastic explosive RDX being perfected there. Although the mills' main purpose was to provide for the military it was also a catalyst in the advancement of explosives for civil use. With the industrial revolution in full swing, gunpowder related products were in great demand for tunneling, mining and quarrying.

During the First World War over 6,000 people worked in the Waltham Abbey factories. However, during World War II much of the production was dispersed due to the fear of enemy bombing. After the war, work at Waltham Abbey resumed but concentrated on research such as rocket fuels and cartridges for firing jet aircraft ejector seats. Despite the innovative research the mills were gradually run down.

The Waltham Abbey Mills turned full circle in 1991 when what remained of research, development and manufacture was privatised and the gunpowder mills closed. Much of the land that had been used for gunpowder making was sold off and developed for housing.

The Mills are now an industrial heritage attraction open weekends and bank holidays throughout the spring and summer months.

We should not leave the Gunpowder Mills without paying tribute to the many terms commonly used today that have their origins rooted in the history of cannons, gunpowder, and gunpowder making.

SON of A GUN, is one of many phrases from old naval days. It was a term that indicated a boy was conceived as a result of a coupling on the gundeck of a warship in the days when women could accompany their men to sea.

A LOOSE CANNON, is used to describe someone out of control, as when the pitch of the sea could cause a gun to roll erratically. In such circumstances a master gunner would call for *A LOAD OF JUNK* to be found such as old rope or rubbish to stuff the barrel and stop the cannon ball falling into the sea.

Primed and ready for action

A *FLASH IN THE PAN* which nowadays might describe failure after a showy start, derives from the small amount of powder in the ignition pan burning with a flash but failing to ignite the main charge; it could be fatal in battle. If one is *OVER A BARREL*, it would mean a hopeless situation with no way out. In the navy it would mean being flogged while tied to the barrel of a gun. The shout of *HANG FIRE,* the order to delay lighting the charge to fire the cannon, has come to mean wait! Let's think it through. Where *STICK TO YOUR GUNS* meant maintain your position under fire, we now mean make a decision and don't change your mind. And to be *HOISTED BY ONE'S OWN PETARD* was the end, blown sky high by the petard; a hand held bomb - a phrase now used to denote a plan that backfires on the perpetrator.

Three subjects are linked to Sir Eliab Harvey of Rolls Park, Chigwell.

1. The Essex Sea Fencibles - probably the least known unit in the history of Britain's defences,

2. *HMS Temeraire* - a ship of war launched in 1798 and built from oak cut in Hainault Forest, made famous by J.M.W. Turner's painting *The Fighting Temeraire* which hangs in the National Gallery in London.

3. The Battle of Trafalgar 1805 - England's most celebrated naval victory.

As the 18th century closed Britain was again embroiled in war with France. The threat of a seaborne invasion was very real which led to the creation of a coastal defence force known as the Sea Fencibles. The entire English coast facing the European mainland was covered by the scheme, as was Lands End and the whole shoreline up as far as Bristol. The Sea Fencibles were a nautical Home Guard manned by part-time volunteers. Essex Sea Fencibles' zone covered the Essex side of the River Thames in the south of the county and ran around the Essex shoreline to Harwich.

The force comprised about 1500 men divided into small units, each serving their own community. Most of the volunteers lived in shacks on the coast and eked out a living from fishing and bait digging. One of the great advantages of joining the Sea Fencibles was that it exempted its members from being impressed into the navy. This was a boon for any man living near the sea. The fear of the navy's strong armed press gangs turning up unannounced was very real.

Eliab Harvey's background could not have been more different from that of the average Sea Fencible. He was born into a privileged family at the huge Rolls Park estate that once dominated much of Chigwell. Harvey was educated at Westminster and Harrow. He enrolled in the navy whilst still a pupil, though he never went to sea whilst at school. When his elder brother William died suddenly, Eliab, just 21, inherited the estate plus a vast fortune.

The next year Eliab Harvey became MP for Maldon. Parliamentary duties didn't interrupt his naval career and after four years he resigned the seat. By the age of 35 he was in command of the *Valiant*, a 74-gun ship of the line. He saw action in the West Indies but unfortunately became ill after contracting dengue fever in Jamaica which forced him to return home in late 1798.

Although still poorly, Harvey had sufficiently recovered to beg the Admiralty to find him something to do. As going back to sea was out of the question, their ingenious solution was to offer him a part-time job as Captain of the Essex Sea Fencibles.

For Harvey this arrangement was ideal. He could divide his time between recuperating at home in Chigwell and, when required on field duties, could stay in one of many comfortable lodgings scattered around the Essex coast. Although the situation was ideal for his circumstances, command of the Sea Fencibles offered Harvey little or no excitement especially as the threatened invasion never materialised.

The Fencibles were never called out in defence of the realm nor took part in any meaningful action. It soon became apparent to Harvey that being in charge of a bunch of part-timers was quite different to life in the navy. Much to his disgust, the iron discipline that ruled a 'Man-o-War' could not be enforced on civilian volunteers. What the Fencibles thought of Harvey is not known.

Many of the Fencibles who lived on the Essex Coast were, in all probability, involved in smuggling in one form or another. They benefited enormously from the Navy's distribution of weapons, offers of sea combat, signals training and official issue of tots of rum. Furthermore volunteers were paid one shilling a day when they attended!

Eliab Harvey had fully recovered by the end of 1799 and was back at sea again. In 1803 he was appointed Captain of the *Temeraire*. On the 21st October 1805 Harvey joined Nelson at the battle of Trafalgar. It could be said that the *Temeraire* not only saved the day but also Nelson's ship the *Victory*, which had come under attack from the French ship *Redoubtable*.

Today the *Victory* is preserved as a monument in Portsmouth's Royal Naval Dockyard. The *Temeraire* survived until 1838 and would have been completely forgotten had it not been for the painter J.M.W. Turner. He witnessed the ship, now no more than a rotting hulk, being towed by a steam tug, up the River Thames from Sheerness to a breaker's yard at Rotherhithe. This was the inspiration that led him to create *The Fighting Temeraire*, one of his best known paintings.

As for Eliab Harvey he was promoted to the rank of Rear Admiral. Shortly afterwards he was dismissed from active service following accusations that he had insulted his commander before a naval action on Basque Roads in the Bay of Biscay. He returned to his Rolls Park estate, his wife Louisa and their nine children and resumed his seat in Parliament. However, Eliab Harvey was still a hero to many. The public outcry at his treatment by the admiralty led to his reinstatement and eventual promotion to full Admiral, although he never went to sea again.

With the threat of invasion over, the Essex Sea Fencibles faded into obscurity and were disbanded in 1810. It is presumed the volunteers returned to their previous way of life.

Royal Small Arms Factory and a Small Island on the River Lea

Enfield Island Village, managed by the Enfield Island Trust, is a relatively new development on the site of the former Royal Small Arms Factory which supports a community of three thousand or more people. It lies on an island between the River Lea Navigation Canal and the Cattlegate Flood Relief Channel. Part of Essex until 1994, the village is now in the London Borough of Enfield.

Two hundred years ago in 1812, when the Napoleonic wars still had three years to run the Crown acquired land on the east bank of the River Lea to build an ordnance and small arms factory. Co-incidentally this site was just south of the Waltham Abbey Gunpowder Mills described on page 70. The Government of the day had been heavily criticized by the military over the poor quality and high cost of weaponry available to the armed forces. Until 1812, most weapons had been supplied from Birmingham's 'Gun Quarter' where small companies manufactured various components for other companies to assemble. These groups eventually came together to form BSA, the *Birmingham Small Arms Company*.

The marshy island site chosen for the Royal Small Arms Factory (RSAF) was ideal. The island location offered a degree of security. There was water power to drive machinery and to carry barge transport of raw materials from, and finished weapons to, sailing ships on the Thames. Completed in 1816, the factory gradually began to produce small arms and even swords were made from 1823.

The RSAF pioneered the use in Britain of machinery for the production of interchangeable parts for small arms. The Crimean War in 1853 created a surge in demand, steam power was introduced and a new machine shop was built by the Royal Engineers. Production soared and by 1887 there were 2,400 employees.

Quite a community grew up around the factory with many of the workers living in purpose built cottages on site. There was a school, a church, a fire brigade, eventually a police station, and of course several public houses.

The RSAF became famous for its designs and none more so than the *Lee Enfield Rifle* designed by James Paris Lee in 1895. This rifle went into production four years later and, together with the Enfield Revolver, was to become the standard British Army issue for decades to come.

The advent of World War I brought further rapid expansion. The same thing happened in the build up to World War II. To cope with demand, Enfield designed weapons were also being manufactured at other sites less vulnerable to enemy bombing in this country and overseas, notably in Canada.

All weapons designed at the factory were identifiable by having the word Enfield or the letters EN in the name, for example the *Bren, Sten and Tanden* guns, among others.

Decline set in during the 1950s and by 1963 half the site was closed. The RSAF was decommissioned by the Ministry of Defence in 1984 and privatised as Royal Ordnance PLC. Closure was announced on 12th August 1987. The site was bought by British Aerospace (BAe) and all the machinery and equipment auctioned off by November the following year. BAe then formed a joint venture with the property company Trafalgar House to develop the site. The picturesque situation of the site, with the River Lea and Lea Valley Park to the West and Sewardstone Marsh and Epping Forest to the East, made housing development and the creation of an urban village a very attractive proposition. Adjacent to the village is *Gunpowder Park,* an area that was once used as a testing ground for ordnance and explosives.

In 2010 a barge was moored in the millpond in front of the historic RSAF workshops as a heritage feature. As far as is known the barge was never used for RSAF purposes, formerly being the *Fairview,* a disused narrow boat. Following a makeover the barge was given a new name, *Harold Turpin,* the co-inventor of the sten gun.

Some of the original RSAF factory buildings were kept and converted for use as workshops and retail units. The original 1856 machine shop, now a listed building, has been completely renovated and redeveloped as the commercial centre of the Island Village. The central clock tower of this building houses a *Thwaites and Reed* clock which pre-dates London's Big Ben by three quarters of a century. Installed around 1783 in the original factory it is certainly the only piece of original equipment on the site which is still working.

On September 23rd 1828 the dilapidated remains of the Royal Manor at Havering-atte-Bower was sold at public auction. The successful bidder was Hugh McIntosh who had made his fortune from excavating the East India and London Docks. After more than 800 years, from the time of Edward the Confessor before the Norman Conquest, the special connection between Havering-Atte-Bower and the Crown was severed.

Havering-Atte-Bower was once the site of one of the most prestigious and luxurious Royal residences in England. Situated 350 feet above sea level, the palace had at least 26 rooms, a chapel, extensive kitchens, a gatehouse and a large inner court yard. It was originally sited beside the Village Green and surrounded by 1300 acres of parkland and forest within the former Royal Liberty of Havering which also included the parishes of Romford and Hornchurch. It is now part of the greater London Borough of Havering. The Palace had commanding views west towards London and south towards the River Thames and Kent.

The first Royal connection comes from a legend that records the returning of a ring in Havering to Edward the Confessor after he supposedly gave it to St. John the Evangelist, disguised as a beggar or a pilgrim.

Following the defeat of Harold at the Battle of Hasting in 1066 the manor passed to William the Conqueror although there is no record of him visiting Havering.

A Royal Palace in Essex

The first King known to have regularly visited Havering was John (of Magna Carta fame). Between 1203 and 1214 he visited the palace twelve times. In 1262, John's son and successor Henry III bequeathed the palace to his Queen, Eleanor of Aquitaine. Although it was commonly known as 'Kings House' the residence subsequently belonged to the queen consort or dowager.

In the 14th century the Essex Royal Palace was a favourite place of King Edward III; he made over 30 visits and frequently stayed for weeks at a time. His grandson Richard II only visited rarely, briefly staying in the summer of 1381 to deal with the aftermath of the Peasants revolt. Fortunately for him Havering Palace was not sacked during the revolt.

Richard was there again in 1397 en route to Pleshey where he planned the arrest of his Uncle, Thomas of Woodstock. (See page 42) Henry VIII took a particular liking to Havering as the hunting was considered excellent. He frequently held court there. A regular visitor was Richard Riche, who lived at Leez Priory near Chelmsford, acquired along with many other manors in Essex during his role in the dissolution of the Monasteries.

Queen Elizabeth I carried on the Tudor tradition of regularly coming to Havering. The Palace was usually her first or second stop on her 'Progressions' into the Eastern Counties. At the time of the Spanish Armada in 1588, preparations were made for the Royal Palace to serve as a strategic command post should enemy forces land in Eastern England.

James I, the first Stuart King who followed the Tudors in 1603 also frequently came to Havering Palace and visited at least once a year during his 22 year reign. He too enjoyed the hunting. Havering was conveniently close to London yet was far enough away to escape the demands of government. James's son, Charles I, was the last monarch to stay at Havering and following his execution the Palace began to deteriorate. Oliver Cromwell's austere regime had little love for vast Royal Residences. In their view there were too many and they cost a fortune to upkeep. By 1650 Havering Palace was described in a survey as 'a confused heap of ruinous decayed old buildings'. Two years later the park was sold off in two lots. Much of the best woodland was cut down to provide timber for building ships for the navy. In 1660 the Monarchy had been restored and Charles II was on the throne. An Act of Parliament returned the Havering Palace lands to the Crown and as a consequence some of the tenants were evicted. Although Charles' queen, Catherine of Braganza, in effect now owned the estate, the Royal Family never again returned to reside in Havering.

Over the next 100 years parcels of land from the former Royal estate were leased or sold off. The former Palace was vandalised and salvageable building material was removed for use elsewhere. New stately houses sprang up on the former Royal lands. On the 2nd October 1801, the six year old daughter of George IV, Princess Charlotte of Wales, accompanied by her governess, visited the Bower House, a mansion built by Sir John Smith Burges, a director of the East India Company. Princess Charlotte had stopped at Havering en-route from bathing at Southend, the new fashionable watering place, on the orders of her doctor.

In 1938 Essex County Council bought a large area of the once royal estate and the three public parks; Havering Country Park, Bedfords Park and Pyrgo Park. They are all that remain of the former royal hunting grounds enjoyed by Monarchs through the ages.

The Lady on the Five Pound Note

Elizabeth Fry has adorned our £5 note since 1992 in recognition of her work in prison reform. She was born in Norwich in 1780 to wealthy, middle class Quakers, John and Catherine Gurney. In 1800 Elizabeth married Joseph Fry, the son of a successful Essex merchant family who were also Quakers, and came to live in Plashet House, in East Ham, the Fry family home.

In 1813, Elizabeth Fry, who was now a Quaker preacher and had already given birth to eight children, made her first visit to Newgate Prison* on the instigation of a family friend, Steven Gellet. As a child in Norwich, Elizabeth had accompanied her mother collecting clothes for the poor and visiting the sick. None of those experiences prepared her for the horrors of Newgate. She found women, and their children, living thirty to a cell in such squalor, filth and deprivation that she resolved to devote her energies to improving their lot.

During the next three years she organised friends to collect clothing for the inmates. She also had two more children and suffered the death of her daughter Betsy. By 1816 she had become a frequent visitor and with eleven other Quaker women formed the 'Association for the Improvement of the Female Prisoners in Newgate'. They established a school, with a teacher elected from the inmates, organised chapel and held regular Bible readings. A system of supervision by matrons and monitors was provided along with materials for compulsory sewing duties where the women could make items to sell.

Fry was opposed to the death penalty and campaigned vigorously for its abolition. At that time there were over 200 offences, including the passing of forged notes and stealing clothing, which carried the ultimate penalty. Through her brother-in-law, Thomas Fowell Buxton the MP for Weymouth, she was invited to address the House of Commons.

Whilst impressed with her charitable work, the majority of MPs believed that her views on capital punishment were misplaced. She pleaded with the Home Secretary, Lord Sidmouth, for the lives of two women condemned for forgery. He would not budge and warned Fry that her ideas were dangerous as they would, "remove the dread of punishment in the criminal classes".

Undeterred, Fry continued her campaign visiting prisons throughout the country. However, prisons were not her only targets for reform. After seeing convicts taken to ships for transportation in open carts with hand and leg shackles, she managed to change the way they were treated by arranging closed carriages to protect them from the missiles thrown by the mob.

* *Newgate Prison was demolished in 1902 and most of the women prisoners were move to Holloway. The Central Criminal Court the 'Old Bailey' now stands on the site.*

78

Visiting the convict ships became another regular duty for one of Fry's committees. Robert Peel, who succeeded Lord Sidmouth as Home Secretary, was more sympathetic. He allowed many 'Fry inspired' improvements to be included in his 1823 *Gaols Act*.

Another area that interested Fry was the training and standards of nursing. In 1840 she set up training courses at Guy's Hospital. Fry nurses were held in high esteem and Florence Nightingale was influenced by Fry's views on the training of nurses. She took a group of Fry nurses to the Crimea to nurse sick and wounded soldiers.

Queen Victoria, nearly forty years younger than Fry, was an admirer and supporter of her charitable work and they met on a number of occasions. The Queen wrote in her journal of Fry as, "a very superior person".

Elizabeth Fry's influence was not confined to England. Towards the end of her life she travelled in Europe visiting many of the royal families to explain her work. In fact the King of Prussia visited the Fry family home and dined with her.

The Lady on the £5.00 note (In East Ham Library)

Elizabeth Fry died on 12th October 1845 after a short illness. It would be difficult to disagree with June Rose who wrote in her 1994 book, *Prison pioneer, the story of Elizabeth Fry*, "Over two hundred years after her birth, she seems a brave and modern woman, battling with the injustices of her time". Her popularity may perhaps be measured by the fact that, although Quakers do not have funeral services, over 1000 people stood in silence as she was buried at 'The Society of Friends' graveyard in Barking.

Plashet means 'an enclosure in the wood'. Plashet House was demolished in 1883. Six years later the Vicar of East Ham acquired the grounds for use as a public park having obtained a grant of £3,000. Plashet Park was opened in 1891. Still a public park today, it is managed by the London Borough of Newham.

Rocket Man

Lieutenant-General Sir William Congreve should not be confused with his eldest son, Sir William Congreve. Sir William senior supervised the Royal Gunpowder Mills at Waltham Abbey (see page 70). His son Sir William junior was an inventor and rocket designer who built rockets in his private factory on West Ham marsh adjacent to the River Lea at Bromley-by-Bow. The factory opened in 1809.

The missiles became known as the *Congreve rocket* and were fired in several military engagements during the Napoleonic wars, both on land and at sea. Modified 'civilian' versions were used for whale hunting.

As would be expected, due to the family connection, the rockets used gunpowder purchased from the Royal Gunpowder Mills further up the River Lea at Waltham Abbey. By today's standards the rockets were crude and looked much like a gigantic modern firework. The Congreve Rocket had a maximum range of just over a mile with the largest weighing 32 pounds (14.5 kgs). Its head was three feet long. It then carried a stabilizing stick which measured another 15 feet. These rockets were notoriously inaccurate, being easily blown off course by the wind, and were prone to blow up on ignition. The propulsion system in the head accounted for nearly all the gunpowder used. As a consequence there was little explosive left to cause damage even if the rocket hit its target. However, as a new weapon, the noise, the glare and incendiary effects caused panic amongst the enemy who had not come under this form of assault before.

Growing improvements in artillery soon rendered the Congreve Rocket obsolete and it was another 150 years before rockets were effectively used again in the latter stages of the Second World War. Although militarily redundant, Congreve's rockets were adapted for use as flares.

The Congreve rocket was only one of many scientific inventions created by Sir William junior. In 1815 he patented a 'Hydro-Pneumatic Lock" for canals and apart from perfecting numerous improvements to the manufacture of gunpowder, he introduced a new type of banknote paper which would make forgery much more difficult.

Congreve's West Ham Rocket factory has long been demolished. In 1872 it was replaced by the Bromley-by-Bow gas works. The gas holders that still stand there have grade II listed status and are used today for storing natural gas.

Sad Days at High Beech
My sleep is restless and I feel my power ebbs away.
The forest trees hem me in and keep me at bay.

Alfred, Lord Tennyson is one of England's most celebrated poets. Born in 1809, on his death at 81, he was buried in poets' corner at Westminster Abbey. His best remembered poem, *The Charge of the Light Brigade,* was published in 1855 as a memorial to the suicidal charge of the British light cavalry at the Battle of Balaclava in the Crimean War a year earlier.

At the age of 20 Tennyson won the Chancellor's Gold Medal at Trinity College Cambridge. However, following the death of his father in 1831, he left Cambridge without completing his degree. Two years later Tennyson published his second book of poetry but it was panned by the critics, some of whom took delight in the severity of their reviews. This hurt Tennyson badly, so much so that he published nothing for nine years, although he continued to write. In 1833 he was further traumatized by the sudden death of his friend Arthur Hallam at the age of 22.

In 1837 Tennyson became engaged to his childhood sweetheart, Emily Sellwood, but then inexplicably he moved to High Beech House on the edge of Epping Forrest, whilst leaving Emily in Lincolnshire. He was to spend three years at High Beech with his mother, generally feeling sorry for himself. He wrote often to Emily saying how he missed her and how awful life was at High Beech. Emotionally and financially these were difficult years for Tennyson. He claimed he could not afford the train fare to visit Emily. Suffering from depression, he stayed for two weeks as a guest in Dr. Matthew Allen's High Beech Asylum. He reported that mad people were the most agreeable and reasonable persons he had ever met. Tennyson later regretted his acquaintance with Dr. Allen. Whilst apparently not having money for a train fare, he nevertheless managed to invest his family's money in a woodcarving scheme proposed by Dr. Allen. He lost everything and as a consequence plans to marry Emily were postponed again.

If High Beech and Epping Forest provided a setting to match Tennyson's mood, it was a productive one. It was there that he began writing his epic poem *In Memoriam*, a tribute to his friend Arthur Hallam.

In 1840 Tennyson left Essex and moved to Tunbridge Wells in Kent where he published two volumes of poems which met with immediate critical acclaim. He married Emily in 1850 and was created Poet Laureate. During the next forty years he produced a body of work that has made him the second most frequently quoted writer after Shakespeare. For all the sadness Tennyson felt in Essex his stay there proved a significant turning point in his life.

The Biggest Fishing Fleet in the World.
In Barking!

Records show that Barking was home to 14 fishing smacks in 1660. By 1814 there were 70 and in 1833 the fleet had grown to 123. By 1850, at its peak, there were more than 220 boats, arguably the biggest fishing fleet in the world.

A Barking fishery, probably limited to the River Roding, existed since 1086 and by the 14th century salt water fishing had become a thriving industry in Barking Creek. Fish stock conservation was in the news then as much as now. In 1320, several Barking fishermen were prosecuted by the City of London authorities, the conservators of the Thames, for the illegal use of nets with too fine a mesh. Barking men were similarly charged in 1349 and again in 1406. There were riots when officials seized their nets.

As the population grew so did the fishing fleet. By the 1700s the boats were sailing out of Barking Creek to venture as far as Iceland in the summer. The main type of boat used was the "Well Smack" the "well" being a large pool of water held in the body of the boat. During a typical Icelandic trip the boats would make three catches. The first two would be gutted and wet salted on board. The last catch would be kept alive in the well until the boat arrived back in Barking. This round trip could take about fourteen weeks depending on the weather.

In the beginning of the 19th century, Scrymgeour Hewlett and his son Samuel, founders of the *Short Blue Fleet*, began to revolutionise the fishing industry at Barking. Samuel Hewlett recognised that the long voyage delivering the catch back to Barking was uneconomic. He devised a system known as "fleeting". The smacks would fish as before, but the fish would then be packed in boxes of ice and loaded on to fast boats called 'cutters' that would ferry the catch back to port. This allowed the smacks to remain in the northern grounds, fishing continuously, for up to six months. To make this system work another innovation was required to supply the ice. Initially the ice was harvested in winter from the marshlands in the surrounding area and then stored in the great ice house that Hewlett had built in Barking. Later he installed the first ice making plant. This system of fishing was so successful that it was quickly copied by all the other fleets and became the industry standard.

During the wars and conflicts of the 17th and 18th centuries, as well as fishing, the smacks were frequently called upon by the Royal Navy to act as auxiliaries.

The decline of Barking's fishing industry began in the mid 19th century after the building of railways provided a direct link for the North Sea ports to London and Billingsgate Market. In 1863, a great storm off the coast of Holland caused huge damage to the fleet and the loss of 60 fishermen.

Following this disaster, the *Short Blue Fleet* of Hewlett & Co. transferred to Gorlestone, in Norfolk, though they kept a ship repair yard in Barking until 1899. Many other fishing companies also moved their business to the east coast ports of Grimsby and Great Yarmouth and by 1900 Barking, as a working fishing port was no more.

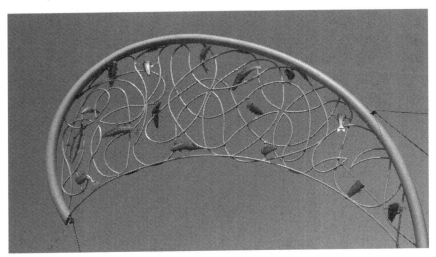

'The Catch'. Fishing nets on a roundabout at Fanshawe Avenue!

Today there are still a few clues to this once thriving industrial heritage, mainly street names such as Whiting Avenue and Fresh Wharf Quay. One well known pub, 'The Fishing Smack', was built in the 1850s in Fisher Street which in the 1450s was called Fish Row but is now known as Abbey Road South. Destroyed by an explosion and rebuilt in 1903, this once popular pub was closed in 2003, demolished in 2008/9 and the area redeveloped for housing.

In 2002 a new memorial to Barking's heritage was erected, Loraine Leeson's great sculpture 'The Catch' is a public artwork for Barking Town Centre. It sits on the roundabout at the end of Fanshawe Avenue at the junction with Longbridge Road. It represents two fishing nets tossed upwards to form opposing wave shapes. The structure, made from aluminum, incorporates fish leaping from the net as well as Celtic motifs reflecting Barking's Saxon beginnings.

PC George Clark
- Buried in God's Little Acre

On the evening of 3rd July 1846, four days after he had been reported missing, the mutilated body of PC George Clark was discovered in a hedge at Thorntons Farm, approximately two miles north of Dagenham Village.

Dagenham in 1846 was a rural area of scattered farmhouses and rustic workers' cottages in among cornfields, lakes, streams and ponds. At its centre was Dagenham Village with a population of just over 2000. Six years earlier the Metropolitan Police jurisdiction had been extended to cover Dagenham. This had caused some local misgivings. Some regarded the police as simply another state instrument of suppression while local ratepayers considered professional police an unnecessary expense. A catalogue of incidents in the early years of the new police force had reinforced these sentiments. In the latest incident, at Dagenham in the spring of 1846, three constables had been sacked for being drunk on duty and making a false arrest. They were replaced in May that year by the nineteen year old Clark, PC Isaac Hickton, transferred from Stepney, and the newly trained PC Jonas Stevens. They joined the existing PCs John Farnes, Abia Butfoy and Thomas Kimpton under the supervision of Sergeant William Parsons. Dagenham was part of 'K' Division headquartered in Ilford.

PC Clark was assigned the 'Eastbrookend' beat, which he patrolled nightly between 9:00 pm and 6:00 am. Starting from Four Wants crossroads, his lonely route headed along Dagenham Road towards Eastbrookend Farm, the farmhouse which became the 'Farmhouse Tavern'. He continued straight ahead into 'The Chase', now part of Eastbrookend Country Park, to check on Hooks Hall Farm before doubling back to the Dagenham Road. Stopping just short of Thorntons Farm at Rush Green, he would then return the same way to Four Wants. The last part of his beat would take him north towards Becontree Heath before returning again via Frizlands Lane and Oxlow Lane to his original starting point at Four Wants.

PC George Clark began his shift at 9.00pm on Monday 29th June. He was seen at 10.30pm by a Luke White who was returning home to Oxlow Lane. He was not seen alive again. When he didn't report back the next morning, Sergeant Parsons ordered a search at around 9.00am. The first priority was to check all the ponds and drainage ditches. In recent years five police officers had drowned on night duty. The long night shifts took their toll. In the pitch dark, tired (or sometimes drunk) officers could stumble into a deep ditch or pond and never get out.

As the days wore on the searchers became increasingly anxious. In the seven weeks PC Clark had been at Dagenham he had gained a reputation as a cheerful, conscientious officer. As he was soon to be married, enquiries were made at his home in Bedfordshire in case he had returned there unexpectedly.

On the fourth day, meticulous searches having found nothing, police and civilian helpers arrived at Thorntons Farm, Rush Green, the home of Elizabeth and Ralph Page. PCs Butfoy and Kimpton dragged the farmyard pond to no avail. Mrs. Page then told them of another smaller pond on the edge of her property. The two police officers were taken there by her 12 year old son, William. As the three approached they became aware of a strong unpleasant smell which led to the horrific discovery of a badly decomposed, mutilated body with hardly any recognizable features. In this isolated spot, a quarter of a mile from the road and a long way from his beat, the search for PC Clark was over.

All the above has been substantiated but from then on what witnesses recalled at the inquests and who is supposed have said what to whom and when became confused and conflicted. In all there were six inquests and two autopsies. After the first autopsy P.C. Clark's remains were buried but then dug up for a second autopsy. Whilst the inquests were proceeding the press ran a series of sensational stories dwelling on the conflicts between the witness statements and the perceived failing of the police.

From the very first inquest there were differences between Kimpton, Butfoy and William Page's statements on the position of Clark's body and the location of his cutlass. Kimpton even omitted to say that Page was there. Robbery had been ruled out since Clark still had money and his stopwatch in his pockets. His cutlass and staff were found at the scene. The only item never discovered was his hat.

At the second inquest Mrs. Page claimed Kimpton had told her that he was covering for Sergeant Parsons who was indisposed on the night of the murder. Parsons vehemently denied this and even claimed that he had seen PC Clark at 1.00am that morning. His story and movements were backed up by all the Dagenham Constables. Nevertheless Mrs. Page stuck to her story. The press had a field day with this. Not only was it normal practice for separate beat officers to meet at prearranged points and times to report and pass on messages but the Sergeant was supposed to be on duty all night supervising and coordinating their movements.

Whilst the inquest revealed many inconsistencies between the various witnesses, the murder investigation itself was making little headway; numerous suspects were questioned, all to no avail.

The investigation was not helped by a newspaper appeal for information getting the date of the murder wrong. With the passage of time between the murder and the discovery of the body, the perpetrators would have had plenty of time to dispose of any bloodied clothes and murder weapons. In fact no murder weapons were ever found.

Nearly three weeks after the murder a reward of £100.00 was offered. With still no progress the Metropolitan Police decided to send two detectives, Edward Kendall and Jonathan Whitcher, to head the investigation.

Then on August 17th a bombshell dropped. PC Abia Butfoy, who had previously undertaken the beat of the deceased, went to see the police commissioners in Whitehall. He told them Sergeant Parsons had not been on duty as he claimed. He and Parsons, with two officers from a neighbouring force, had embarked on a marathon drinking session during the day. As result Butfoy was excused duty and Parsons arranged for Thomas Kimpton to cover for him. He further stated that Kimpton and Isaac Hickton would say whatever Sergeant Parsons told them to as they were frightened of him.

All the while the detectives were following up leads that took them ever further from Dagenham. The reward offered had produced little useful evidence other than a series of attention seekers and time wasters.

The 22nd September 1846 saw the convening of the sixth and final inquest. Coroner Charles Lewis' verdict was that PC George Clark was willfully murdered by persons unknown. He concluded that Sergeant Parsons was not on duty and Kimpton and Hickton had continually lied to support him. Parsons, Kimpton and Hickton were immediately suspended and placed under house arrest. After lengthy deliberation the Attorney General decided that all three men were to be indicted for perjury and conspiracy.

There then followed great embarrassment for the police when the indicted officers promptly escaped house arrest and fled. Kimpton gave himself up quite soon. With Parsons and Hickton still on the run, another reward was authorised although Isaac Hickton surrendered voluntarily in June. A year had now passed since the murder of PC Clark. In July 1847 Kimpton and Hickton were brought before Judge Baron Parker at Chelmsford assizes. Judge Parker had a reputation for going by the book and handing down severe sentences. Both men were duly convicted of perjury and sentenced to be transported for seven years.

Time was running out for the former Sergeant Parsons. He had made his way to Lincoln but was arrested by two undercover police officers following a tip off. Brought back to London, he spent eight months in Ilford Gaol before coming to trial in the spring of 1848.

Appearing before Lord Justice Thomas Denman, Parsons stuck to his story. Incredibly, after listening to the prosecution submissions, the judge stopped the trial and ordered a verdict of not guilty. Parson walked free. Despite this verdict there was no immediate prospect of release for PCs Hickton and Kimpton. They had as yet not been transported and their appeals were rejected. Hickton later had his sentence reduced, partly on the grounds of ill health, and was released in July 1849. The outlook though for Kimpton was grim. He was serving his time in Woolwich on a prison hulk that had been subject to several deadly outbreaks of cholera. Yet following another appeal he was pardoned. In the meantime Parsons had remarried and immigrated to Canada.

All the other officers serving at Dagenham at the time of PC Clark's murder had been dismissed. PC Abia Butfoy, who had dramatically testified against his fellow officers in 1846, was later classed as a lunatic and committed to Colney Hatch Pauper Lunatic Asylum, where he died in 1853. As for the murder of PC Clark the case remained open.

Eleven years later in 1857, a Mrs Mary Ann Smith was interviewed following reports that she had information on the murder. She claimed her late second husband, William Page, along with farm labourer George Blewitt, 16 year old George Chalk and a man named Ned Wood were caught red handed by PC Clark in the act of stealing grain from the farm of Thomas Waters Brittain. The resulting skirmish led to the murder. Unfortunately for George Blewitt he was the only suspect still alive and living locally. Once again Detective Jonathan Whitcher came to Dagenham to pursue the investigation. Blewitt was arrested. However Mrs Smith's statements were deemed unreliable and Blewitt was freed at a pre-trial hearing. The other living suspect, George Chalk, had apparently moved to Australia and was never traced. Thus after twelve years the murder of PC George Clark remained unsolved (as it is today). There were many theories and suspects. It seems that despite the undoubted pressure on Detective Jonathan Whitcher to get a conviction; he was meticulous in his methods, no short cuts were taken and all leads pursued vigorously, there was no justice for PC George Clark. He was laid to rest in Dagenham Parish Church. The monument shown on the left stands appropriately at the entrance to 'God's Little Acre'.

SACRED

TO THE MEMORY OF
GEORGE CLARK
LATE A POLICE CONSTABLE
OF THE K DIVISION OF
METROPOLITAN POLICE
WHO WAS INHUMANLY AND
BARBAROUSLY MURDERED
IN A FIELD AT EASTBROOK
END IN THIS PARISH
WHILST ON DUTY ON THE
NIGHT OF THE 29TH OR THE
MORNING OF THE 30TH JUNE
1846
AGED 20 YEARS

HIS UNIFORM GOOD
CONDUCT GAINED HIM
THE RESPECT OF ALL
WHO KNEW HIM AND HIS
MELANCHOLY END WAS
UNIVERSALLY DEPLORED

Christmas Day in the Workhouse

Prior to 1834 each parish had to take care of its poor. Romford was no exception and the amount of the poor rate was always a bone of contention for those that paid it. For the workhouse inmates, their Christmas diet was like any other day, the extra expense of seasonal fare being considered unacceptable.

The Romford Poor Law Union, formed in 1836, brought the poor of ten parishes; Barking, Cranham, Dagenham, Hornchurch, Havering-atte-Bower, Rainham, Romford, Upminster, Great Warley and Wennington, under the responsibility of one Board of Guardians. With the new organisation came some enlightened thinking. Within three years the board had bought a five acre site at Oldchurch and built a 'state of the art' new workhouse with a capacity for 450 people. The 'enlightened thinking', to some of the public, may have been a step too far when, in 1841, there appeared a report in the Essex Standard stating that, 'On Christmas day, the 400 inmates had been given 240 plum puddings, with a total weight of 600 lbs'. The Guardians withstood the criticism of wasting ratepayers' money and the practice of allowing inmates to celebrate Christmas like this was established for future years.

The workhouse, of necessity, had its own infirmary. In time it came to treat not only the residents but also the poor generally. This aspect of its work gathered such a reputation that, in 1893, a hospital was added. Experience gained by the staff during and after the Great War led to its recognition as a respected medical institution.

In 1924 the hospital was expanded, becoming bigger than the workhouse itself. The Poor Law Union was dissolved in 1930, the institution being taken over by Essex County Council. In 1935 responsibility for Oldchurch Hospital was given to the Public Health Committee. It was much enlarged and grew to become a major regional hospital and a nationally respected centre of expertise in Neurosurgery.

Most of the central cruciform block, a highlight of the original Francis Edwards design, was dismantled in 2000 to make way for a temporary single story building and a car park. The one 'N' shaped block still standing is in a sorry state. It backs on to the appropriately named Union Road and is fenced off, waiting an uncertain future. The remaining Oldchurch buildings have since been totally demolished and the site is currently being redeveloped with apartment blocks and 'key worker' housing. The hospital, now under the Barking, Havering and Redbridge NHS Trust, was closed in 2006 and the patients transferred to the close by, new state of the art, Queen's Hospital.

Poles Apart

Pole Hill in Chingford stands eight miles north of the Greenwich Observatory on zero degrees longitude. At its highest point, 91 metres (299 feet) above sea level, it was the highest visible point due north from the observatory.

In 1824 a granite obelisk was erected, under the supervision of the Astronomer Royal John Pond, for use as a reference point by geographers working at the observatory to check that their instruments were correctly set.

Twenty-six years later, further calculations led to an adjustment of the Greenwich Meridian and as a consequence the obelisk on Pole Hill was judged to be 19 feet (6 metres) out. In 1850, another smaller pillar was put up in the correct position close to the original. Its prime purpose was not to mark the meridian's change but to indicate the top of the hill for Ordinance Survey mapping purposes. The smaller pillar is more commonly known as a trig or triangulation point and its positioning on the new meridian is pure coincidence.

The revised Greenwich Meridian was adopted by an international treaty in 1884 and is still in use today. Nowadays tall trees on the lower slopes mean that it is virtually impossible to see Greenwich from the base of either obelisk. However, on a clear day there are excellent views of the River Lea valley, its reservoirs and the taller buildings in London.

There are two plaques on the original obelisk; the larger one records its erection in 1824 and the subsequent moving of the Greenwich Meridian. The second plaque, set higher up and somewhat difficult to read, states that Pole Hill was home to TE Lawrence. Thomas Edward Lawrence, who was better known as Lawrence of Arabia, owned 18 acres of land at the top of Pole Hill in the 1920s. Apparently he intended to build a house there and use it as a base to print books. Neither the house nor printing press came to fruition. Pole Hill is now owned and managed by the Corporation of London.

Poles apart on Pole Hill

LOST: 'Doctor Livingstone I presume'

At the age of 27, the famous explorer and missionary Doctor David Livingstone went to Africa. He travelled down the great Zambezi River to discover 'The Smoke that Thunders,' which he renamed Victoria Falls after the then Queen. Two years before his death, after a long search, the journalist Henry Morgan Stanley met Livingstone in 1871 with the famous phrase, 'Doctor Livingstone I presume'. During his 30 years in Africa, Livingstone crossed the continent from the Atlantic to the Indian Ocean, in the process walking some 5,000 miles. Although he died in Africa, his body was brought to England to be interred in Westminster Abbey.

A self-educated Scot from Blantyre, Livingstone trained as a doctor in Glasgow. In 1838 he was accepted as a probationer by the 'London Missionary Society'. He was then sent to study under the Rev. Richard Cecil in Chipping Ongar, Essex. He lodged with other students in what are now called the 'Livingstone Cottages' in Ongar High Street.

During that time his colleague and fellow probationer, Joseph Moore, recorded an incident, which, in view of his future achievements was surprising to say the least. One November day David Livingstone set off on foot to London to visit a sick relative. Fellow students marvelled at the energy and drive that would be needed to walk this distance. After seeing his relative Dr Livingstone returned via Edmonton where he apparently stopped to render assistance to a lady who had fallen off her horse. Dr Livingstone helped the lady to the nearby Cook's Ferry Inn that once stood beside the River Lea. Once content the lady was in good hands, Livingstone resumed his journey. He would have more or less have followed the course of the present day North Circular Road to Woodford before joining the Chigwell then the Abridge roads towards Ongar.

However, with night falling and a thick fog descending, the Doctor lost his way at Stanford Rivers, not far from Ongar. After some time walking round in circles he managed to find a lamppost on which he climbed to get his bearings. Eventually, with the clock striking 12 midnight, David Livingstone made it back, much to the relief of his fellow students. Nevertheless, he was ribbed mercilessly in the following days. David Livingstone left Ongar for the last time on December 30th 1839 to continue his medical studies in London. Whether he walked there is unknown.

The lady falling off a horse incident has never been verified. Whilst the distance from Ongar to Edmonton is perhaps only 40 miles return, the roads in 1838 were poor and there was little or no street lighting, so completing the journey in one day was nevertheless quite an achievement.

Thames Barge

Every day hundreds of heavy goods vehicles thunder along the roads of Essex taking goods into London and beyond. Comparisons between a 40-ton truck and a sedate Thames sailing barge may seem absurd. Yet 100 years ago the sailing barges on the waterways of the Essex coast and the River Thames were the HGVs of the day, carrying the essentials to build, repair, fuel and feed the capital.

Today there are only about 30 seaworthy sailing barges left which are used for recreation, charter work and racing. At one time at least 5000 barges worked in and around Essex and as far up river as the Pool of London. The writer H Rider Haggard observed in his 1902 book *Rural England* the barges' ability to penetrate far inland, 'On the distant deep some sails and in the middle marsh, a barge gliding up a hidden creek as though she moved across a solid land'.

The barges, with their shallow draft, were robust and relatively inexpensive to build. They could carry large and bulky cargoes which made them cost effective. Familiar sights were the 'stackies', barges loaded with hay stacked up to 20 feet high. In order to navigate it was necessary for one man to stand on top of the stack and then pass instructions to his fellow crew member manning the tiller who could not see where he was going. A barge carrying 100 tons of cargo was usually crewed by two. An equivalent load on land would have required a hundred horse-drawn carts plus one hundred drivers!

The first Essex sailing barge would seem to have been built in Rettendon in 1791 and the last in Mistley in 1928. The Thames Barge came of age during the Napoleonic Wars. Surprisingly it not only survived the advent of steam but barge numbers increased.

The mid 1800s saw the highest number of Thames Barges in service. This period coincided with the great era of railway building which in turn was the biggest factor in the barge's demise. Ironically it was often the barges that carried the materials to strategic points, thus speeding railway construction.

In the First World War sailing barges made significant contributions to supplying troops and in the Second World War they played a key part in the evacuation of Dunkirk.

In 1930 new maritime safety standards were introduced that required additional crew and therefore increased costs. In the end the barges could not compete with the modern transport alternatives; the railways or the articulated truck. Notwithstanding this there were still barges carrying commercial cargoes when Neil Armstrong set foot on the moon.

The Destruction of Hainault Forest

Today, Hainault Forest Country Park, south of Chigwell Row and bordered by Romford Road to the west, occupies approximately 300 acres. It was originally part of the great forest of Waltham and Essex. Seven hundred years ago this great forest embraced the whole of the county of Essex.

Over the centuries the boundaries of the forest gradually shrank as it succumbed to an ever expanding population needing houses and agricultural land to feed its people.

Although reduced in size, by 1849 Hainault Forest still covered a huge area of *Metropolitan Essex*, from Wanstead to Abridge, occupying some 17000 acres – over fifty times greater in area than the existing forest today. Furthermore, nearly all the forest was open to the people.

Hainault Forest was a prime source of oak used for building warships for the navy. Timber from the forest had been used to build the *Victory* and the *Temeraire*. This era was coming to an end and new ships were being constructed from iron. Sail was giving way to the age of steam. For years the Government had been under intense commercial pressure from developers and interested landowners to turn the forest over to them and keep the public out. The Crown could no longer justify reserving the vast forest for hunting (for a privileged few) nor could the Government use the excuse of the navy needing the wood.

As early as 1817, the *Commissioners of Woods* applied for an Act of Parliament to enclose part of the forest and do away with the commoners' rights in the forest. The attempt caused public uproar. The bill was eventually approved by the Commons although its passage was bumpy. It ran out of time and couldn't be put before the House of Lords, so it failed.

Despite the failure of the Parliamentary bill many illegal enclosures of the forest were made despite the best efforts of the forest keepers to prevent it. Frequently the keepers were bribed to look the other way or in extreme cases threatened by landowners. Yet where forest keepers were able to, the enclosure fences were torn down and the offenders prosecuted.

Following a court case in 1848 the *Commissioners of Woods* asked for 'all persons who had or claimed encroachments to notify them by giving details' and then 'requesting them to make a fair offer to buy the rights from the Crown'. The Commissioners subsequently produced a report that advised Parliament that 'disafforestation', as it was called, should be undertaken. The forest was considered 'waste'. Opponents described the report as factually inaccurate and legally dubious. However this time, and out character, Parliament acted swiftly.

It ignored the howls of public outrage that followed and passed the 'Disafforestation of Hainault Forest Act' in the summer of 1851. The ink was hardly dry on the Royal assent before the destruction of the forest began. Within six weeks 3000 acres of woodland were cleared. Specially built steam powered machines were used. They had chains that could encircle the trunk and then uproot the tree whole. An estimated 100,000 trees were felled and sold off during this time.

The destruction had its supporters. Not surprisingly, John Alison the farmer responsible for clearance and creating replacement roads and farms was quoted as saying "I hope to see the adjoining forest treated in the same way soon. It would be a great service to me, as well as to the whole neighbourhood". Other comments were highly critical. One described the disafforestation as "state sponsored vandalism on an unprecedented scale".

Whilst the destruction may have been achieved in record time the clearance was another matter. A contemporary description mentions 'scores of fine trees lying side by side in the forest stripped of their bark like heaps of bones bleaching in the sun'. Removal of the timber was chaotic, taking months of day and night working.

Many wagon loads of timber were stolen en-route to Barking and hundreds of trees were left to rot where they had been felled.

The cleared land was then drained to become three farms; Forest Farm - now home to Forest Farm

Foxburrows Farm - Hainault Country Park

Peace Garden; Hainault Farm which became an aerodrome for the duration of WW1 and Foxburrows.

Today Foxburrows is one of the main attractions of the Country Park. Now managed by the London Borough of Redbridge, it has a 'rare breeds' zoo, a café and many events are put on throughout the year to attract visitors.

The Cathedral of Sewage

Just over a javelin's throw from the new London Olympic stadium in Stratford stands the Abbey Mills pumping station which officially opened for 'business' on 30th July 1868. The inauguration then was almost on a par with the 2012 Olympics opening ceremony. The building was a triumph of extravagant Victorian flair with flourishes of French Baroque, high ornamental windows, beautifully sculptured masonry, striking mosaics and lavish wall tiles. Two Moorish style chimneys, each 190 feet high, stood guard at either end. The inside was a showcase of beautifully crafted ornate iron work.

Abbey Mills was strategically sited at the junction of three major sewer networks that ran west to east, serving London north of the Thames. The station's task was to pump effluent up forty feet and drain it into the newly built northern outfall. This in turn would take all the sewage of north London to Barking Creek where it would be stored temporarily and then flushed into the Thames on the ebb tide. Such was the extravagance of architecture at Abbey Mills (no doubt created to disguise its real purpose) it soon became known as the *Cathedral of Sewage*.

By the end of the 1840s the population of London was nearly three million. There was no coordination in dealing with waste. In the capital eight separate bodies dealt with drainage matters and each jealously guarded their own territories. As a consequence there was no proper sewer network. Each different authority set its own standards that were often at odds with their neighbours. Many homes and businesses had private cesspits that constantly overflowed in heavy rains which in turn polluted rivers and local reservoirs. With the arrival of the new 'water closet' (flushing toilet), that replaced the old fashioned chamber pots, the problems were compounded as millions of extra gallons of foul water and excrement poured into the already creaking infrastructure.

In 1849 Parliament authorised the creation of the Metropolitan Board of Sewers to replace the separate bodies dealing with London drainage. The constantly changing management of the new Board proved ineffective and within a few years it was replaced by the Metropolitan Board of Works who did their best, against much entrenched opposition, to bring order to a chaotic situation.

Between 1831 and 1854 nearly 40,000 people died in three major cholera epidemics in London. Today it is universally accepted that cholera is linked to contaminated water and poor sanitation. However, that was not the case during the 1850's.

Many eminent people, including Florence Nightingale, were convinced that health problems were the result of breathing bad air – the so called *miasmatic* theory.

A Professor of Chemistry, Henry Booth, even made the astounding claim that "from inhaling the odour of beef the butcher's wife obtains her obesity". Despite the cholera deaths and the chaos in London's drainage system, improvements moved at a snails pace. Whatever scheme was mooted, and there were many, all were delayed by vested interests or infighting on the part of those who had proposed new schemes. Numerous critics described the construction of new sewers as unnecessary, expensive and unable to solve the 'imaginary' sewage problem anyway. A prominent barrister, J Toulmin Smith, circulated a document in which he described the Metropolitan Board of Works as illegal and pernicious. He said such central bodies were contrary to the Magna Carta and the Common Law. Anybody who complains about the work of today's 21st Century bureaucrats could well learn something from Toulmin Smith.

The summer of 1858 was one of the hottest on record. The Thames had become a large open-air sewer. During July the incoming tide brought mounds of rotting sewage right up to the doors of the Houses of Parliament. The smell of untreated sewage was so bad that the chamber had to be evacuated. Government ground to a halt.

Tentative proposals were even made to move Parliament and the Law Courts out of London. Members of Parliament could now no longer ignore the filth on their doorstep. The Press described the episode as 'The Big Stink'. It was the final straw and something really had to be done.

So suddenly, after years of procrastination, heads were knocked together, red tape was magically cut and funding put in place. The Chief Engineer of the Metropolitan Board of Works, Joseph Bazalgette, was put in charge of building a vast network of sewers.

It was hoped to rid the capital of its sewage nightmare once and for all. The new sewers would be underground or enclosed which would solve the problems of both smell and disease. Over an eight year period 1,000 labourers built more than 85 miles of brick sewers using the new Portland cement.

The Northern Outfall Sewer still performs its duties faithfully as it has done for the last 150 years. It runs from Hackney Wick and then alongside the Olympic Park at Stratford and on to Plaistow and East Ham, terminating at Beckton. An embankment conceals the route of the Northern Outfall for most of its journey. It has since been landscaped and turned into a motor-vehicle-free walking and cycle path lined with grass and shrubs and is now part of London's Capital Ring walking and cycling route.

The dumping of sewage in the Thames ceased in 1887. Instead barges were used to take it out to sea and dispose of it there. In 1998 dumping in the sea ceased and after treatment the solid matter is now incinerated.

Today the *Cathedral of Sewage* is used only as a standby. It was replaced in 1994 by a new pumping station next door to it. The original pumping station had two tall chimneys, one on either side of the main building, whose function was to expel the exhaust fumes from the pumping machinery. At 190

feet in height it was feared that these could provide navigational landmarks for enemy bombers during the Second World War. Accordingly both chimneys were demolished.

Bazalgette and his team made great progress in building proper sewers for London. As far as the Parliamentarians were concerned the 'big stink' had ended. London's public health problems however were far from over.

Denial

Although the Northern Outfall Sewer had essentially been completed in the summer of 1865, one year later an average of 50 people a day were still dying of cholera in East London. The undoubted culprit of the outbreak was contaminated water.

Although suspected, the establishment of the day denied this. It was described as the 'final catastrophe of cholera in London' and the capital's forth cholera epidemic in 35 years. The death toll for the week ending 28th July 1866 was 818 and for the 4th August it was 916.

Riding on Joseph Bazalgette's Northern Outfall Sewer

Apart from a huge new London-wide sewage system having been built, the Metropolis Water Act, dating from fifteen years earlier in 1851, expressly prohibited water companies from supplying water taken from uncovered reservoirs within five miles of St Pauls. Nearly all the deaths recorded during the outbreak of 1866 occurred in areas where water was pumped by one company, the East London Waterworks.

The head office and main reservoir of the East London Waterworks originally straddled the River Lea at Old Ford, just over three miles from the City of London. As people died by the score and medical facilities were overwhelmed, the finger of suspicion pointed at the Old Ford reservoir. At the time new sewage mains in Bow and Stratford had not yet been connected to the greater London network.

As a consequence the lower reaches of the River Lea were severely polluted from local sewage discharges. Added to this was the increasing quantity of industrial waste that was being dumped into the river from the factories that lined the banks of the Lea. With each new tide mounds of putrid slime were deposited as the water retreated.

Rather than offer any help to the suffering, or even an in depth investigation of what might have gone wrong, the East London Waterworks Company chose to deny any responsibility for the cholera outbreak and to go on the offensive. They even went as far as to suggest that the victims were responsible for their own fate.

On the 2nd August 1866, the company's chief engineer Charles Greaves wrote to *The Times* stating categorically that its waters were completely safe. Later he publicly added that not a drop of unfiltered water had been supplied by the company for several years 'for any purpose'. A week later another engineer wrote that overcrowding, poor drainage and poor diet amongst the local inhabitants were the most likely causes of the cholera outbreak. He said that the East End was populated by dock labourers, sailors and the mechanics in the new factories – just the social groups whose poverty, irregular lives and under developed sense of personal hygiene made them susceptible to disease.

Victorian Street
Water Pump

After peaking in August the outbreak declined during September. So far the epidemic had killed nearly 4,500 people. In November an enquiry was convened by the Board of Trade chaired by a Captain Tyler. Once again the East London Waterworks Company used every trick in the book to disclaim any responsibility, liability or even regret for what had happened.

Several eminent 'expert' medical witnesses were called on behalf of the company, including Henry Letheby, the medical officer of the City of London. He began by refuting the principal that cholera could be water borne and emphasised the *miasmatic* theory that the deaths were in the main caused by bad airs.

It was then argued that local water storage systems, tanks or water fountains could be poisoned as they were not cleaned properly. Once again it was implied that the victims were at fault as they lived such debauched lives in unsanitary conditions. The water company claimed that teetotallers were immune. More astonishingly the East London Water Company stated that as there were areas where they distributed water that hadn't recorded any deaths it couldn't be possible that the company's water was contaminated.

Nevertheless notices were put up all over the East End imploring the populace to boil water before drinking it. Despite continuing company obstruction and protestations, evidence began to emerge of serious irregularities. One group of angry consumers displayed decomposed eels that had emerged from water supply pipes.

In December 1866, a bombshell dropped when the chief engineer Charles Greaves did an about turn and admitted that water from uncovered reservoirs and the polluted River Lea had been fed directly into the city without purification. A company foreman, and then a carpenter testified that during high demand in the summer months sluice gates had been opened on at least three separate occasions thus allowing water 'vulnerable' to contamination to top up the main reservoir.

The enquiry dragged on for well over a year. The Chairman castigated the East London Waterworks for having breached the Water Acts of 1851 and 1852. He said their actions were indefensible. In the end there were no sanctions and no record of prosecution of company directors or of any compensation paid. In fact there seemed to be a degree of satisfaction all round that this most recent London epidemic was less deadly than the previous three!

Although John Snow and William Budd had both published theories of cholera being a waterborne disease fifteen years before the most recent outbreak occurred, the medical profession as a whole did not accept the thesis until Robert Koch identified the actual germs in the 1880s.

The Old Ford reservoir closed completely following the cholera outbreak. It was filled in and redeveloped. The area has since been cleared again and much of it lies under what was main warm up area for the London 2012 Olympic athletes.

Polluted waters originally not believed to be a source of cholera!

In 1902 the East London Waterworks company was taken over by the Metropolitan Water Board which in turn became part of Thames Water, founded under the terms of the Water Act 1973.

Thames Water was privatised as Thames Water Utilities Limited in 1989. It was subsequently acquired by the German utility company RWE who sold it in 2006 to the Australian consortium, Kemble Water Limited.

The Father to Nobody's Children

Against the wishes of his father Thomas John Barnardo, aged nineteen, left his home in Dublin and travelled to London. He wanted to study at the Mission Training School in Stepney before setting out for China where he hoped to become a missionary.

Barnardo arrived in East London in 1866 amidst what was described as the 'final catastrophe of cholera in London' which was claiming at least fifty lives a day (see page 94). The area where Barnardo took lodgings was described as utterly squalid, unhealthy, stinking and crime ridden. Few outsiders chose to visit, let alone live, there. There were an estimated 30,000 plus deserted children roaming the streets of the capital with no homes or regular shelter to go to. The cholera epidemic only exacerbated their misery. After personally witnessing 16 people die in one day Barnardo wanted to help. His studies were put on hold and he abandoned his plans to go to China. He started to teach in one of the so called 'ragged schools' in Mile End. Everyday he came into contact with what he thought were the most deprived children in London who, in theory, had a home of sorts to go to. However, at the end of one school day in December, he was approached by one of the pupils, Jim Jarvis, who pleaded to stay at the school overnight as he had no mother and his home was a hay cart just off the Strand. Barnardo took the boy in that night and Jim Jarvis told of the hundreds of other children in the same predicament. This encounter led to Thomas Barnardo's first move into childcare when he set up a home called the Juvenile Mission for destitute boys in Stepney. Within five years the Mission was the largest and fastest growing in East London. Barnardo was gifted with an enormous range of talents, especially a fanatical drive to get things done and an extraordinary flair for getting publicity and raising funds.

In June 1873 Thomas Barnardo married Syrie Elmslie, who shared his aims and beliefs. The wedding was much to the dismay of Syrie's affluent family who considered Barnardo, at the age of 28 an unsuitable match, as he had no profession, no settled home, no stable income and little prospect of an inheritance. However one of their wedding presents was a 15 year lease on a large house, Mossford Lodge at Barkingside now in the London Borough of Redbridge. It was given by John Sands, a solicitor and admirer of Barnardo's work. The couple set up home there and by October that year, Thomas had adapted a coach house on the estate to be a home for twelve destitute girls. The initial 12 girls very soon grew to approach 60. Bringing up this number of motherless street girls under one roof soon became an impossible task. Barnardo's plan was not working.

Thomas was horrified by what he described as their 'vile conversation that propagated and intensified evil'. Not one to give up, he decided that a different approach was needed which would give the girls a semblance of a home life. The idea for a village with separate cottages took shape. After a period of strenuous fundraising Barnardo bought the freehold of the house and grounds. The following year the foundation stone was laid for the first cottage. Initially fourteen cottages were built and on July 9th 1876 Dr Barnardo's first 'Girls Village Homes', was opened by Lord Cairns, the Lord Chancellor.

These fourteen cottages were the first phase of what would eventually become 'The Village Homes'. By 1879 all 30 of the planned cottages were built, each catering for between 10 and 20 children under the care of a 'House Mother'. The site continued to expand with more cottages and eventually catered for a population of over one thousand. In its layout 'The Village' mirrored the ideas of the 'garden city' movement with the cottages set around two greens. There were two schools, a church, a laundry and a hospital, making the community virtually self contained.

The Barkingside experiment was so successful that other homes were opened across the country. At the time of Barnardo's death, on September 19th 1905, the organisation was running more than ninety homes caring for over eight thousand children. During his lifetime some 60,000 children had been not only given a home

The Barnardo Memorial in Barkingside

and an education but trained to allow them to lead useful and purposeful lives. Sadly successful 'do gooders' are not without their critics. From the day he started work with children Barnardo attracted criticism from jealous rivals, certain sections of the church and even the Guardians of the workhouses who believed his methods were the wrong way to deal with the 'undeserving poor'.

Several letters, in the main anonymous or written under pseudonyms, appeared in the local press questioning what Barnardo was spending all the charitable donations on. Barnardo didn't help his case. He now had two homes, a carriage, driver and several servants. The charity's accounts were always late and he tended to be exceptionally intolerant of any criticism. He had little hesitation in forcefully attacking his opponents and their motives. From 1872, Barnardo insisted that he was called Doctor and recklessly claimed to have a Medical Doctorate from a German University which turned out to be bogus. Many of the children given a new start in life were 'boarded out' with families in Australia, New Zealand, Canada, or South Africa. Barnardo was accused of sending children abroad, as it was cheaper than keeping them in Britain, and doing it without the consent of their parents. For publicity purposes a pioneering scheme was introduced for all children to be photographed exactly as they were found on arrival and again years later on leaving the homes. A sort of 'before and after' register which showed dramatic changes in some children. Barnardo was then accused of mistreating children and faking the photographs.

To refute all these allegations Thomas Barnardo, instead of suing for libel, opted for arbitration under an Order of Court. In October 1877 the Arbitrators were unanimous in their verdict; there was no evidence to support the serious charges laid against him. Although he had left medical school without qualifying, and despite the bogus Medical Doctorate mentioned above, Barnardo succeeded, in 1879, in becoming a fellow of the Royal College of Surgeons in Edinburgh.

When Thomas Barnado died, on 19th September 1905, his charity was almost £250,000 in debt, an astronomical amount for the time. Despite this, the organisation adapted and expanded. At its peak in 1933, Barnardo's had 16,000 children in care, housed in 188 homes. Long term residential care was discontinued in 1979. In 1991 the Village Homes were closed and some of the land sold for development. The house, Mossford Lodge, where it all started was demolished to make way for Redbridge Magistrates Court, which opened in 1977. Barkingside, however, remains the headquarters of the Barnardo organisation. Today the charity runs hundreds of projects to provide short term residential care followed by long term fostering and adoption. There is also a huge emphasis on removing children from sexual exploitation.

The work Barnardo began continues, not just in the United Kingdom but in many countries across the world. Thomas John Barnardo's memorial was unveiled in 1908 in the grounds of the former village home where it still stands. Although Thomas is remembered as *The Father to Nobody's Children*, he and Syrie in fact had seven children of their own.

Triumph and Disaster in Bow Creek

December 1860 was one of the coldest for 50 years. Bow Creek, opposite today's O2 arena, where the River Lea joins the Thames, was thick with ice. On land frozen snow covered the shipyard and icicles hung like daggers from roofs and pipes. Frost encrusted cranes sparkled as if decked in gems. Against this backdrop, the Thames Iron Works, just inside Essex, was to be the setting of not just a national first but an international one too.

It was the 29th of the month and hundreds of braziers blasted out heat as two thousand men worked like demons to ensure the vessel would be ready on time. Crowds of spectators of all ages, including old men and young babies wrapped against the winter's chilling bite, grew by the hour. There were thousands scrambling to find a vantage point. Inside the dock the hull of the *Warrior* rose tall. Every launch from the shipyard was an event in itself but this one was going to be a celebration of national pride and triumph.

Sir John Pakingham MP stepped up to perform the launch ceremony; the *Warrior* however refused to move. Despite dozens of burning braziers placed close to the hull, the iron keel would not budge. Tugs were called in to give extra leverage and shipyard workers on the upper deck ran from side to side trying to rock the vessel free. After 20 minutes, and accompanied by a great cheer, the *Warrior* finally broke away and eased down the slipway.

The launch heralded a new chapter in maritime history. At a stroke all existing warships became out of date. The *Warrior's* vital components, main guns, engines and boilers were encased inside an armoured iron hull. The revolutionary design offered power from both steam and sail. New breech loading guns and a powerful engine meant that the ship could outrun and outgun all others. At 10,000 tons it was one of the biggest ships afloat. It was remarkable that a vessel of such size could be launched in the confined area of Bow Creek. By way of comparison the *Warrior* is almost the same size as the World War II cruiser *HMS Belfast* that is permanently moored in the Thames opposite the Tower of London.

Nearly 40 years later, disaster struck the Thames Iron Works. The *Albion* was a first-class cruiser which the Admiralty had commissioned at the height of the Anglo-German naval race. The launch was due to take place in the summer of 1898 on the 21st June. Thirty thousand spectators had crammed into the shipyard to watch the Duchess of York perform the launching ceremony. Parallel to the *Albion* was a temporary slipway 'bridge'. Two hundred spectators, desperate to get a good view of the launch, had forced their way onto it despite desperate warnings from the police and yard workers that it was extremely dangerous.

As had been the case with the *Warrior,* the launch was beset with problems. Following three failed attempts to smash a bottle of champagne against the hull, which is always a sign of bad luck, the Duchess finally cut the cord and the *Albion* slid down the slipway slowly gaining speed.

The momentum of the vessel as it hit the water created a huge wave which raced across the narrow Bow Creek and engulfed the temporary slipway bridge, smashing it to pieces, and throwing the spectators into the river. Their cries of panic were drowned out by the cheers of the main crowd applauding the launch who were completely unaware of the catastrophe, as were the Duke and Duchess of York.

It was at least ten minutes before news of the accident filtered through to the yard managers. Nearby spectators and workers begun immediate rescue efforts and some dived into the muddy waters to try and pull out survivors. The newly formed ironworks ambulance corps was soon on the scene. Yet, despite their best efforts, 38 people, including women and children, died in the incident.

Inscription at Canning Town Station

For half a century the Thames Iron Works had been the most important shipyard in the country. During the 75 years of its life, until it closed in 1912, over 600 ships were built - from small cutters to great dreadnoughts. At its peak 7000 workers were employed there.

Vessels destined for Japan, Portugal, Sweden and Germany featured prominently in its order book. One ship, the cargo-passenger-gunboat *Yavari*, was even crated up in kit form and sent to Lake Titicaca, two miles above sea level in Peru, where it was to be assembled. Mules were used to carry the ship's sections on the last leg of the journey up the high mountain passes to get to the lake.

The *Albion* disaster was the beginning of the end for the shipyard. Ship building ceased in 1911 following the completion of the *Thunderer,* then the navy's biggest warship. Its construction bankrupted the yard. The Thames Iron Works could not compete with the rapidly expanding shipyards of the north-east of England who had better access to coal and iron and longer slipways.

Nearly all physical traces of the Thames Iron Works at Bow have now disappeared. The buildings have long gone and been replaced by warehouses. The site is cut in two by the lower River Lea road crossing. On the western side of the River Lea, on Trinity Buoy Wharf, heritage plaques recall the shipyard. At the entrance to Canning Town station, on the edge of the original site is an inscription carved in concrete by Richard Kindersley that gives a potted history.

Nevertheless, the Thames Iron Works legacy lives on. West Ham United Football Club (The Hammers) had its origins in the yard's social club. Crossed Hammers like those used in ship construction appear on the club's logo. Should the reader care to travel further afield - to Peru and onwards to Lake Titicaca - the *Yavari* is still there. It claims to be the oldest surviving single propeller iron ship that remains in working order.

Despite all the hype at its launch the *Warrior* had an undistinguished career. Within a decade the ship was obsolete. Never once had it fired a shot in anger and it soon fell victim to rapidly evolving warship technology. In 1883 the *Warrior* was withdrawn from sea service, stripped and used as a depot ship. It was then sold and for 50 years was used as a floating oil jetty in Pembroke Dock in Wales, renamed *Oil Fuel Hulk C77*.

In August 1979 the Maritime Trust rescued the *Warrior*. Taken to Hartlepool, it was restored over eight years at a cost of £10 million. By contrast, in 1860 the cost of building the *Warrior,* including guns and initial coal supply was £390,000.

The Warrior berthed in Portsmouth Harbour

Today the fully restored *Warrior* can be seen in Portsmouth harbour close to the other legend of British naval history - Nelson's *Victory.* As for the *Albion*, she saw service in the Mediterranean during World War I and was then sold for scrap in 1919.

Hitchcock's Psycho montage at Leytonstone Tube Station

An Essex icon. The Ford Capri, made in Dagenham on show at Valence House

Abbey Mills Pumping Station Stratford. The Cathedral of Sewage

The Thames Sailing Barge.
The HGV of the 19th century

A Ford Zodiac Mk 4. It would really fit
in a matchbox!

The Olympic Rings on a barge in the Royal Docks by City Airport awaiting their move to Tower Bridge

The Peoples Forest

On Saturday May 6th 1882, Queen Victoria alighted from the Royal Train at Chingford Station having travelled from Windsor. Chingford station and its approaches were bedecked with flowers to mark the occasion. From Chingford the Queen moved on in a horse drawn carriage to High Beech where an amphitheatre had been put up for an audience of 2000 people. There the Queen addressed the crowd and formally declared "It gives me the greatest satisfaction to dedicate this beautiful forest to the use and enjoyment of my people for all time". From that time it became *The People's Forest*.

The Great Royal Forest of Essex, or the Kings Forest or Waltham Forest, was so named in the 13th century when Henry III gave the area legal status. The King reaffirmed most of the forest rights laid down in the *Magna Carta* which permitted commoners to graze cattle, pasture swine (known as pannage), collect firewood or cut turf for fuel. They could also gather food - generally edible nuts and berries. However, the hunting rights were reserved for the Crown. Commoners were strictly forbidden from hunting and if caught poaching faced severe penalties. Waltham Forest was a huge area covering some 17000 acres in Metropolitan Essex. The word 'forest' can be confusing and was then taken to mean areas of land reserved for royal hunting where forest laws applied, but did not necessarily mean land that had trees on it.

What remains of this once great forest, lying in the north and east of the London Borough of Waltham Forest and into today's Essex, is now known as Epping Forest. It stretches from Forest Gate in the south for approximately twelve miles north to Epping and at its widest point is not more than two to three miles. Although mostly wooded it also has areas of grassland, heath, rivers and ponds. It is protected by the *Epping Forest Act of 1878*.

The area has been the subject of settlement since Saxon times and was always looked upon as a sustainable source of food and fuel to be conserved. Nothing changed much until Oliver Crowell became Lord Protector. He regarded Royal Hunting for the privileged few with disdain. He believed the forest should be harvested for its raw materials. With the expansion of the navy the forest was naturally an ideal source of timber. Cromwell had no particular feeling for the 'commoners' ancient rights in the forest and seemed quite happy that his supporters could enclose areas of the forest for their own use or for more intensive and sustained forms of agriculture.

In the early 18th century much of the forest was lawless. It was infested by criminals and thieves. Notorious villains like Dick Turpin and his gang hid there.

Feeling threatened, the big land owners enclosed more and more of the forest and employed their own men to protect their homes and families.

New threats to the forest were given extra impetus with the coming of the railways. In the mid 19th century, the rapid expansion of Walthamstow and Leyton made them virtual suburbs of London. The edges of the forest were increasingly becoming attractive for wealthy merchants and officials who wanted to build larges house in the countryside whilst still retaining good access to central London.

Epping. The forest for all

All the time the forest was being eaten into, a growing resistance movement to the enclosures was building. It was led by Thomas Willingale (see page 110). He was determined to preserve his ancient lopping rights and received considerable backing from Parliament and the City of London Corporation.

To this day Epping Forest is managed, under the terms of the Epping Forest Act, by The City of London Corporation who act as Conservators of the Forest. Commoners, that is, people that own more than half an acre of land within a Forest parish, still have the right to graze cattle. Cattle grids are installed on all the roads leading into the forest to keep animals in and hopefully prevent traffic accidents in the neighbouring built up areas.

In 1963 the London Government Act created a new local government structure for the capital in what is now Greater London. When the act came into force in 1965, The London Borough of Waltham Forest was formed by absorbing the three Essex boroughs of Chingford, Walthamstow and Leyton.

Thomas Willingale – the Lopper of Loughton

The Epping Forest that remains today might have been lost as a public open space if it had not been for the efforts of one man, Thomas Willingale.

In the 16th century the forest was still a Royal preserve known as Waltham Forest. The forest rights were regularly updated and renewed by the Crown. The first Queen Elizabeth had confirmed the charter that gave rights to householders who lived in and around the forest. They could cut wood for fuel and graze their cattle but as previously mentioned they were strictly forbidden to hunt deer or catch game. This was the exclusive privilege of the King or Queen of the day.

Strict rules were laid down for the practice of cutting wood, known as lopping. Lopping was permitted on Mondays only between 11th November and St George's Day, 23rd April. Lopping could only be carried out by one adult per household. Wood acquired had to be removed on sledges, not wheeled carts, and no more than two horses were allowed to draw the sledge. It was forbidden to lop branches lower than seven feet from the ground. The wood obtained was to be burnt as domestic fuel and could not be sold or used for any trade purpose.

After the Tudor period, although the forest was nominally Royal, the influence of the crown was waning. The word of the monarch was no longer absolute and Parliament was becoming the commanding voice in state affairs. As London expanded, more and more of Waltham Forest was fenced off and enclosed. Trees were cut down to make way for housing, industry or agriculture. In 1858 the increasing costs of maintaining the forest forced the Crown to sell off some rights. It also disposed of 1400 acres to William Whitaker Maitland, the then Lord of the Manor at Loughton.

His grandson, the Reverend John Maitland, decided he would sell much of his manor for housing and ban lopping from the estate. Legend has it that one year later Maitland tried to end the lopper's rights by inviting all commoners to a supper at the local King's Head public house on 11th November. His intention was that by midnight they would all be too drunk to start lopping and thus forfeit their rights. Thomas Willingale, one of those invited to the King's Head, suspected treachery was afoot. He firmly believed that if no one started lopping at the appointed hour commoners rights would be lost forever.

Willingale jealously guarding these rights handed down from Queen Elizabeth, discreetly excused himself before midnight. He went to the forest, lopped off a branch and returned with it in triumph thus ensuring the lopping rights were still intact.

Maitland, with the clandestine backing of the local board of works, decided to prosecute Willingale and the loppers. For 10 years a legal game of cat and mouse went on. Thomas died in 1870 but his son, Sam, took up the standard of the loppers. Over the years several fines were imposed on the Willingales. Most of these were not paid and Sam even spent some time in prison for non-payment. The case became a cause célèbre and was viewed as a David and Goliath contest. The Willingales attracted considerable moral, and then financial, support from the City of London and the House of Commons. There was still lingering outrage at the way much of Hainault Forest had been destroyed 20 years earlier. Now alarm bells were ringing at the way huge areas of Epping Forest were being fenced off for the personal gain of a few rich land owners whilst the public at large were denied access.

Thomas Willingale lopping.
Entrance to the Lopping Hall in Loughton

The tables were turned and Maitland was confronted by a series of legal challenges undertaken by the Corporation of London which culminated in the passing of the *Epping Forest Act of 1878*. Amongst other things the act declared that all the enclosures made by land owners in the previous 25 years were illegal and henceforth the forest was to become a public open space.

The lopping rights ended too but the 'loppers' were financially compensated. A sum of money was also put aside to build the Lopping Hall on Loughton High Road. The forest had been saved and unwittingly the *Lopper of Loughton*, Thomas Willingale, had been its saviour.

An oak carved plaque displayed in the Lopping Hall celebrating Thomas Willingale's efforts disappeared during renovations in the 1960s. He is remembered in Loughton by a street named Willingale Road and Thomas Willingale School in The Broadway.

William Morris

His colours reflect the landscape, Of Essex rolling downs.
Each thread or blade of grass And stitch of golden corn.
(Christine Billington 2006)

William Morris was born in 1834, at Elm House in Walthamstow, to prosperous middle class parents. His father's rising fortunes allowed a move from this house, when William was six, to the far grander Woodford Hall. Eight years later, after his father's death, the family moved again to the smaller, but still quite grand, Water House. This, the only one of the three still standing, is today the home of the William Morris Gallery in Lloyd Park Forest Road, Walthamstow.

Morris left Walthamstow for Oxford University in 1853. It was there that he became lifelong friends with Edward Burne-Jones and later with the pre-Raephelite Brotherhood, all of whom were influential in his later life. Despite wealth and a privileged upbringing, he later embraced the ideas of Karl Marx and became a founding member of the Socialists. He had seen the way that the industrialisation of the nineteenth century had dehumanised production with its emphasis on the 'division of labour'. His answer to what he saw as 'the dull squalor of civilization', was to turn away from mechanisation, seek inspiration from history and nature, and draw heavily on the experiences of his Essex childhood.

In the 1830s Walthamstow was little more than a village, bounded by the River Lea and its marshlands to the west and by green fields and forest to the north and west. Elm House stood on the rising ground of Clay Hill with views up the Lea valley to Epping Forest two miles away. It was not a 'Grand' house but it stood in its own grounds. With its white panelled hall, wide carved staircase and its garden of flowers, mulberry bushes and rows of elm trees it was a place with lots of scope for William's imaginative young mind to develop.

From a young age Morris was interested in romantic tales of chivalry, knights in shining armour, fairies and heroic deeds from history. When the family moved to Woodford Hall he had not only a garden of his own but a large estate and a park to roam as well. He had his own pony and even a suit of armour in which he acted out heroic deeds. Riding around the estate and the surrounding Essex countryside, he also acquired a love of hunting, shooting and fishing.

Although the family fortunes changed when his father died the move to the smaller Water House made little difference to Morris's life.

The house was, and still is, impressive. With its spectacular black and white marble entrance leading to a massive chestnut staircase, it was a smaller version of Woodford Hall. It was a moated house, the moat at the rear being some forty feet wide with an island in the middle.

William and his siblings fished the moat for perch and pike, skated on it in winter and lived out games on their own adventure island. It was an ideal environment in which to indulge fantasies absorbed from his reading of tales of medieval chivalry, such as the novels of Walter Scott and the Arthurian legends.

In later life Morris was to say of Epping Forest that, as a boy he knew it 'yard by yard from Wanstead to the Theydons, and from Hale End to the Fairlop Oak'. Through the forest he came to know the trees, the shapes of their leaves and the birds and wildlife that inhabited them. He was familiar with the rivers and marshes and the fish and waterbirds of the Lea and its tributaries.

Morris was fascinated by the ancient earthworks in the forest; Loughton Camp, an early Iron Age encampment, and Ambresbury Banks, an Iron Age hill-fort, both reputedly once fortified by King Arthur as a defence against encroaching Saxons.

He discovered Queen Elizabeth's Hunting Lodge at Chingford, originally built as a grandstand from which Henry VIII could watch the hunt on Chingford plain. Going inside, his imagination was fired by the faded greenery of the tapestries hanging in the medieval manner and the sheer romanticism of the place. All these experiences and scenes from his early years provided images that would be drawn on again and again in his designs.

After graduating from Oxford he became an artist but design was his real forte. A natural business man, he set up workshops to produce things by hand. Morris described his works as creating beauty, while blending usefulness, truth to material and sound design. His products were an immediate success. His designs of wallpapers, fabrics, furniture and interior decoration made a worldwide impact which is still being felt today.

During the 1880s a number of young men developing their interest in traditional hand crafts came together to form what became, 'The Arts and Crafts Movement'. William Morris is often associated with the Arts and Crafts Movement and although he was not its founder, he was certainly its inspiration.

The William Morris Gallery was opened on Saturday 21st October 1950 by Prime Minister Clement Attlee and is the only public museum devoted to Morris and his works.

Steam Trams for Portugal

Monkhams Lane, situated close to Buckhurst Hill, runs in a south easterly direction between Lord's Bushes and Knighton Wood, both detached parts of Epping Forest. Today Monkhams Lane separates the London Borough of Redbridge and Essex proper. It is a pleasant forest track popular for dog walkers and joggers that gently slopes down towards the River Roding. The Corporation of London manage the open space and enforce strict byelaws which include not only a ban on motorised vehicles but cycling too!

One hundred and forty years ago Monkhams Lane was used for a very different purpose. At that time Britain was the 'Workshop of the World' and the lane was the site of an experimental iron rail track, laid on flat timbers for approximately one mile. In December 1872, a 4-2-4ST steam tram locomotive called 'Cintra' was trialled to ascertain if it could pull two carriages, each holding 18 people, up the 1 in 20 incline to test the power of the engine. The tests took all day with the engine chugging back and forth, sometimes reaching speeds of 20 miles per hour. The event was watched by hundreds of curious spectators.

Monkhams Lane had been chosen as its terrain was considered similar to that of the steam trams' eventual destination. The end customer for the engine was the Lisbon Steam Tramways Co. Ltd in Portugal where it was to be used on the Lisbon – Torres Vedras line.

The engine was one of 16 especially built by Sharp, Stewart & Co of Manchester for the Portuguese Company.

Although the trial at Monkhams Lane was successful, the engine, the first in a series, never arrived in Portugal. Following the tests it was loaded on to the *SS Northfleet* which sank following a disastrous collision in the channel which claimed 300 lives.

The further 15 locomotives were eventually delivered to Lisbon but the

A 4-2-4ST Steam Tram Locomotive

Lisbon Steam Tramways Co. Ltd went out of business two years later. With the passing of the Epping Forest Act in 1878 Monkhams Lane was no longer deemed suitable to test steam engines. The iron rail tracks were torn up and since then the route has not been disturbed by puffing steam engines.

DATE	EVENT
1800	*Britain captures Malta.*
1803	*Henry Shrapnel invents the Explosive Shell*
1805	*Battle of Trafalgar*
1810	*First public Billiard room opens in Covent Garden*
1812	*British PM Spencer Percival is assassinated in Parliament*
1815	*Battle of Waterloo*
1820	*Birth of Florence Nightingale*
1828	*Trial begins of Bodysnatchers, Burke and Hare*
1830	*Last person put in pillory in England*
1831	*Charles Darwin embarks on voyage of the Beagle*
1832	*First Great Reform Act*
1837	*William IV dies, Victoria becomes Queen.*
1838	*Public Record Office is established*
1840	*Queen Victoria marries Prince Albert*
1841	*Britain claims sovereignty over Hong Kong*
1843	*Dickens 'A Christmas Carol' published.*
1844	*YMCA founded in London*
1845	*Potato crop fails causing famine in Ireland*
1860	*Abraham Lincoln elected 16th US President*
1865	*Abraham Lincoln is assassinated*
1867	*Dominion of Canada created*
1870	*Death of Charles Dickens*
1874	*Disraeli becomes Prime Minister*
1876	*Alexander Graham Bell invents Telephone*
1878	*First electric street lights in London*
1883	*Buffalo Bill's 'Wild West Show' opens in London*
1885	*John Boyd Dunlop patents the Pneumatic Tyre*
1883	*Buffalo Bill's 'Wild West Show' opens in London*
1888	*Jack the Ripper murders six women in London*
1889	*Cecil Rhodes obtains royal charter for British South Africa Company*
1890	*Death of Vincent van Gogh*
1891	*Edison patents movie camera*
1892	*Keir Hardie becomes first Labour M.P.*
1894	*Blackpool Tower opens*
1895	*Trial of Oscar Wilde begins*
1899	*Siege of Mafeking begins*

Disaster at Gallions Reach

Tuesday September 3rd 1878 began as a bright, sunny, late summer day that attracted hundreds of Londoners to take advantage of the nice weather and embark on a Thames Pleasure Steamer for a day trip to Rosherville Gardens at Gravesend. The day however was to end in tragedy and the largest ever loss of life from a single incident in the UK.

At 10:30 on that fateful morning the *SS Princess Alice* left Swan Pier near London Bridge on a routine trip to Gravesend and Sheerness. Numbers were uncertain since only adults paid the two shillings for a ticket, children were not counted. Returning that evening passengers were in good spirits, a band was playing and there was singing and dancing as the ship approached the final leg of the journey.

At 19:40 that evening the ship had entered Gallions Reach and was within sight of North Woolwich Pier, the destination for some passengers, when a much larger vessel was seen approaching in the centre of the river from upstream. The *S.S. Bywell Castle* was an iron hulled collier displacing nearly 900 tons. She had just been repainted in dry dock and was bound for Newcastle. In command was Captain Harrison who was accompanied by an experienced Thames river pilot.

As both vessels approached Tripcock Point, Captain Harrison, on the bridge of the *Bywell Castle*, saw the *Princess Alice* make for the north bank of the river. Accordingly he changed course to pass on her port side, the correct procedure. At this point the master of the *Princess Alice*, Captain William Grinstead, became confused by the *Bywell Castle's* maneuver and altered course to try to cut between the bigger ship and the south bank. This led her directly into the path of the huge collier. Captain Harrison immediately ordered engines to reverse but it was too late. The iron hull of the unladen *Bywell Castle* was riding high in the water and struck the *Princess Alice* near her starboard paddle wheel. Being a wooden boat of only 250 tons and with more than 750 passengers so very low in the water, the pleasure steamer had no chance. She was effectively sliced in two and sank within four minutes. The *Bywell Castle* which was relatively undamaged immediately lowered three boats and let down ropes over her bows to assist rescue. Her whistle attracted other boats from shore. Rescue operations continued through the night. It is thought that somewhere between 590 and 640 lives were lost that night. There was no definitive figure since there was no accurate record of passenger numbers. Some bodies were never found. They may have been swept down stream by the tide or buried in the Thames mud. Of the dead recovered 120 were never identified. Altogether only 69 people were saved.

One of the contributory factors to the high death toll was that one hour before the collision millions of gallons of raw sewage were released from the outfalls at Barking and Crossness, making that section of Gallions Reach the most polluted stretch of water in the country.

While a handful of people swam to the shore, many of those not trapped in the boat and dragged down may have been suffocated or choked by the poisonous water. A contemporary report states that when the flood gates are opened, twice in every 24 hours, ' ...there is projected into the river two columns of decomposed fermenting sewage, hissing like soda water with baneful gases, so black that the water is stained for miles and discharging a corrupt charnel house odour.'

A mass burial and funeral service, which thousands attended, was held on September 9th at Woolwich Old Cemetery where a large stone Celtic Cross still stands as a memorial. The monument was paid for by donations of sixpence (2½p) from 23000 people.

An inquest was held that recorded a verdict of death by misadventure, whilst accepting that the collision was an accident. Both captains were criticised; Harrison for not stopping his engines earlier, and Grinstead for not stopping and not staying on course for the north bank. A later Board of Trade Inquiry came to more or less the same conclusions as well as criticizing the amount of passengers on the *Princess Alice*. New rules were passed into law in 1880 which included mandating vessels always passing port to port; numbers of lifebelts stowed on board and stricter controls on passenger numbers.

Another recommendation was that the Metropolitan Police should equip its Thames division with steam launches since up until then they had only had rowing boats.

Despite these recommendations, over a hundred years later on 20th August 1989 history was to repeat itself. The *Marchioness*, a light pleasure boat with 131 people on board, sank after being in collision with a much bigger, iron clad dredger, the *Bowbelle*. On that night 51 people lost their lives.

WOOLWICH FERRY

The Woolwich Free Ferry was opened by Lord Roseberry, Chairman of the then London County Council (L.C.C.), on March 23rd 1889. It is difficult to believe that it was established as a free ferry and to this day there is still no charge for passengers, cars or commercial vehicles.

The Woolwich Ferry leaving Essex for Kent

It appears the Victorians were not nearly as mercenary as the Normans who established a crossing point at Woolwich nearly 1000 years ago. Hamon Dapifer, the Sheriff of Kent seized North Woolwich and made it part of Kent so he could collect the taxes and tolls from the cross-river traffic on both sides of the river. (See also page 30 Detached Woolwich).

The new free ferry was launched amid much celebration with bunting, bands and a procession preceded by mounted police. Of the three ships linking Woolwich to North Woolwich only one, the *Gordon*, named after General Gordon of Khartoum, was in service that weekend. She would later be joined by *Duncan*, named after Col. Francis Duncan, and *Hutton*, named after Sir John Hutton Chairman of the L.C.C.

118

Crowds clamoured to take advantage of the first free trips across the river. Great Eastern Railways brought 25000 people to North Woolwich in that weekend alone, most of them intent on riding the ferry.

These twin paddle steam ferries displaced nearly 500 tons and measured 164 feet in length but had a draught of only four feet to cope with the rise and fall of the tide. They were licensed to carry 1000 passengers, with room for 15 to 20 vehicles.

By 1930 the original boats had been gradually replaced by four similar paddle steamers at a cost of £74,000. These were the *Squires*, the *John Benn*, the *Will Crooks and a* new replacement *Gordon*. Each vessel was coke-fired and grossed 625 tons. However, the ferries could not be loaded to full capacity due to the limited depth of water at the loading pontoons. The paddle steam era for the Woolwich Ferries ended during the 1960s. The old ships were despatched to Belgium to be scrapped. During their life time they had covered four million miles and carried nearly 180 million passengers.

The paddle steamers were replaced by three new diesel powered ferries - *John Burns, Ernest Bevin* and the *James Newman* pictured on the previous page. New loading ramps were built to allow for bow/stern, roll on/roll off loading. Each was licensed to carry 500 passengers and vehicles, provided the combined weight was no more than 200 tons. The ferries could proceed equally well in either direction, were highly manoeuvrable and able to leave the terminals whatever the state of the tide.

These boats are still in service today. They are named after three politicians connected in some way with Woolwich or the River Thames. John Burns was an enthusiastic student of London history and the Thames. Ernest Bevin was the son of an agricultural labourer who became a trade unionist before entering Parliament as a member for Woolwich, and between 1945 and 1951 he was Foreign Secretary. James Newman was a school teacher by profession. He was a member of the Woolwich borough council for many years and mayor from 1923-25. In 1948 he received an OBE in recognition of his service to local government.

Throughout their 120 years of service the Woolwich Ferries have only been stopped by fog or the occasional breakdown. During the war the ferry was available whenever it was needed. For a while during the blackout, navigation lights were extinguished which made steering difficult.

In April 1965 North Woolwich became part of the London Borough of Newham.

When the Whales Came

Just after midday on Thursday 19th January 2006, a Northern Bottlenose Whale was spotted swimming in the Thames close to the Thames Barrier. It was described as dark grey and approximately 20 feet long with a rounded dorsal fin.

Early the next day the whale was again seen, initially at Greenwich, then at around 10.00am, further up river close to Westminster. It soon attracted crowds of sightseers and the world's media was not far behind.

It is not known what had caused the whale to swim up the river. As the river grew shallower the ability of the whale to find its way back to the open sea would be difficult. Therefore, the chances of survival were slim. In fact the whale was stranded more than once as the tide receded. By the following Saturday morning the whale's fate had become the focus of international attention. The *Los Angeles Times* reported "Whale of a good show in London" and a Spanish newspaper ran a headline "A whale visits Big Ben". By lunch time on the same Saturday the whale had even managed to reach Battersea Bridge.

A rescue plan was put into effect, jointly undertaken by the British Divers Marine Life Rescue and the Zoological Society of London. The animal was 'captured' and carefully hoisted onto a specially prepared barge to be taken back to the open sea. However, during the early evening the whale began convulsing and died shortly afterwards. The cause of death was put down to severe dehydration and kidney failure.

The plight of the whale so inspired a Southend Poet, Derek Adams, that he penned the poem seen on the left, which won first prize in a competition to become BBC Wildlife Poet of the Year of 2006.

Odysseus in London

Secured on the deck,
watched over by a crew
who cannot hear the
beep... ping,
beep... ping
of the siren's voice,
but it's too late: the sonar's song
has gripped your cetacean heart,
led you through shipping lanes
down narrowing curves
that echo Eustachian tubes.
The call is fading now,
drowned by the constant
thump-thump of the engine,
those monitoring your heart
might just pick up its echoes
before they see that long flat line;
Ithaca still beyond the horizon.

Derek Adams

Over the years whales have been seen in the Thames many times. On 27th November 1899, a large female rorqual whale appeared at North Woolwich between the Albert Docks and Barking Creek. A photograph taken at the time suggests this particular specimen was over 60 feet long.

Sadly the Victorians showed none of the compassion that was evident in 2006. It seems that once the whale was spotted it was immediately pursued. A steam tug took up the chase which was described at the time as 'exciting'. The tug eventually managed to ram the whale and push it onto the shore at Woolwich Arsenal. The injured creature was then set upon by the crew with hatchets and crowbars until it was killed. Later the deceased behemoth was towed to the north bank, by the Royal Victoria Gardens (originally Pavilion Gardens) and beached. The body attracted huge crowds, many of whom waded into the mud and hacked pieces off as souvenirs. Passengers travelling on the Woolwich Ferry would have had grandstand views not only of the initial chase but also of the hacking to death of the whale, its movement to the north bank and the crowds who came to take souvenirs.

The dead animal, which was discovered to be a female, was found to have been carrying two young, both over 10 feet long. One of the stillborne infants disappeared mysteriously but the other was purchased by a Mr White, the landlord of Pavilion hotel. He took the baby whale and covered it in a black preservative acquired from the Beckton Gas works. For three months the body was displayed in a tent behind the hotel where visitors could pay to see it. It was a very popular exhibition and profitable too for the landlord. The Pavilion Hotel has since been demolished.

After a few days the mother's carcass began to rot. The Council ordered its removal and the whale was towed down river to Price's Oil Works in Erith where it was cut into pieces and boiled up.

Suffice it to say the cause of death was obvious. However, much like the incident in 2006, there was no obvious explanation as to why such a huge creature should make its way up the River Thames.

Moby Dick, Whalebones, and the night Oliver Cromwell Died

The *Moby Dick* public house, at the junction of Whalebone Lane North and the A12 Eastern Avenue, was officially opened by the Mayor of Dagenham, Councillor Mrs Mary Bredo, on 8th July 1959.

The Hollywood film *Moby Dick* starring Gregory Peck had been released in the UK two years earlier and what with the *Moby Dick's* location on Whalebone Lane the accompanying publicity couldn't have been better.

Directly south of the *Moby Dick* is the *Tollgate Inn*, at the junction of the High Road, A118, in Chadwell Heath. This occupies the site of the ancient toll gate at the tenth milestone on the old Roman road from London to Colchester. The area also boasts a Whalebone House, Whalebone Cottages, Whalebone Grove and Whalebone Avenue all of which occupy land once part of the Whalebone House Estate.

The clues to the uses of so many references to 'Whalebone' can be found at Valence House Museum in Dagenham where two bones from the lower jaw of a common Greenland Whale are displayed. In the 17th century bones formed an arch by the octagonal Toll-House on the High Road where they remained until the house was demolished in 1870. They were then transferred to nearby Whalebone House to form an arch at its entrance gate. There they stood until the house was hit by bombs in 1941. The bones were then removed to Valence House for safe keeping. After the war they were erected either side of the entrance to the museum. Over time the bones deteriorated and they were taken down and stored in the basement. In 2010 Valence House museum benefited from a substantial refurbishment and the bones were taken out and restored to their best condition. They are now on display in a sealed glass cabinet on the ground floor of the museum.

Where these bones came from is shrouded in mystery. Although London had a thriving Whaling industry in the 17th century, a persistent local legend has it that the bones came from a whale that was stranded in the Thames at Dagenham as a result of a great storm on September 2nd 1658, the night Oliver Cromwell died. Dr. Howell in his 1678 work, *Ancient and Present State of England* supported the date of the storm and the sighting of a 'Whale of very great length and bigness'.

Daniel Defoe also wrote in his *Tour through the Island of Great Britain*, published in 1724, of 'The Whalebone', a roadside Inn at Chadwell Heath. He drew parallels with the 'monstrous' Oliver Cromwell and a monstrous creature – a whale.

Defoe wrote that the Inn was "so called because the rib-bone of a large whale, taken in the River Thames, was fixed there in 1658, the year Oliver Cromwell died, for a monument of that monstrous creature, it being at first about eight and twenty foot long".

We now know that they were jawbones and did once belong to a Greenland Whale. Since Greenland Whales have never been known to visit our shores, it seems unlikely that these bones came from one stranded in the Thames anywhere near Dagenham.

Nevertheless in the 17th century many Greenland Whales would have been brought to the Greenland Dock at Rotherhithe from the Arctic grounds by whaling boats. Maybe that's also a clue?

The Moby Dick and Hotel on Whalebone Lane

It is a curious coincidence that Herman Melville, the author of the book *Moby Dick* on which the film was based, used facts gleaned from the true account of a whale attacking a ship taken from the 1921 book *Shipwreck of the Whaleship Essex* by Owen Chase.

There the parallels end as the *Whaleship Essex* sailed from Nantucket in Massachusetts, although it must be said it was colonists from Essex in England who were responsible for Essex becoming a place name in the USA.

Unlike many contemporary public houses, the *Moby Dick* in Whalebone Lane North is still going strong. It has a fine restaurant and a hotel has been added alongside.

The Greatest Show on Earth
(in Ilford)

At 4.00am, on Tuesday 21st June 1904, three specially chartered trains edged into Ilford station having travelled down from Chelmsford overnight. It was described by the *Ilford Guardian* as the most remarkable train freight ever to be brought to Ilford by the Great Eastern Railway Company. It was an exhibition that had no counterpart in the world. The three trains totalled three quarters of a mile in length and consisted of 49 railcars.

Buffalo Bill's Wild West show and his Congress of Rough Riders had arrived in town. As it became light a true spectacle unfolded as 500 horses and 800 people, many already in their stage costumes, disembarked and made their way on foot southwards along Ilford Lane to the Kingsfield Estate. They were accompanied by an authentic wagon train carrying the marquees, side stalls, props and even the seating needed to run the event – and the show hadn't even started yet!

William Frederick "Buffalo Bill" Cody was a former US cavalry soldier, frontier scout and hunter. However, he made his name as a showman and built his reputation as one of the most colourful figures of the old American west. Quite how much of his past was true and how much was woven into legend is difficult to distinguish. Following the success of Cody's American shows he brought the show to Europe where his tours included the British Isles on several occasions.

Two actual shows were planned for Ilford, the first for 2.00pm and the second for 8.00pm. Advance tickets were on sale from Rockley's Piano Warehouse at 151 High Road, Ilford and prices ranged from four shillings to seven shillings and sixpence, the most expensive in the house. Lower priced tickets of between one and four shillings could only be purchased on the day from the ticket booths.

The show opened with a cowboy band playing a lively rendition of the 'Star Spangled Banner' which was immediately followed by a parade on horse back which included 100 Indian braves in full war paint. There followed Colonel William Cody 'Buffalo Bill' himself, astride a magnificence white steed. He cantered to the head of the parade and raised his hand. There was immediate silence. He greeted the audience with a welcoming smile, doffed his hat, bowed and declared the show open. Immediately the Indians galloped around in full war cry and the audience cheered. From that point the programme moved into full swing. No time was wasted and each different performance moved seamlessly from one to the next.

First up were displays of horsemanship not only from veterans of the old west but also riders who had joined 'Buffalo Bill' around the world, including Cossacks, Japanese, Arabian and Mexicans. The Mexicans showed off their amazing lassoing and rope skills. A stunning display of taming bucking broncos followed. Then, taking centre stage, the unmatched shooting skills of Johnny Baker who could shoot white balls tossed into the air from any angle even if he was riding backwards on a horse at speed or even standing on his head. Next followed Carter the Cowboy cyclist who would make a daring leap through space as he rode down a chute and jumped 50ft on to a lower platform whilst firing his pistol at a target high above his head. This was a new sensational item on the programme that bought the house down.

However, the main attractions as usual were those that were most eagerly awaited - the Wild West spectaculars which always began with a parade of the US 7th Calvary. There followed a re-enactment of the journey of the pony

express though hostile territory and the dramatic mock attack on the 'Deadwood Stage'.

The 'grand finale' of the evening was a staged battle scene from 'Custer's Last Stand' or the 'Battle of the Little Big Horn' in which Custer's entire command of 300 men was trapped and then annihilated by Sioux Indians.

During the performance the audience was mesmerised and when it was over they rose to their feet to cheer and clap with gusto.

With the show over once again, 'Buffalo Bill' appeared at the head of the 7th Cavalry. He thanked the spectators for coming and then saluted them, as did the performers before departing into the wings. Again the audience rose to its feet and the applause was unrestrained.

For Colonel William Cody it had been another tremendous performance that had left the spectators ecstatic. With great efficiency the marquees were dismantled and the wagons loaded. It had been a long day, in fact by coincidence the longest day of the year. Buffalo Bill headed the return procession along Ilford Lane back to Ilford Station and started preparing for the next venue in St Albans. After all the show must go on!

Britain's First Aerodrome (in Dagenham)

The early 1900s were exciting times for would be aviators. In 1908 the *Daily Mail's* prize of £1000 for the first cross channel flight was a great encouragement to this embryonic industry. Members of the 'Aeronautical Society' (it didn't become 'Royal' until 1918) had been anxious for some time to establish a permanent base where they could test and develop their aircraft. On 25th January 1909 the search was over. The society's 'Experimental Ground Committee', chaired by Major B.F.S. Baden-Powell, leased a two acre stretch of land on the banks of the Thames at Dagenham at a cost of £50 per annum.

It was rough, reclaimed marsh land and criss-crossed with drainage ditches. The area, known as 'The Dagenham Breach', had suffered from many floods and tidal surges since the 17th century which had left a large lake surrounded by marshland. So the 'Experimental Testing Ground' was not everyone's ideal choice. However, it was a secluded spot and had good transport links via the London, Tilbury and Southend Railway at Dagenham Dock. The site was cleared and sheds were erected to serve as hangers.

Baden-Powell, the brother of the Chief Scout, was the first aviator to use the new facility. He brought his small untested 'Quadruplane' and housed it in one of the sheds. He was soon followed by a series of aircraft pioneers who tested a number of weird and wonderful contraptions of all shapes and sizes, many of which never left the ground. One of the first arrivals was Frederick Handley Page who went on to successfully build a range of military and commercial aircraft, including the Halifax bomber that was manufactured in large numbers during the Second World War.

Page's first effort was a tandem biplane designed by G.P. Deverall Saul. The machine was built in Woolwich and taken to Dagenham where it was tested on a trolley towed by a car to aid the aircraft's engine. The structure was built of wood, mainly hickory, and rested on two long skids. It was recorded as having made several brief and short hops which, though by no means successful flights, were encouraging enough for its owner to commission the building of a two-seater version.

In an effort to promote itself, the Aeronautical Society arranged an open day for members and their guests, as well as representatives of the press. They would see for themselves the benefits of the 'first Experimental Landing Ground in the country' and witness flying displays.

The members were brought to Dagenham by the 'Aeronautical Special Train' (a grandiose term for open goods wagons from which passengers had to alight by ladders!) but the visitors were soon disappointed.

The unfavourable weather ruled out any flying displays and interest was limited to inspection of the aircraft being exhibited. Many of them, it was reported, had their engines running, which considerably irritated fishermen in the nearby Dagenham Breach. There was further disappointment for the photographers and reporters when it was found that an airship created by another pioneer, Mr C. A. Moreing, was not even inflated.

Overall the day was not a success. After inspection of the grounds some members were unimpressed with its potential. There were comments that the site was impractical and far too small; by way of comparison Southend airport, not large itself, is 150 times the size of the Dagenham site. Within a year most of the aviators had left. Only Moreing's airship remained stored in a special hangar. That too was removed in 1910 and the 'Experimental Landing Ground' fell into disuse.

Handley Page's tandem biplane. It achieved little more than a hop skip and jump

However, Handley Page must have felt that the area had much to offer. That same year he took a lease on land adjacent to the society's grounds. Stretching from Dagenham Dock to Barking Creek, the strip was flanked by the London, Tilbury and Southend Railway. He also had flying rights along the north banks of the Thames. Workshops erected on this site became his first factory and it was here that the company, Handley Page Limited, was established.

In January 1910 Handley Page bought three of the redundant aircraft sheds from the Aeronautical Society for £40. These allowed him to start work on his own monoplane, the Type A or HPI 'Bluebird'. However, there are no records of any successful flights at either of these two sites. All Handley Page's successful test flights were carried out at a sports ground at Fairlop. In 1911/12, the company transferred to a new site at West London.

The 1920s saw what might have been the site of the first aerodrome in Britain sold by the land owner Samuel Williams to become part of the U.K. base of the Ford Motor Company.

The Wilderness Eton Manor
To strive, to seek, to find, and not to yield
from Ulysses by Alfred Lord Tennyson

The Wilderness once occupied a triangular wedge of land between Ruckholt Road in Leyton, the Temple Mills rail marshalling yards and the A12. Its western boundary was the oddly called Quarter Mile Lane close to the River Lea. Opposite the site is the New Spitalfields Flower and Vegetable market that opened in 1991. In 2012 the *Wilderness* firstly became the Olympic training and accreditation area and was then converted to the Paralympic tennis courts. It is somewhat odd to call an area in East London the *Wilderness* but when the site was acquired on behalf of Eton Manor for sports, that was the nickname it was given (due to the scruffy nature of the land) and it stayed for 40 years.

Eton Manor as a boys' club began life in 1909 under the patronage of Gerald Wellesley, an 'Old Etonian' and the grandson of the Duke of Wellington. The boys' club was described 'as an institution in Hackney Wick run for the very roughest class of working boy'. With the help of fellow 'Etonians', a purpose built complex was opened in 1913 in Riseholme Street on the disused Manor Farm – hence the name Eton Manor. From the very beginning Eton Manor offered a wide range of sporting and educational activities. As the membership role grew, drama, music, first aid and even mechanics were added. The club premises had one of the finest libraries in East London. Professional tutors, some even from Eton College, were brought in to teach the more academic subjects and expert coaches were on hand to assist with the different sports offered. Such was the popularity of the club that waiting lists were soon in place. The club's sporting achievements were making headlines too and 'respectable middle class' families now wanted their children to enrol.

In 1930, thirty-two acres of 'rough ground' at Leyton were acquired and the *Wilderness* came into being. Over the next few years the ground was developed into a sports complex of football pitches that alternated as cricket pitches in the summer, two rugby fields, a netball court and a bowling green. A full size athletics track, with spectator seating, was built as were a pavilion, changing and shower rooms, a gymnasium and a café. Eton Manor came to be one of the most prestigious and comprehensive sporting venues in the UK.

In 1951, Eton Manor was the first club in Britain to be equipped with floodlights and the first to host a floodlit track meeting. Many of the countries leading post-war athletes competed at Eton Manor. Most notable were Roger Bannister who later broke the four minute mile and Chris Brasher who went on to win the 3000 metre steeple chase at the Melbourne Olympics.

The club had several footballs teams. Eton Manor was also the adopted 'home' ground for other local boys' teams. One of the reasons for its popularity was that coaches and even sometimes players from Leyton Orient or the Arsenal would be on hand to referee or give advice. The Leyton Orient ground at Brisbane Road was close by and within earshot of the *Wilderness*. When the 'O's were playing at home the Eton Manor footballers could follow the course of the game by the cheering.

Perhaps one of the most dramatic games for the players of Eton Manor was on Saturday 8th September 1962. Leyton Orient had been newly promoted to the First Division and were at home to Manchester United. Kick off for the Eton Manor games was 2.00pm. As soon as their games were finished there was an almighty stampede to get changed and then rush up to Ruckholt Road across the railway bridge to get to Brisbane Road. At the Orient ground 30 to 40 breathless teenage boys suddenly appeared. Kick off there had been at 3.00pm. It was the usual practice to open the gates just after half time and the boys were able to creep in, for free, in twos and threes to see Leyton Orient beat Manchester United by a single goal.* What a day it was.

Sadly the end for Eton Manor came just a few years later. Membership had suddenly declined and in 1967 the Riseholme Street headquarters was compulsory purchased and demolished to make way for the A102(M) East Cross Route to the Blackwall Tunnel. The *Wilderness* gradually fell into disuse, Eton Manor was disbanded and the various sporting sections dispersed. Once the site was cleared, the area became the temporary home of the 'Construction College East London'.

Eton Manor's name lives on though. The football club's ground is now located in Waltham Abbey. The Rugby Club, Eton Manor RFC, moved to Wanstead where its new ground is called the *New Wilderness*. Eton Manor Athletics Club is somewhat more nomadic. Since moving from *the Wilderness*, they train in and around the Lea Valley and Hackney Marshes.

Post 2012 Olympics it is planned that Eton Manor will again be a mix of sporting facilities for local and regional communities where the facility will be owned and run by the Lee Valley Regional Park Authority.

Engraved on the wall at the entrance to the new Eton Manor ground is a brief poetic history of the *Wilderness* and Eton Manor written by Poet Laureate Carol Ann Duffy.

Leyton Orient survived one season in the First Division (the equivalent of today's premier league) before being relegated. However, as well as beating Manchester United they beat Liverpool too in their one glorious season in the top flight of English soccer.

The Three Week Election

December 3rd 1910 was the first day of voting for the second General Election held that year. *In Metropolitan Essex* balloting took place in both West Ham North and West Ham South on the 3rd December, in Walthamstow on the 10th December and in Romford on the 17th December. That year the majority of people were still ineligible to vote. Only three out of five men were registered and women were excluded. Intriguingly, a candidate could stand in more than one place during the same election. If defeated in the constituency where polling had finished first, he could move on and campaign in another which voted later.

This second election had been called because of the failure of the two principal parties, the Conservatives and the Liberals, to agree on reform of the House of Lords and home rule in Ireland. Yet, again the December result was again inconclusive.

Although the Conservatives won slightly more of the popular vote, they ended up with one less seat than the Liberals' total of 272 and far short of the number needed to form a majority in Parliament. The fledgling Labour party returned 42 members, an amazing result considering that they had only contested 56 constituencies. Nationally just over five million votes were cast; just 28% of the adult population. One of the few things the parties agreed on was that the electoral register was hopelessly out of date. In Essex it was estimated that 50,000 eligible electors were disenfranchised, although of those actually entitled to vote, the turnout was recorded as 80%. After the December 1910 election all UK elections were completed on the same day.

The December results in *Metropolitan Essex* produced no change from the earlier ones held over three weeks in January and February 1910. In West Ham South, Will Thorne was returned for the Labour Party. Thorne, originally from Birmingham, was sent out to work at the age of six since his family was on poor relief. By the age of nine he was working in a brick works which required a four mile walk to the site. At the age of 25, in 1882, he moved to London and found work at the Beckton Gas Works. Will Thorne was instrumental in founding the Gas Workers and General Union which soon had 20,000 members. He later became its general secretary. He served on West Ham Town Council and for a time became its Mayor. First elected to Parliament in 1906, he remained a serving member for the area until 1945.

On the other side of the tracks of the London, Tilbury and Southend Railway line, was the West Ham North constituency won by Charles Masterman for the Liberals. Masterman's background compared to Will Thorne's could hardly have been more different.

130

Masterman came from a privileged background and graduated from Christ's College, Cambridge. He went on to work as a journalist promoting social reform. Like Thorne he was first elected in 1906. Sensationally the Masterman result was declared void in January 1911 "because of corrupt practices and bribery on the part of the successful candidate". The voiding of the result and the corruption allegations didn't thwart Masterman's ambitions though. He made a rapid come-back in July 2011 when he won a by-election in neighbouring Bethnal Green. During the First World War he served as head of the British War Propaganda Unit although his political career faded after that.

Adjacent to West Ham North, Walthamstow was gained for the Liberals by John Simon. Also from a well-to-do background he attended Wadham College, Oxford and went on to be a successful lawyer. A year after the 1910 December election, he bought the now grade II listed Fritwell Manor in Oxfordshire which became his family home.

Like Thorne and Masterman, John Simon first entered Parliament in 1906. He rapidly rose through the ranks to become the 1st Viscount Simon. During his career he held the offices of Home Secretary, Foreign Secretary, Chancellor of the Exchequer and Lord Chancellor. Although he lost his seat immediately after the First World War and no longer represented Walthamstow, he returned to Parliament in 1922 to represent Spen Valley in Yorkshire.

Further to the east in *Metropolitan Essex,* Romford was a huge Parliamentary constituency that in 1910 encompassed Havering, Dagenham, Barking, East Ham and parts of Ilford. In December 1910, John Henry Bethell, another Liberal, was re-elected. Originally from a modest background in Cheshire where his father was a gardener, as a boy he was a brilliant student who won a scholarship to King's College, London.

On completing his studies, John Bethell worked as an auctioneer, living in lodgings in West Ham. By 1901 he was married and owned a large house in the Romford Road. He described himself as a Land Agent & Auctioneer working on his own account. Bethell cut his teeth in politics when he became Chairman of the East Ham Ratepayers' Association. He then served on West Ham and East Ham Councils and was mayor of both twice. From 1918 he represented the new seat of East Ham North where he worked tirelessly to help servicemen, returning from the Great War, to find work. His parliamentary mail was enormous, about 20,000 letters a year. In 1922 he became Baron Bethell of Romford.

Silvertown (1917)
London's biggest explosion

Between 1800 and 1900 the population of West Ham increased by a factor of forty, standing not far short of 300,000 in 1901. One of the major stimulants to this growth was the *Metropolitan Buildings Act of 1844* which restricted noxious trades, such as chemical manufacture, west of the River Lea in Metropolitan London.

The parish of West Ham, east of the river in Essex, lay just outside these boundaries. With rail and river transport facilities provided by the new docks and railways, West Ham developed rapidly. Hundreds of factories were established in the parish, taking advantage of the less stringent planning regulations. With the factories came the workers and West Ham became an important manufacturing centre with a teeming population.

In 1894 the chemical firm, Brunner, Mond & Company, opened a factory in Silvertown initially to produce soda crystals and later caustic soda. By 1912 lack of demand led to the closure of the factory.

Two years later saw the outbreak of World War I. In 1915 the military were in crisis with a severe shortage of reliable high explosives. The Brunner, Mond factory, which was lying idle, was adapted for the purification of the high explosive T.N.T. History was repeating itself; 200 years earlier the Crown acquired the Gunpowder Mills at Waltham Abbey to solve a similar crisis. (see page 70)

The Ministry of Munitions was established. Its task was to improve the supply and quantity of high explosives. At the time little was known about the methods of large scale purifying of T.N.T. Until 1915 it had been regarded as relatively safe which is perhaps a contradiction in terms. It was recognised, however, that the purification of T.N.T was far more dangerous than its actual manufacture so the Ministry deemed that purification should be carried out in separate, and preferably isolated, factories.

Despite the above recommendation and the objections of the Brunner, Mond management, Lord Moulton, the Director-General of the Explosives Department, persuaded the company to begin T.N.T purification at Silvertown - by now one of the most densely populated areas of the country.

For two years purification of T.N.T proceeded without incident. By the beginning of 1917, the First World War (which, in August 1914, was hoped to have been to be over by Christmas) still had no end in sight.

On 19th January 1917, work at the factory went on as normal. The factory was working 10 hour shifts and producing nine tons of explosive per day. Sometime around 5pm a small fire broke out near a loading hoist. The fire brigade were called and attempted to extinguish the blaze.

At 6.51pm a devastating explosion ripped through the plant and at 6.52pm the chemical works were no more. The *Stratford Express* reported "The whole heavens were lit in awful splendour. A fiery glow seemed to have come over the dark and miserable January evening, and objects which a few minutes before had been blotted out in the intense darkness were silhouetted against the sky".

The blast destroyed or severely damaged 900 properties in the immediate area with another 60,000 being damaged to some degree. The explosion was heard 100 miles away. A gas-holder on the Greenwich Peninsula exploded as a consequence and eight million cubic feet of gas created a huge fireball. The blast also badly damaged a large plywood factory, a flour mill and 17 acres of warehouses in the docks. The Silvertown Fire Station, which had been completed three years earlier, was wrecked along with the firemen's houses.

Sixty-nine people were killed outright in the explosion including Dr Andreas Angel, the plant's chief chemist who was helping to subdue the original fire. Ninety-eight were seriously injured and of those four later died raising the death toll to 73. Another 328 were slightly injured and between five and six hundred people were treated for cuts and bruises. The death toll might have been far higher had it occurred earlier in the day when many more people were on site or working in the neighbouring businesses.

Repair and rebuilding work was an immense task complicated by the fact that there was still a war on. The government chose to take on the job of rebuilding ruined homes rather than, in its view, 'give the money to unscrupulous private landlords'.

By mid-February 1917, more than 1700 men were employed in repairing houses and by August most of the work was complete.

A somewhat non-descript memorial (shown left), situated underneath the Docklands Light Railway on the North Woolwich Road is all that remains to commemorate the tragedy. No actual cause of the accident was ever identified. Enemy involvement was ruled out. To this day, the site of the Silvertown factory is still more or less derelict.

After the end of the First World War in 1918, the Prime Minister, David Lloyd George, promised to make Britain "a place fit for heroes to live in". The country was suffering an acute shortage of housing particularly for working class people. In response to Lloyd George's promise the London County Council (LCC) took up the challenge and embarked on a plan to turn the slogan 'Homes for Heroes' into reality.

In 1921 the LCC purchased the Valence Estate in Dagenham in order to build what was to become the biggest public housing development in the world; 'The Becontree Estate'. In the next eleven years, over 20,000 houses were built, becoming the home to a population of some 100,000 people. The estate takes its name from the ancient administrative area of the Becontree Hundred in which the borough of Barking and Dagenham is situated.

One of the stipulations that the LCC laid down from the beginning, in line with their East End slum clearance program, was that only London residents would be allowed to rent these new homes. As well as building houses, a major objective of the plan was to improve the social fabric of society. There was strong 'official' disapproval of the perceived drinking habits of the working classes. The existing public houses were often no more than drinking shacks, some without even mains water, and were considered breeding grounds for a variety of social ills. As the Becontree estate developed these were to be demolished and replaced by a selected number of suitable 'salubrious licensed refreshment houses where social intercourse and entertainment could take place'.

The initial building of the Becontree Estate required 3000 acres of land. The dilapidated Valence Estate, along with its manor houses, derelict farm cottages and neighbouring market gardens, were purchased at an average cost of £100 per acre. During the course of the construction more than 10,000 workmen were employed. A special railway line was laid which had its own jetty on the Thames where much of the bulk material was brought in by barge.

The first houses were completed in November 1921. A blue heritage plaque on a house in Chittys Lane commemorates this. Many of the first homes did indeed go to 'heroes'; soldiers who had fought in the war.

The average cost of building each home was estimated at £750 although these prices more than doubled once the mammoth project was underway.

Many of the families re-housed found the move to Becontree an entry to an undreamt of new way of life. It was a life with privacy, their own front door behind which was a bath, an indoor toilet, running water, fireplaces, gas and even electricity. Private gardens were also something most had not experienced previously. There were strict rules governing the upkeep of the gardens with tenants being obliged to maintain their gardens to the required standard. To encourage this, prizes were given for the best kept gardens. Candidates were selected by the weekly rent collectors. In the early 1950s the first prize was £20, a large and very welcome sum of cash. On the other hand tenants who continually left their gardens untidy could face penalties.

Many of the front gardens today have been paved over to provide off street car parking. In the 1920s and '30s working class ownership of cars was not considered a possibility. In fact the LCC initially would not sanction the installation of telephone lines to the estate as such luxuries were deemed well beyond the needs of the new Becontree residents.

Despite early problems caused by infrastructure inadequacies - at one time there were only four secondary schools for a school age population of 25,000, Becontree Estate has been a major town planning success. Authorities from across the world came to study the project to find solutions to their own social housing problems. Gradually Becontree's transport links were improved, more schools were built and more shops sprang up. Even the somewhat ham fisted attempts at social engineering were overcome.

Very few of Becontree's selected 'salubrious licensed refreshment houses and places of social intercourse and entertainment' have survived into the 21st Century. 'The Royal Oak' has since been demolished as has 'The Merry Fiddlers', where Max Bygraves began his singing career - it is now replaced by a petrol station. The 'Ship and Anchor' is currently boarded up. The 'Robin Hood', originally let to the 'Improved Public-house Company Ltd' a pet project of Sir Sydney Nevile, the managing director of the brewers Whitbread, closed in 2005.

The Valence estate once dominated Dagenham. All that remains today is Valence House, a listed timber building, partially surrounded by a moat, set in Valence Park in the middle of the Becontree Estate. It was purchased by Dagenham council and served as its Town Hall until 1937. It has since been fully restored as a museum and is home to the Borough Archives.

Mr and Mrs Robinson come to Dagenham

"History is more or less bunk", said Henry Ford in an interview with Charles Wheeler for the Chicago Tribune on May 25th 1916. Yet history will no doubt show that Ford made a significant historical contribution to the development of the small Essex town of Dagenham.

Ford had been producing the 'Model T' since 1913 at Trafford Park, Manchester. After the 'Great War' demand was such that to meet it a new factory was needed. After a nation-wide search for a site, Dagenham riverside, where Samuel Williams owned much of the land, was finally settled on. His Company's development of Dagenham dock, providing shipping access together with good road and rail links, made it Henry Ford's preferred site. In 1924 Ford bought five 500 acres from Samuel Williams and the 'Ford Dagenham Car Plant' was under way.

In 1928 Henry Ford decided to come to England and inspect the new project. He and his wife, Clara, set sail on the White Star liner *Majestic* for Southampton, travelling incognito as Mr and Mrs Robinson, maybe to avoid publicity since, though highly successful, Henry Ford was not universally popular. While here he met King George V and Queen Mary and the leading politicians of the day.

Henry, impressed with the new project, appointed Sir Percival Perry to re-launch 'Ford Britain' as the hub of his new European organisation. In December 1928 Ford Motor Company Limited (UK) was floated. In May 1929 a ground breaking ceremony took place on the Dagenham site where Henry's son Edsel, aided by his grandson Henry Ford II, cut the first sod on the reclaimed marshland. Sir Percival Perry was unhappy with the Dagenham site preferring one in Southampton. He described Dagenham as 'almost the worst possible choice' from both a manufacturing and marketing perspective. The site was marshy, still subject to flooding and used as a rubbish dump for London. On the edge of the site was a 40 acre lake that was the remains of the Dagenham Breach (see page 66).

Despite Perry's misgivings, work on the new factory progressed smoothly. The new plant included its own foundry, coke ovens, gas plant and power station. The factory also had the largest private wharf on the Thames.

Production began in 1931. Workers were hired locally as far as possible but two thousand key workers, their families and furniture were brought on special trains from Manchester and other workers came from Ireland. On arrival, however, they found that housing was in short supply. Many new employees were left to their own devices to find accommodation and the lack of housing provision led to Ford suffering its first strike.

On 1ˢᵗ October 1931, the Managing Director of Ford Dagenham, Roland Hill, drove the first vehicle off the assembly line, a Fordson AA truck. Yet Ford's first years at Dagenham were memorable only for the financial losses incurred due to lack of demand owing to the depression. The first quarterly production figures recorded 4,500 trucks and just five cars. The figures were so bad, despite the huge investment that had been made that Henry Ford even considered closing or mothballing the plant

Later in the nineteen thirties, things began to improve with the introduction of a new small family car, the Ford Model Y. With the advent of World War II, the company switched to production of vehicles for military use. Ford's contribution to the war effort was so important that workers needed permission to leave; even to join the forces. By 1951, despite post war shortages, the hugely successful 'Consul and Zephyr' range came into production and Ford was employing upwards of forty thousand people to cope with demand.

By 1996 ten million vehicles had been built at Dagenham. Their names - Anglia, Cortina, Capri, Sierra and Mondeo - were all famous in their day. Yet on the 20ᵗʰ February 2002 car production ceased. The last vehicle off the line was a Ford Fiesta.

The name Ford is inextricably linked with the development of modern Dagenham.

A Ford Mondeo Diesel Engine
Made in Dagenham – exported worldwide

Part powered by three wind turbines, the plant now contains Ford's designated world wide centre of excellence for the design and manufacture of diesel engines and employs 2000 people. Approximately one million engine units are made per annum of which 80% are exported.

It is interesting to note that Henry Ford was keen on recycling back in 1930. He decreed that his Dagenham power station should burn the rubbish dumped locally by the London County Council (LCC) - approximately 2000 tons a week. Apparently the arrangement stopped in 1939 when, allegedly, the LLC demanded payment for its rubbish.

The Great Escape

In June 1939, twenty Dagenham Girl Pipers, all under the age of 15, left Dover to travel to Liège in Belgium to perform at the *Exposition Internationale de la technique de l'eau*, (the International Water Exhibition). The group was led by the band's founder, the Reverend Joseph Waddington Graves.

Only a month earlier the German Führer, Adolf Hitler, had announced the incorporation of parts of Czechoslovakia into the German Reich in defiance of the Munich agreement signed in September 1938. The British Prime Minister, Neville Chamberlain, on his return to London, had famously waved a piece of paper in front of the world's press saying he had achieved 'peace with honour and peace in out time'.

The girls' visit to Liège was a great success and as a token of appreciation the Mayor of Liège presented the pipers with a newly born black-footed billy goat. It was agreed that the baby goat could act as the band's mascot. The goat was escorted through Belgium and passed through their customs at Ostend and was shipped safely to Dover. However, on arrival the British authorities immediately declared the goat an alien and despite desperate pleas to Whitehall it was sent back to Belgium. What happened to the goat after that is not known.

With war clouds massing over Europe and Anglo-German diplomatic relationships hostile and strained, the Reverend Graves decided to embark the girls on another European tour after consulting with the girls' parents. So, in July 1939, the Dagenham Girl Pipers set off into the heart of Nazi Germany on a scheduled twenty-five town tour of southern Germany. As was now becoming the norm, everywhere the band played they were cheered, welcomed with flowers, chocolates and souvenirs. In Friedrichshafen, close to the Swiss border, local storm troopers staged a social evening for the pipers' benefit and the girls actually partnered the troopers in the dancing.

In Friedrichshafen the British Vice Consul issued a blunt warning to Mr Graves that the pipers should cut short their tour without delay or they would risk being interned or even imprisoned in Germany for the duration of the war. Mr Graves made secret plans to return the girls to Dagenham. On the 6th August 1939 the band marched to Friedrichshafen's railway station, apparently to take a train to their next venue. Yet, notwithstanding the shrill protests of some of the more observant girls that they were boarding the 'wrong' train, they headed for Luxembourg and onward to England. Just over three weeks later Germany and the United Kingdom were at war.

It is hard to believe that, on 2nd October 1939, a month into the war, the Reverend Graves then received a heavily censored letter from Stuttgart offering the Dagenham Pipers a contract to appear in Cologne!

50-year-old Reverend Joseph Waddington Graves; the inspiration and founder of the Dagenham Girl pipers, had been a Captain in the Canadian army. He had also worked as detective in a jewellery store and performed as a rodeo rider. He had escaped unscathed from a plane crash and had suffered knife wounds in an incident in New York. On his travels he had visited Korea and Siberia. During his time in the Canadian Army he enrolled at Yale University and gained a divinity degree. In 1920 Graves arrived in London as an ordained minister and became the warden of the Robert Browning settlement in Walworth.

Dagenham in 1930 was rapidly expanding especially with the arrival of the Ford Motor Works. The enormous Becontree housing estate was under construction. The Reverend Graves had a fascination with highland pipe music and, almost on a whim, put forward a suggestion to his new congregation that they could form a bagpipe band that could run alongside the usual scouts, brownie and guide activities. To his surprise the proposal was enthusiastically taken up and an Aberdonian Pipe-Major, G. Douglas Smith, agreed to train the band in piping and marching skills.

Twelve girls enrolled and the first full practise session was put together in October 1930. Over the next 18 months intensive rehearsals and band practice took place. The numbers grew and new Highland outfits were acquired. In April 1932, the pipers gave their first concert to a group of parents and close relations. The milestone in the band's history came on 20th May 1932 when the Dagenham Girl Pipers gave a press and tea concert on a specially erected stage next to the Osborne Hall in Becontree. Not only did the press turn up in droves but so did film crews. The concert was a sensation and reports on the novelty of a girl piper band from Dagenham, performing flawlessly to great acclaim, were carried in over 100 newspapers both nationally and internationally.

Soon invitations for the pipers to tour flooded in. In their heyday separate groups of Dagenham Girl Pipers toured not only all over the UK at the most prestigious venues, but also in Europe, Africa, India, the USA, Canada and Australia.

October 2010 witnessed the 80th anniversary of the founding of the famous Dagenham Girl Pipers' Band. A special commemoration event was held at the *Daggers* stadium in Victoria Road, Dagenham. Although reduced in size and now part-time the band is still successful today.

DAGENHAM GIRL PIPERS.
"THE PIPE MAJOR."
Copyright
J.W. Graves, Dagenham.

Pipe Major Edith Turnbull

140

Gone to the Dogs

Although greyhound racing was pioneered in England in the 1890s it didn't take hold. It was then developed in the USA after an American called Owen Patrick Smith invented a mechanical hare which could run in a circular path. Smith seems an odd person to have invented such a contraption as he disliked bookmakers and was opposed to any form of gambling.

Organised greyhound racing then re-crossed the Atlantic and a track using the American model with an 'electric hare' was set up at Bell Vue in Manchester. Another was opened in the White City Stadium in London and by the early 1930s a boom in stadium building was taking place. In their heyday, during the 1950s and 1960s, nearly 80 greyhound racing stadiums were licensed across the country. Some of the bigger race meetings attracted crowds of 100,000. Around Metropolitan Essex greyhound racing stadiums were built at Hackney, West Ham, Romford, Walthamstow and Clapton.

Attendances at greyhound stadiums began to drop with the opening of betting shops in 1961. Further declines were recorded when racing was allowed to be televised in the betting shops. With satellite technology, punters were able to get a huge choice of events without going anywhere near a dog track. As a result, despite their many innovative attempts to diversify, one by one the stadiums began to close.

West Ham (Custom House) Stadium opened in July 1928. Although designed by Archibald Leitch, whose credits included Anfield and Highbury football grounds, it had no connection with West Ham Football Club. It was huge and could accommodate 100,000 people. The track itself was the largest in Britain with a circumference of 562 yards. West Ham Stadium originally stood in Prince Regent Lane close to where the present day Prince Regent Docklands Light Railway Station stands. The stadium, in its attempt to diversify, also staged motor cycle speedway and was home to the *West Ham Bombers* but the dogs came first. Sir Louis Dane, the Chairman of Directors, was quoted as saying, "We are a Greyhound Racing Company and the dogs are the most important and our first interest". West Ham Stadium closed in May 1972 and was demolished to be replaced by housing. Some of the local streets are named after former speedway stars who rode there.

Clapton Stadium adjacent to the River Lea, held its first greyhound meeting on 7th April 1928. Prior to that it was the home ground of Clapton Orient Football Club, who subsequently moved to Leyton, and were renamed Leyton Orient. Clapton Stadium closed in 1974 and was later demolished. Again the site has since been developed for housing.

Walthamstow Stadium (*the Stow*) was opened in 1933 by the former White City booking making supremo William Chandler and was recorded as having a bigger income from gambling than any other dog racing track in the UK. Walthamstow also hosted motor cycle speedway racing for a short while, and later stock car racing. The last greyhound race was held in August 2008. Currently the stadium is boarded up and site is scheduled for redevelopment. It is little known that a teenage David Beckham worked there, part time, collecting glasses.

'The Stow' closed in 2008

Hackney Stadium was in Waterden Road, midway between the River Lea and the Lee Navigation, sandwiched between Stratford and Hackney. The stadium opened its doors for greyhound racing in 1932 and three years later motor cycle speedway racing was added. The stadium was the home to the *Hackney Wick Wolves*, the *Hackney Hawks*, the *Hackney Kestrels* and the *London Lions* in succession. Much like the other greyhound stadiums, Hackney suffered a severe downturn during the seventies and eighties but somehow kept going through a very loyal, but increasingly elderly, fan base. As a last gamble, in 1994, the owners embarked on a £12 million rebuild of the stand together with a new restaurant and a rebranding as the London Stadium. The new stadium welcomed a host of dignitaries to its opening a year later; sadly they were to learn that the track had been placed in receivership on the same night.

The London Stadium struggled on for another two years with little success. During the rebuild and upgrading it had managed to lose nearly all of its former loyal customers and failed to attract enough new ones. In January 1997 the stadium closed it doors for the last time. It was left derelict for six years until it was bought by the London Development Agency and demolished in 2003.

The location of the London stadium in Waterden Road was interesting. Opposite it were the headquarters of the Hackney Sea Cadet Unit also known as the training ship *TS Jervis Bay*. This occupied a brick building constructed to look like a ship complete with a mock funnel. Further south along the road was the confectionary maker Clarnico. Most of the remainder of Waterden Road consisted of small factories, workshops and warehouses. One plant made manure out of fish bones. Locals nicknamed the area around the Waterden / Carpenters Road junction as 'Smelly Lane'. As a contrast the area immediately behind the *Jervis Bay* contained several allotments and a large sports field. Strangely there was also an ex-army Bailey Bridge that spanned the River Lea.

Although the dogs have gone, sport has returned to the site with a vengeance. Waterden Road runs through the middle of the 2012 Olympic site. The Handball Arena now stands where the greyhounds once ran.

One greyhound stadium still survives in *Metropolitan Essex;* at Romford, owned and operated by one of the UK's largest betting shop and casino operators. The first greyhound race took place in Romford on June 21ˢᵗ 1929 beside the Crown public house in London Road. The present stadium, on the opposite side of London Road, was opened in 1933. It has had its fair share of ups and downs. However unlike other, now defunct stadiums, Romford is compact with a crowd limit of just over 4,000. It is hemmed in on three sides by the railway line to the south and residential roads to the east and west. Access to the stadium is gained by a narrow lane, running parallel to Cromer Road, from the A118, London Road. With this formula it seems that, for the time being the future of greyhound racing in Romford is secure.

Evacuation

In September 1939 Goodmayes Infant and Junior School, in Aithrie Road Ilford, was due to open for the new term. However, the declaration of war on 3rd September changed everything. Like many other schools in the capital it was to be closed and the children evacuated to the country. Evacuation was an integral part of the Civil Defence scheme which had been drawn up two years earlier. Despite the Prime Minister's 1938 assurances of "Peace in Our Time", Civil Defence Planning had continued. In what was known as *Plan 2* the country was divided into three areas – evacuation, reception and neutral. In *Metropolitan Essex*, Dagenham and most of Ilford were initially classed as 'neutral' areas. Barking, West Ham, Walthamstow and the built up areas closer to central London were classed as evacuation zones where well rehearsed dispersal plans were already in place.

In both Dagenham and Ilford there was a great deal of apprehension. Although classed 'neutral' both boroughs were built up and home to industries that many thought would be prime targets in an enemy bombing campaign. For the people and their civic leaders it was a most unsatisfactory situation and as a result of sustained local pressure, evacuation status was reluctantly granted to both areas. For the staff, parents and pupils of Goodmayes School it was all very confusing. The evacuation plan necessitated a lengthy and complex registration process. It was made worse by the lack of information and no one having a complete picture of what was going on.

To be fair the country was facing an unprecedented situation. Evacuating more than three million people - primary school children, mothers with pre-school children and babies, pregnant women and the disabled was a logistical nightmare. With the rumour mill in top gear forecasting imminent bombing and poison gas attacks, the evacuation became all the more urgent.

Official lists stated what each evacuee should take with them. Top of the list was the gas mask. Additionally a suitcase was needed to hold spare clothing, a towel, soap, toothbrush, comb, waterproof boots and food for the trip. This was a problem in itself as many families had only one suitcase, if any, between them and very little in the way of spare clothing. Even if all the requirements could be met the smaller children were unable to lift the packed suitcase! Every child also required an identity card. Getting these processed quickly and then issued was another ordeal. The children had no idea where they were going or how they were getting there. The destination was the 'country' but nowhere specific was mentioned. They had also been told, unofficially, that they would be sleeping in a barn for at least one night on arrival until their billets had been sorted out.

The favoured evacuation route was by ship from Dagenham Dock. The General Steam Navigation Company's eight vessels, including the *Medway Queen* and *Royal Sovereign*, would take the evacuees to Yarmouth, Lowestoft or Felixstowe. On the day designated for evacuation children were to meet at their school with their suitcase, collect an identity card and shipping ticket, then take a bus to Ford's jetty at Dagenham Dock. It was decreed that embarkation had to take place early in the morning, before the working day began so as not to interfere with Ford's war production. However the plans kept changing. In one instance children escorted by their parents arrived at the docks in the pouring rain only to be sent back to re-register. To add to the confusion once evacuation began, the Ministry decided that the total number of evacuees should not exceed 20,000 due to billeting shortages.

Throughout September and October 1939 there was no bombing. The great calamity everyone expected hadn't happened. Many evacuees came back within a week preferring to face the danger from the *Luftwaffe*, than endure the poor food and accommodation at their destinations. The so called 'Phoney War' continued until April 1940. As more and more evacuees came back to Dagenham and Ilford, Goodmayes School reopened. Attendance was patchy; there were still lots of evacuated children that had stayed away. Classes were split up and amalgamated as necessary. There were also fewer teachers, some were absent supervising the evacuated children and others had joined the forces.

On the 7th September, a year after war had been declared, the German Air Force made its first sustained bombing raid on the capital. The 'blitz' began in earnest and the Ministry implemented another evacuation, *Plan 4*, soon to be followed by *Plan 5*. This time the plans were more comprehensive and all the metropolitan boroughs were better prepared. Yet Goodmayes School stayed open throughout the war. Even during the height of the bombing the school managed to run 10 classes. Lessons were often disrupted when the sirens went and everyone hurried to the shelters which was fun at first. The school numbers continued to fluctuate with some pupils leaving to be evacuated only to be replaced by others returning. Many evacuees came back after May 1942, but there was another mass evacuation in August 1944 (in fact greater than the one in 1939) when the capital came under sustained attack from the VI flying bombs. This time the 'well oiled' evacuation procedures ran efficiently. All the evacuees had returned by 1946.

Goodmayes School originally opened in 1910 and still functions in the same place. Today the infant and junior sections have been combined. During the 'blitz' in London 20,000 people were killed, 40,000 injured and one million homes were destroyed or badly damaged.

Swords should be beaten into ploughshares when wars end - so pleaded Isaiah the Prince of Prophets. Sadly, on far too many occasions, his plea has been ignored and the opposite has happened. With the outbreak of the Second World War furniture makers converted their production lines from making kitchen cabinets to turning out war machines.

One of the best examples of this was the 'Wooden Wonder' – or the 'Mosquito' - an aircraft whose fuselage and wings were made entirely of wood. Wood had already been used by aircraft maker de-Havilland for the DH88 Comet, which had won the prestigious 1934 London-Melbourne air race. The Mosquito had been on the drawing board since 1936 in response to the Air Ministry requisition number P.13/36 specifing the manufacture and design of a twin-engined bomber for world wide use. The declaration of war in 1939 gave urgency to its development and to meet the substantial production planned, the Air Ministry and de Havilland turned to the UK's wooden furniture industry. In a short time thousands of carpenters were retrained to build wooden aircraft bodies.

The majority of Mosquitos were finally assembled in de Havilland's two plants in Hatfield and Leavesden. However, in order to avoid a single catastrophic attack from the German *Luftwaffe*, production of component parts was spread between more than 200 sub-contractors. One of the biggest of these, a sub-contactor for Mosquito fuselages and wings, was the high-class domestic furniture maker, F. Wrighton & Sons Ltd. In 1933, the company, which had a long history of building furniture, had moved into the Billet Works, a six-acre site in Billet Road, Walthamstow, just east of the River Lea. With the declaration of war, Wrighton Aircraft Ltd, was formed as a subsidiary company. Furniture making virtually ceased in Walthamstow during the war years and on July 8th 1944, despite regular disruption from bombing, Wrighton produced their 1000th mosquito fuselage.

Made in Walthmamstow Fuselage No 1000.

After the war Wrighton Ltd returned to furniture making. In 1958, Len Aarons, who now lives in Los Angeles, went on an organised school trip to the Wrighton plant and he recalls a thriving, well lit factory, with lots of cheerful people happily putting together one cabinet after another and working their way through vast piles of stored timber. At that time Wrighton Aircraft Ltd was being maintained but it finally closed in 1967 with the furniture factory closing shortly after. F. Wrighton & Sons suffered the fate of most of the other quality furniture makers that the Lea Valley was known for; the increasing competition from mass produced and 'flat pack' furniture. Wrighton furniture is today sought after by collectors and there is even a piece of their kitchen furniture in the Victoria & Albert museum

Today, parts of the Billet Works still stand. There is, in fact a small furniture outlet on the site that is not connected to the original Wrighton & Son. In the main the site is occupied by more grounded forms of transport such as bicycle sales

Facia of the Billets Works in 2011

and motor vehicle repair and storage. The remains of the Billet Works are in all probability likely to be demolished in the foreseeable future and the site cleared for housing.

As for the de Havilland Mosquito, the first operational sortie of the took place on 20th September 1941. It was a successful photo reconnaissance (PR) mission, flown by Squadron Leader Rupert Clerke, who photographed harbour facilities in enemy-occupied South West France. The Mosquito went on to become one of most versatile aircraft employed in World War II. Over 7,500 of the aircraft were built and, apart from being used for photo reconnaissance it was adapted as a night fighter, a light bomber and a pathfinder. It ended the war with the lowest loss rate of any aircraft in RAF Bomber Command.

The Mosquito was the star of the fictional book by Frederick E. Smith, and subsequent 1964 film, *633 Squadron,* which depicted attempts to destroy a German V-2 rocket fuel plant in Norway.

From the late 1930s onwards Dagenham's 'May and Baker Ltd' was synonymous with M&B tablets. In 1938 it first produced M&B693' the wonder drug in fighting infectious diseases from sore throats to pneumonia.

The efficacy of this drug received a huge boost from Winston Churchill in 1943. He was struck down with bacterial pneumonia and in an extremely poor condition until treated with 'M&B693'. After recovering, on the 29th December 1943, the prime minister told the nation:-

"This admirable M&B, from which I did not suffer any inconvenience, was used at the earliest moment and after a week's fever the intruders were repulsed. I hope all our battles will be equally well conducted. I did not feel so ill in this attack as I did last February. M&B did the work most effectively. There is no doubt that pneumonia is a very different illness from what it was before this marvellous drug was discovered"

The drug Sulphapyridine, discovered by May & Baker's research and development team at Dagenham, was logged in their Test Book on 2nd November 1937 under Code No M&B693. Together with M&B760, (Sulphathiazole, developed a year later), these were the forerunners of today's antibiotics.

Both products were very effective as treatments against infections and with the advent of the Second World War both were needed in far greater quantities than during peace time. Medical production was put onto a war footing to ensure supplies would meet expected casualties. M&B693, as well as being the first powerful treatment for pneumonia, could also prevent the growth of bacteria in wounds which often led to gangrene. During the conflict many thousands of lives were saved by what was being hailed a 'wonder drug'.

On a lighter note it was reported in the *Glasgow Evening News*, in January 1944, that M&B693 had saved the life of Nero, the Royal Circus lion, who had contracted pneumonia.

The May & Baker company was started in 1851, unsurprisingly by a Mr. May and a Mr. Baker in Wandsworth. From an initial specialism in chemicals derived from Mercury and Bismuth, the company grew into other branches of chemicals including pharmaceuticals. In 1919, the company purchased the 60 acre Stockvale Farm site in Dagenham from the Essex based Tiptree Jam maker Wilkin and Sons for £11,000.

May and Baker had already begun to specialize in pharmaceuticals and pesticides when in 1922 it was taken over to become part of the Rhone-Poulenc group who kept the May & Baker name.

The group went on to establish the new May and Baker factory in Dagenham where manufacturing, research and development began in 1934. During the 1930s, the factory doubled in size to occupy a huge site stretching from Dagenham East station for nearly a mile eastwards next to the railway line.

During the next 65 years products from this plant included pharmaceuticals, veterinary medicines, agrochemicals, photographic and industrial chemicals. The big breakthrough for the R&D team came in 1937 with the synthesizing of M&B693.

After the war, the Company expanded world wide and underwent a series of mergers. By 1999 the Dagenham site produced only pharmaceuticals and a merger with Hoechst changed the name to Aventis. Within, a year research and development was transferred abroad. 2004 saw another take over by the French and the name was changed to Sanofi-Aventis.

The May & Baker site, which at its peak employed 4000 people, had won the Queen's Award for Industry three times for technological innovation. In 1974 they were granted a royal warrant to supply agricultural herbicides to HM Queen Elizabeth II. In spite of these awards and the illustrious achievements of the past, in 2009 Sanofi-Aventis announced that May & Baker Dagenham – it is still known as this by the local community despite the new name on the gates - will close in 2013. There are plans to turn part of the site into an industrial park. The existing sports ground and club house will remain.

On July 2nd 2010 the 'National Chemical Landmark' plaque (opposite) was presented to Sanofi-Aventis by the Royal Society of Chemistry as a tribute to the valuable research and manufacturing activities at the Dagenham site. The plaque was unveiled by the Mayor of Barking and Dagenham, Councillor Nirmal Singh Gill.

RSC Advancing the Chemical Sciences

National Chemical Landmark

Dagenham Site

In recognition of the pioneering research and manufacturing work carried out at the May & Baker (sanofi-aventis) Dagenham site in a wide range of chemical and pharmaceutical fields since 1934. These products continue to benefit patients and their quality of life around the world.

2 July 2010

It is understood that the plaque will continue to be displayed on the site to commemorate the significant contribution of May & Baker to medical history and also to the development of Dagenham.

An original laboratory sample of 'M&B 693' may be seen on display in the Science Museum in London.

Jerrycans, Helmets, Bread
and Parachutes

During the Second World War it was critical that the fighting forces on the front line were equipped with not only enough weapons and ammunition to attack the enemy but also the necessary logistical backup to keep them going through thick and thin. In providing this backup, factories in Dagenham

played a key role in helping to furnish the needs of the armed forces while also providing essential supplies for the home front.

The Ford Motor Company was a key supporter of the war effort by supplying armoured tracked vehicles as well as engines for all kinds of military trucks. They also, during the war years, built 120,000 agricultural tractors. Other figures for industrial production during this period are equally impressive.

*20 Million,
Made in Dagenham*

The factory next door to Ford's, Briggs Motor Bodies Ltd, in peacetime produced car bodies and truck cabs for other vehicle manufacturers. However, following the fall of Dunkirk, the Ministry of Supply deemed the helmets of the armed forces not fit for purpose.

Briggs rose to the challenge to supply newly designed helmets and by the war's end had produced 11 million. In the same period they also manufactured 20 million jerrycans for fuel as well as 8 million ammunition boxes.

The Kelsey-Hayes Wheel Company, adjacent to Briggs, supplied wheels to the motor industry. During the war, in addition to producing over two million wheels of all shapes and sizes for land vehicles and aircraft, Kelsey-Hayes turned to manufacturing machine guns.

11 million made

At Dagenham Dock, Southern United Telephone Cables Ltd manufactured over 25 million miles of telephone line, essential for communications.

May and Baker Ltd, the pharmaceutical company (see page 148) made 550 million 'Quinacrine' anti-malaria tablets. The mattress maker, Springcot Ltd in Whalebone Lane made 750,000 parachutes and nearly 200,000 sleeping bags. On the food front W.J. Barton Ltd, whose Bakery used to stand between Kemp Road and Turnage Road baked over 50 million loaves.

In the 1950s, Briggs and Kelsey-Hayes were both subsumed into the Ford empire. Barton's Bakery, (famed for its wartime coconut macaroons), along with its high street outlets, closed in 1981. In 1984 the bakery was leased to Barking College for use in its Youth Training Programme. The college vacated the premises two years later following difficulties with government funding. The bakery has since been demolished and the site redeveloped for a combination of light industry and housing.

After the war Springcot Ltd continued to manufacture sisal products such as rope, twine and general cordage. The company became a casualty of fierce competition from overseas and the business closed at the end of the 1960s. The factory was demolished and replaced by a DIY store which in turn was replaced by the current occupants – a fast food restaurant.

Even the mighty Dagenham Ford works has undergone substantial change since its heydays of the post war years. As we have seen on page 136, cars or indeed any vehicles are no longer made there, only diesel engines.

During the early summer of 2012 one of the now vacant car compounds on the Ford estate was put to good use. Mostly in continual rain, it served as a rehearsal arena for volunteers taking part in the Olympic Games opening and closing ceremonies.

The 2012 London Olympic Park covers an area the size of Hyde Park. During the Games athletes ran, jumped and swam in places that were once home to industries long since gone from East London. In many cases the manufacturers have left the British Isles altogether.

The northern boundary of the Olympic Park is bordered by Eastway, a busy route that takes road traffic in and out of central London. Just inside the park, by Eastway, is the purpose built Broadcast and Media Centre which served as a base for the estimated 20,000 reporters, photographers and journalists who covered the Olympic and Paralympic Games.

Forty years ago the same site was a thriving manufacturing hub where *Lesney Matchbox* toys were designed and made in their millions. The company *Lesney Products* was formed on January 19th 1947 when two unrelated Smiths; Leslie and Rodney, raised £600 to form a die casting business. The name *Lesney* was a composite of the two men's names.

The company started life in a disused public house in Edmonton called *The Rifleman* that cost £100 per annum to rent. The basement was adapted to accommodate a compressor and the ground floor was used for die casting and storage. *Lesney* began by making components for industry. That same year Rodney Smith introduced Jack Odell, an engineer he had worked with at another die-casting company. Odell needed somewhere to place his die casting machines. He initially rented space in the Lesney building but before the year was out he joined the company as an equal partner.

Usually trade slowed down just before Christmas, so the partners looked for something else to do. They tried their hand at making a range of die cast toys as a stop gap. This proved to be a turning point in the company's fortunes and in 1948 *Lesney* had eight employees as well as the three partners. They continued supplying non-toy die-castings to industry as well as developing a range of toys that included mechanical animals, horse drawn carts, toy guns and even handcuffs. Seeing an opportunity at the 1951 Festival of Britain they began to work on a large - nearly 16 inch - scale model Coronation Coach. Unfortunately with the outbreak of the Korean War the use of Zinc for toys was banned. The coach project was abandoned and trade fell off. The future looked bleak to Rodney Smith and he left the company in 1951.

A year later the war ended, the ban on Zinc was lifted and King George VI had died. Realising that the coronation of Elizabeth was imminent the Coronation Coach project was revived. It proved popular and some 30,000 were sold.

This success inspired a miniature version - 4½ inches long - of the Royal State Coach. This was released in 1953 and proved immensely popular. Over one million models were sold and the success was a major turning point in the company's fortunes.

The next major success for Lesney was the Matchbox brand. It had a strange beginning. The story goes that Jack Odell's daughter had just started school. The school would only allow children to bring in toys that would fit in a matchbox. Jack Odell made a miniature, scaled down version of a previous larger model, a brass road roller that did just that. When his daughter took this to school it became so popular with the other children that everybody wanted one. Word spread and, realising that they had another success on their hands the name *Matchbox* was soon registered as Lesney's most famous brand name.

In 1957, the company moved to the Eastway site. The Matchbox range of models, all sold in replica 'matchboxes', had expanded and were in great demand. Many other model lines were introduced including the 'Models of Yesteryear' range of classic cars. In 1960 Lesney was floated on the London Stock Exchange. Six years later the Eastway factory employed over 1,000 people and was working round the clock. A fleet of buses were used to bring staff from all over London.

Voltswagen Camper (1970)

Fifty million castings were made annually at Eastway, which in turn fed the assembly plants at nearby Lee Conservancy Road, and further afield at Chingford Mount and Rochford in the east of Essex. In 1966 Lesney was awarded the Queen's award for industry. In 1968 the company gained its second Queen's award for industry and Les Smith and Jack Odell were awarded OBEs.

By the end of the decade *Lesney* was employing over 6,000 people. More than fifty percent of production was exported and the company had big sales offices in the USA and Australia. By any measure the 1960s were the Golden Years for Lesney.

The 1970s saw a reversal of company fortunes. Sales declined sharply in the USA (Lesney's largest market), following the introduction of the 'Hot Wheels' range of miniature cars from toy maker Mattel. It took 18 months of very expensive redesign and retooling for Lesney to come up with a rival product. As a consequence the company finances tipped into loss, and there were also problems with the taxman.

The difficulties multiplied when in 1974 UK production halted completely for three months during the miners strike and the resultant three day week. To compound Lesney's woes the Rochford factory suffered two major disasters in quick succession. A fire destroyed a large part of the factory containing thousands of plastic components and then a flood ruined much of the machinery. For nearly two years one of the key product ranges 'Models of Yesteryear' were not made.

Towards the end of the 1970s the company briefly returned to profit and picked up its third Queen's award for industry. However, more difficulties soon arose. There was a dispute about the use of the Royal Crest that led to an estimated 100,000 models being recalled. Some critically poor investment decisions were made and huge losses were run up on reckless foreign exchange transactions.

A Wheeled Hovercraft (1974)

In 1979 one of Lesney's UK rivals, the pioneer toy maker Meccano's *Dinky Toys*, went into liquidation. Unfortunately Lesney was in little better shape and despite widespread layoffs and sales of its buildings, the company called in the receiver in June 1982. In September that year Universal Toys acquired the Matchbox brand name and remaining assets.

The Eastway plant closed but production continued in Rochford until 1987. Eventually all manufacturing was transferred to the Portuguese colony Macau, now part of China. The Matchbox brand is now owned by the Californian toy giant Mattel Inc.

Over the years the miniature creations of Lesley Smith and Jack Odell have brought joy to countless millions of small (and big) children in almost every country in the world. Even today large sums of money change hands for some of the rarer models. Meanwhile on the former Eastway site, perhaps little ghostly Matchbox vehicles come out at dusk to see what the Olympic Park is all about.

Jim Peters – "I was lucky not to have died that day"

Jim Peters perhaps invented modern marathon running. He turned it from a plodding endurance test into the speed running race that it is today. He broke the world record for the men's race four times in the 1950s, was the first to run a marathon in under 2 hours 20 minutes in 1953. *The International Amateur Athletics Federation*, considered him, along with Abebe Bikila of Ethiopia and Carlos Lopez of Portugal, the three all-time, greatest Marathon runners in the world.

Peters grew up on Dagenham's Becontree Estate. In his youth he played football for Dagenham boys club, alongside Alf Ramsay. As a trained optician, he joined the Royal Army Medical Corps in 1939. He left the army in 1945, returned to work as an optician and took up cross country running with the Essex Beagles club; now the 'Newham and Essex Beagles' who today number Mo Farah and Christine Ohorugu among their famous members.

In 1947, after a disappointing 10,000 metre race at Wembley, Peters was persuaded by his coach and mentor, Herbert Johnston, to extend his distance to the marathon. He embarked on a radical training program, concentrating on speed and stamina. This regime, involving running up to 130 miles in a week, led him to a world record for the marathon with a time of 2 hours 20 minutes 42.2 seconds in 1952. In 1953, running in a pair of Woolworth's 'plimsolls' costing '12 shillings and 6 pence' (62p today), he completed the Polytechnic Marathon in 2 hours 17 minutes 39.4sec, to become the first man to run a marathon in under 2 hours 20 minutes.

His last marathon, at the Vancouver Empire Games in August 1954, is the one Peters is more often remembered for. As he entered the Stadium with a lead of five kilometers and only the 400 metre circuit of honour to go, he began to totter. He had pushed himself too hard in the 75°F heat. It took him eleven minutes to stagger 200 metres with spectators watching horrified. After a dozen attempts to stumble onwards, he fell into the arms of the English team masseur and was stretchered off to hospital. There he spent the next seven hours in an oxygen tent while being fed, intravenously, no less than half a gallon of saline solution and dextrose. Much later in an interview Peters said "I was lucky not to have died that day….I set off too fast in the heat, but that was always my way: to destroy the field". The course was later found to be 27 miles long. Peters had actually covered the standard 26 miles 385 yards before he wilted.

Jim Peters retired in 1972 and moved to Thorpe Bay near Southend where he died in 1999. His optician's practice at 192 High Road Chadwell heath, after three different owners, still trades today as 'JH Peters'.

Wembley, World Cup Final

Football in Metropolitan Essex has contributed to the national game at every level. From schoolboy and Sunday league teams who play purely for love of the game; amateur clubs winning trophies in their league and F.A. competitions, to established major clubs playing at the highest level both nationally and internationally. All this as well as being a major contributor to World Cup glory in 1966!

There can be nothing more joyful to any football fans than their nation not only hosting the competition but then winning the World Cup in front of a home crowd. When the goal scorers and their manager all hale from the same area, the pride in victory would be unparalleled. This situation – a dream to many – became reality at Wembley on the 30th of July, 1966 when a quartet of 'Metropolitan Essex Boys' played a crucial role in what happened next.

RESULT - England 4, West Germany 2

The team manager, Alf Ramsay, came from Dagenham and the Captain, Bobby Moore, who accepted the *Jules Rimet Trophy* for England from the Queen, was a Barking lad. Martin Peters, who scored one of the goals, was from Plaistow, and Geoff Hurst, the hero of the match who scored the other three goals, was considered an honorary Essex Boy since he had spent his best playing years at West Ham. The final was a seesaw match with West Germany taking the lead after sixteen minutes. England then went ahead with goals from Geoff Hurst and Martin Peters but as the seconds ticked towards the end of normal time, disaster struck when the Germans equalised with virtually the last kick of the game.

A talk by the manager Alf Ramsay between full time and extra time was inspirational in lifting the team's spirits. He refused to let the England team dwell on their tiredness and disappointment. Shortly after extra time started Geoff Hurst scored his second goal with a strong shot that bounced on the underside of the crossbar. The German team hotly disputed the goal and the referee was unsure, but the linesman was positive and the goal stood. There was no doubt about the fourth goal, as in the dying seconds of the game Geoff Hurst picked up a pass from Bobby Moore and blasted a shot in from 25 yards. As Hurst was running down the left wing some spectators had come onto the pitch. This prompted Kenneth Wolstenholme, the BBC commentator, looking at the crowd to excitedly shout into the microphone; *"Some of the crowd are on the pitch - they think it's all over,"* then as Hurst's shot hit the roof of the net he completed the sentence with *"It is now"*.

These words have become part of footballing legend and are almost as famous as the result itself. Alf Ramsay, England's most successful manager was knighted in 1970. He suffered a stroke during the 1998 world cup finals and died in 1999. Bobby Moore, manager of Southend United between 1984 and 1986, died of cancer in 1993. Geoff Hurst was knighted in 1998; both he and Martin Peters were given the MBE for services to football.

In 2003 a bronze statute, created by Philip Jackson, was unveiled by the Duke of York opposite the Boleyn Pub on the Barking Road just outside the West Ham United Stadium. It shows Bobby Moore clutching the *Jules Rimet* trophy. He is held aloft by fellow England players Geoff Hurst, Martin Peters and Ray Wilson. There is another slightly unusual sculpture overlooking the A13, on the south east corner of Castle Green adjacent to Gale Street in Dagenham. It was unveiled in 2008 and shows local sporting figures including Sir Alf Ramsay and Bobby Moore.

On page 105 we saw that West Ham United F.C. had its roots in the 19th century Thames Iron Works shipyard on the River Lea. Thames Ironworks F.C was formed in 1895 as a healing mechanism following a bitter strike. The team played on a strictly amateur basis to begin with and many players from the works were on the team. In June 1900, the Thames Ironworks was in financial difficulties. The works team was wound up but immediately re-launched as West Ham United Football Club. West Ham first played at the Memorial Ground in Plaistow but later transferred to a ground on Green Street, Upton Park. All ties with the Thames Iron works were severed in 1904. The West Ham Upton Park ground although located in East Ham is called 'The Boleyn Ground' - named after a tower on Green Street House that stood there until 1955. Allegedly the tower was built for Anne Boleyn's pre-marital liaisons with Henry VIII. Symbolically West Ham's logo today still depicts two crossed hammers, from the shipyard, and a castle, or tower, as background.

During World War II, although regular football league games had been abandoned for the duration of the war an emergency wartime league was set up. Saturday 7th September 1940 was a beautiful late summer sunny day. West Ham were playing Tottenham Hotspur at Upton Park. Around 4.30pm, with Spurs winning 4 -1, sirens sounded and the referee under standing orders blew his whistle and abandoned the match. As the crowds left the ground the engines of approaching aircraft could be heard clearly. The phoney war was over. London was then subjected to its first mass air raid which carried on relentlessly for the following 57 nights.

"The Boy Done Good"

To the north west of West Ham's Boleyn Ground is Chingford, the original home turf of one, David Robert Joseph Beckham, who was born at Whipps Cross Hospital in Walthamstow on May 2nd 1975. He attended Chase Lane Primary School and Chingford High School (Chingford Foundation School) also known as the Nevin, simply because it was in Nevin Road.

Without fail every weekend David's parents took their protégé to practise and play at Wadham Lodge sports ground close to Walthamstow Greyhound stadium. Later the London Borough of Waltham Forest even created a *David Beckham Trail* which showed the parks and open spaces where the young Beckham learned his football craft.

Beckham's parents were fanatical Manchester United supporters and regularly travelled to Old Trafford to attend the team's home matches. Whilst at senior school David won a competition to attend one of Bobby Charlton's football schools in Manchester. The young Beckham had trials with Leyton Orient, Norwich City and attended Tottenham Hotspur's school of excellence but eventually signed for Manchester United on his fourteenth birthday. Following an illustrious career at Manchester United he moved to Real Madrid. Beckham appeared more than 100 times for England as player and captain of the national side. Later he settled with his family in Los Angeles. In January 2013 David Beckham returned to Europe to join Paris Saint-Germain  (PSG) where he played the remainder of the season before announcing his retirement from the game. From humble beginnings David Beckham became one of the most famous sporting icons in the world.

Daggers, Orient and Spurs.

A few miles east of West Ham, on the edge of the Sterling Industrial Estate, is the Victoria Road home of 'The Daggers', Dagenham & Redbridge Football Club which originally was the sports ground of Briggs Motor Bodies. (see page 150). The new club was formed when, in 1992, Dagenham merged with Redbridge Forest Football Club which in turn was an amalgam of Ilford, Leytonstone and Walthamstow Avenue Football Clubs. Leytonstone FC could trace its ancestry back to 1886.

The 'Daggers' forbears lifted the FA Trophy once, the Amateur Cup seven times, the Isthmian League twenty times, the Athenian League six times, the Essex Senior Cup twenty-six times and the London Senior Cup twenty-three times. The club played its first match in the Football League on 11th August 2007 but lost to Stockport County by a single goal. They had to wait three weeks for the first win in this League, a home game against Lincoln City on 1st September 2007. The 'Daggers' were promoted to League One for the 2010-2011 season but survived only one year before being relegated.

Over the decades much has changed in the soccer world. Unlike today's globe trotting football millionaire elite, during the 30s, 40s and 50s nearly all the players were local boys. West Ham United has been in the top tier of the English league for over thirty years. Older fans will recall there was a time when many first team players would travel together with the fans from Hornchurch or Dagenham on the same tube trains to attend the home games at Upton Park. Perhaps during this period it was truly a peoples' game. Today even relative minnows in the football world such as the 'Daggers' draw their team playing pool from all over the world.

Leyton Orient, whose Brisbane Road ground is virtually next door to the 2012 Olympic Park, (see page 129) was formed in Clapton and known as Clapton Orient, apparently derived from the Orient Steamship Navigation Company (The forerunner of P&O). They moved to Brisbane Road in August 1937 and became 'Leyton Orient' after the end of the Second World War, although to the fans they will always be, 'the Os'.

Just over the River Lea at White Hart Lane is Tottenham Hotspur (The Spurs) who have occupied the same ground for over a century. Founded in 1882, the club has been at the top of English Football for most of the time since. Tottenham were the first club in the 20th century to achieve the League and FA Cup Double, winning both competitions in the 1960–61 season. Here we apologise to Spurs fans, the club has been so successful and won so many trophies that unfortunately, to record all their triumphs and rich history would take several more books!

Health and Safety!

In October 1952 officials from the War Office turned up at the Kelvedon Hatch Farm of Jim Parish waving a compulsory purchase order for 25 acres of  his land. Shortly afterwards diggers and bulldozers moved in and began to excavate a giant hole. Today prominent signs give directions to what 'the hole' became: The 'Secret' Nuclear Bunker just off the A128, between Brentwood and Ongar.

It might be more accurate if the signs read, 'This way to the Nuclear Bunker that is no longer secret'. However, the bunker was once one of the most hush-hush places in the land. It is now one of the more unusual tourist attractions in Essex.

As soon as the excavations began, public access to the site was banned, local roads were closed and the designated area was fenced off and patrolled by armed guards. After the hole was dug a succession of builders arrived. They all worked under the cloak of the Official Secrets Act. Each group was closely supervised and as they completed their allocated task they were escorted from the site. The work was so secret that none of workers outside their immediate teams knew what anyone else was doing, or what the final objective of their labour was. Work carried on round the clock through the winter months, much of it in the dark, and the bunker was completed by March 1953. The only visible evidence of this extraordinary effort was a quite ordinary looking bungalow. Yet underneath this innocent façade, descending to a depth of 100 feet, was a three-story bunker encased by 10 feet thick reinforced concrete walls. The entrance was shielded by steel blast proof doors weighing one and half tons each. It was hoped that the bunker and its inhabitants could survive the force of a close proximity nuclear explosion.

The originally purpose of the bunker was to serve as a 'ROTOR' station. ROTOR was a government code word used to describe the upgrading of air defences at the inception of the 'Cold War'. The Kelvendon Hatch location was one of a number built on the eastern side of the British Isles. The Marconi Company installed in each bunker the most up to date radar and communications equipment available.

As the 'Cold War' intensified, and the Soviet Union acquired nuclear weapons, the British Government's response was twofold. Firstly British nuclear weapons were developed and tested and then planning began in earnest as to how the nation would cope with a nuclear war and its aftermath.

The role of the Kelvedon bunker was changed to that of Regional Government Headquarters, with the code name RGHQ 5.1. and £10 million was spent on modifications to it. In the event of the unthinkable, a nuclear attack, the bunker would serve as the control centre for Metropolitan Essex, London and the surrounding area.

The bunker was constructed to accommodate 600 key personnel, including top civil servants, scientists, members of the armed forces, cabinet ministers and even the British Prime Minister of the day. It was designed to be fully self-sufficient, with its own power supply and was stocked with enough food and water to last three months. There was also a 2,500-line telephone exchange and a BBC radio studio that could broadcast to the nation's survivors. There was no provision to take any family members of the bunkers occupants in.

A great deal of thought had gone into the nuclear doomsday scenario. A series of civil defence films were made to explain how the population at large should prepare for nuclear war. Most of these were never shown during the 'Cold War' on the grounds that they might cause panic. If the bomb dropped, scientists in the bunker were tasked to monitor fallout and radiation levels and advise on the risks.

In the event of a nuclear attack it was assumed millions of people would die - but millions would live. However, it was supposed many of the survivors would have a short life expectancy due to severe burns, radiation sickness, lack of medical attention or even starvation.

Armed Guards were to be posted outside to keep unwanted intruders out of the bunker. However just as important the guards were also charged with ensuring the key personnel were kept in! Just how the guards were to survive was unclear!

In 1989 the Berlin Wall came down and two years later the Soviet Union began to break up. The 'Cold War' was effectively over. The Government decided the bunker was no longer needed. The £3 million annual running costs may have speeded this decision.

In December 1994 ownership of the land, including the bunker, reverted to the Parrish family. They have preserved the bunker, which is open to the public, as a historical reminder of what might have been. During its 'operational' lifetime when nuclear 'Armageddon' was a distinct possibility there were just two ways to get in or out of the bunker - the entrance tunnel or the emergency stairs at the rear.

With the 'Cold War' over and the 'Nuclear Bunker' becoming a 'tourist attraction' a third exit was added - on the grounds of health and safety!

CHURCHILL – The Honourable Member for Wanstead and Woodford

On October 31st 1959 Field Marshall Viscount Montgomery, *Monty*, unveiled a statue of Sir Winston Churchill on Woodford Green. The bronze statue stands at the southern end of the green, overlooking the top of Salway Hill. Sculpted by David McFall, it was immediately adopted by Wanstead and Woodford Council to honour Churchill who represented the constituency for 40 years.

Five thousand people were present at the unveiling by Viscount Montgomery. Speaking to the crowd he said: "This famous man to whom this statue is dedicated is still most happily with us, enjoying in dignity and quiet the evening of his splendid life. But that, alas, will not always be so. Future generations will not only need, but will desire to know what he looked like, and it is most fitting that you in Woodford have decided to supply the answer. He has received your unfailing loyalty for more than a quarter of a century. Woodford was his political Alamein."

In reply Churchill, at that time an ailing 85 year old, addressed the audience: "I am most grateful to the people of Wanstead and Woodford for the honour you now do me. It has been a privilege representing you in Parliament."

Winston Churchill had a number of Essex connections beyond the Metropolitan area. On November 29th 1910 Churchill, aged thirty-six and then a Liberal MP and President of the Board of Trade, visited Colchester to support the election campaign of local Liberal candidate Edgar Vincent. The Liberal Government's policies on 'free trade' however were very unpopular and on his arrival Churchill was pelted with fish and eggs by a hostile crowd.

The evening and following day were marred by rowdy scenes which resulted in both Liberal and Conservative campaign offices being attacked. Later, a large group swarmed through the town centre and attacked the Free Trade Shop opposite All Saints Church. The shop was smashed up and all the foreign goods on display were destroyed or looted. Still on the rampage, the angry crowd threatened to burn out, a widow and her young daughter who occupied the flat above the shop.

The widow bravely challenged the demonstrators and although the mother and child escaped unhurt, the flat was later burnt out. Churchill's efforts were in vain as the Liberal candidate lost and a coalition government again took office. Perhaps it is ironic that one hundred years later, in 2010, a coalition Government was formed between the Conservative and Liberal parties.

In April 1914 Winston Churchill had a lucky escape in Essex when a seaplane carrying the future Prime Minister made an emergency landing on the beach at Clacton. In his role as First Lord of the Admiralty, Churchill took a keen personal interest in naval aviation, preferring to fly whenever possible.

Although he had completed training as a pilot, he was forbidden to fly solo due to his important position in government. Churchill left the Isle of Grain air station in Kent and was en-route to inspect the fleet at Harwich when the aircraft, a *Short S74 Seaplane,* developed engine problems. The Pilot, Lieutenant W.J.Seddon RN., brought the plane down along the West Beach at Clacton near the pier. Churchill walked into the town where he spent a couple of hours at the Royal Hotel until a replacement Seaplane arrived from the air station at Felixstowe and he was able to continue his journey.

Winston Churchill is best remembered as the Prime Minister who, in World War II, guided Britain through its darkest hour to victory.

A Pirate is a Pirate?

On Saturday 28th March 1964, during the Easter weekend, a very young Simon Dee, sitting in a cramped studio on the Motor Vessel *Fredrica* anchored four miles off of the Essex coast at Frinton, ushered in the short lived era of offshore pirate radio.

"Hello everybody. This is *Radio Caroline* broadcasting on 199, your all-day music station."

These words became inseparable from the so called 'swinging sixties'. Within a short space of time the airwaves were crowded with wannabee radio broadcasters based on ships or disused wartime forts dotted around the English coast. Apart from *Caroline, Radios London, England, City* and even *Essex,* became "must tune into" locations that succeeded in capturing a substantial segment of the listening audience. Today the 60s 'Radio Pirates' are remembered with a degree of rose tinted nostalgia as many of the first offshore personalities later went on to become respected in the 'legal' broadcasting profession or achieved

success in other walks of life.

Less well remembered is the incident that took place in June 1966 in the village of Wendens Ambo, in the west of Essex, that hastened the demise of offshore broadcasting. Reg Calvert, the owner of *Radio City,* was shot dead by Oliver Smedley in a dispute about the ownership of the assets of the broadcaster. Whilst the sixties may have been 'swinging' and pirate radio the fashionable rage, offshore broadcasting was a jungle of shell companies based in tax havens that paid their staff little or nothing. They failed to pay artists any royalties, regularly infringed copyright

Shot dead. Radio City Boss Reg Calvert

and attracted operators with questionable business ethics who, where necessary, employed a variety of strong arm tactics to get their way.

On August 14th 1967 the Marine & Broadcasting (Offences) Act became law in the United Kingdom which closed nearly all of the offshore broadcasters.

Despite this, 40 years later, James Brokenshire, the Member of Parliament for Hornchurch addressed the House of Commons and highlighted the dangers posed by illegal radio stations and the lack of progress in coming to grips with them. He described them as "a living embodiment of contempt for the law that harms local communities with a wanton disregard of the health and safety of others".

As recently as March 2012 illegal radio broadcasting equipment was seized from the top of a tower block in Havering. A transmitter was found concealed in a ventilation shaft connected to the power supply in a lift motor room. Locks and doors had been smashed to gain access to the roof. The illegal broadcasts caused interference and the set up posed a serious fire risk. Further west in Barking a 'pirate' climbing like 'spiderman' from an upper flat in a tower block to the roof, using grappling irons, had been filmed. Several thousand pounds worth of damage had been caused to the roof and lift winding gear. The flat, which served as a studio, was barricaded with steel doors. On another occasion, in July 2005, London City airport was almost closed because of sustained interference to its air to ground communication system. Shortly afterwards a combined OFCOM and police task force seized 70 illegal broadcast transmitters. The *Times* reported 150 land based 'pirate' radio stations and speculated that one third of them were run by criminal gangs that played music that glamourised gun and drug culture. Police raids were said to have found drugs, guns, ammunition, knives, swords and pirate recordings both on CD and DVD. It was said that some drug dealers would tune in to wait for a coded message or for a

particular song to be played, knowing that would be a signal that their next shipment was ready for collection. In contrast to the 'old pirates' who paid their staff little or nothing the new 'pirates' frequently charged their aspiring DJs a premium for the privilege of hosting the shows.

By the year 2000 several land based legitimate community and commercial radio stations had been established. They had gone through a long process and considerable expense to be licensed. They were naturally incensed if 'pirates' who set up on adjacent channels with poorly configured equipment blocked their signals.

For the legal stations, the close proximity of a 'pirate' would act as a deterrent to existing and potential advertisers if the station could not be heard by its target listeners.

The new pirate phenomenon has ebbed and flowed over the last few years. Although tower block roof security has been upgraded, the new 'pirates' have never been eliminated. OFCOM and the police are locked in a continual game of cat and mouse with pirate broadcasters. As soon as one is closed down another springs up in another location.

Despite the recent nostalgic references in Parliament to the 'pirates' of the sixties, the likes of *Radio Caroline* and *Radio London* were described then by Ministers and Honourable Members in much the same language used about the pirates today. In 1965, Edward Short the Postmaster General, who had responsibility for broadcasting, said the offshore radio stations were "squalid enterprises akin to burglars". Addressing the house he added "it's no use talking about lawlessness in our cities if we are prepared to allow it on the high seas". It is debatable if in 40 years time today's tower block pirates will be remembered with the same nostalgia as the offshore pirates of the sixties.

Although most of the offshore pirates closed by 1967, *Radio Caroline* struggled on for nearly 25 years. The original MV *Fredrica* was replaced by the MV *Mi Amigo*. In March 1980, during a severe storm and still moored off the Essex coast, it broke anchor. The station ceased broadcasting and just after midnight a day later, the sixty year old ship was abandoned. The *Mi Amigo* sank leaving only its mast visible above the waves. In 1983 a new vessel, the converted trawler the *Ross Revenge*, became the new home of *Caroline*. However, in November 1991 this too was abandoned during a gale and ran aground on the Goodwin Sands. Unlike the *Mi Amigo*, it was later salvaged and, at the time of writing, is being restored in Tilbury Docks. *Radio Caroline* is now broadcasting completely legally and can be heard via satellite and the internet.

From Clapton to Chigwell to Clapton

Clapton on the banks of the River Lea is part of the London Borough of Hackney. Hackney has regularly featured in surveys over the last 25 years and is described as one of the most deprived areas in the UK. A dozen miles east of Clapton is Chigwell, which along with Loughton and Buckhurst Hill is part of the so called Essex golden triangle, one of the wealthiest parts of the country.

On November 1st 1968, 21 year old Alan Michael Sugar registered a company called the A.M.S Trading Company in Clapton. Sugar had been a pupil at Brook House School (see page 53). After leaving school he applied for jobs with both IBM and ICL (the then computer industry leaders) but was turned down.

Baron Sugar of Clapton

In April 1980 A.M.S Trading Company or AMSTRAD was floated on the London Stock exchange. Although the country was suffering an economic recession the floatation was a great success. Overnight Alan Sugar became a multi-millionaire.

Sugar's business sense and perception was second to none. He pioneered the mass marketing of consumer audio equipment at affordable prices. In 1985 another breakthrough came with the launch of the innovative PCW8256 word processor.

It is perhaps ironic that although initially rejected by IBM on leaving school, Alan Sugar was able to buy the company's European London headquarters for a figure in excess of £100 million in the 1980s and agree a licence for 30% of their personal computer market.

Less successful was Alan Sugar's venture into football. A fervent Tottenham Hotspur supporter, he teamed up with the former England Manager Terry Venables in 1991 to buy Tottenham Hotspur Football Club. The partnership ended acrimoniously. Sugar sold his share in 2001 and was quoted as saying that his time at Spurs was, "a waste of my life".

Alan Sugar was knighted in 2000. In 2006 his wealth, estimated at £790 million, put him 71st on *The Sunday Times* Rich List. Three years later he received a peerage. Though the Sugar's family home is in Chigwell, true to his roots he was ennobled as Baron Sugar of Clapton. Currently he is probably best known for the hugely popular television programme *'The Apprentice'.*

Snatched from Essex

On April 1st 1965, following the demise of the London County Council, five new London Boroughs were formed that became the core of *Metropolitan Essex*. The western boundary of the greater Essex, that had survived more or less intact for over 1000 years since Saxon times, was radically altered. The county border defined by the River Lea was moved over 12 miles east to align more or less with London's the easterly outer ring road the M25. There are still anamolies though. North Ockendon east of the M25 is in the London Borough of Havering, whilst Purfleet west of the M25 is still in Essex!

The change resulted in long established councils such as Romford, Hornchurch, Chingford, Ilford, Walthamstow, Leyton and Woodford disappearing into the new larger authorities of Havering, Redbridge, Barking and Dagenham or Waltham Forest as the case may be. Even West Ham and East Ham that had functioned with looser Essex ties for several years became part of the London Borough of Newham. At the same time North Woolwich which was part of Kent, although north of the River Thames and geographically in Essex, was transferred to the London Borough of Newham.

The reorganization brought relatively little change to the land area of Essex. The five new boroughs accounted for less than eight percent of the original 'Saxon' Essex. However, for the population it was a different matter. With the new status, at a stroke over one million people, or 40% of the Essex population, became Londoners.

The change had been on the cards from some time. Following the end of World War II it had become clear that the London County Council (LCC), originally formed in 1889 to administer the capital, was too small to cope with the new demands placed on it such as the introduction of the welfare state and chronic housing shortages affecting the capital. Built up London, as it once was, no longer ended at the River Lea where it became leafy rural Essex. The London Metropolitan area of continuous housing, offices and industry had extended to Dagenham and beyond. Capital wide bodies such as education, transport, police and the utilities, many of which were already in existence, needed to be co-coordinated with a measure of democratic accountability. It was also obvious that Essex County Council, administering an area fourteen times the size of *Metropolitan Essex* and based 25 miles away in Chelmsford, was not equipped to manage the diverse challenges of its Essex charges in Greater London.

In 1957, a Royal Commission for Local Government recommended that the LCC be wound up and replaced with the Greater London Council (GLC), a body with more powers to administer the larger area.

Eight years later, following what seemed to be interminable delays, petty disputes and much local infighting and haggling on the finality of the new boundaries between 'Essex' and London, the new Greater London Council (GLC) began work in 1965.

Newly created Barking and Dagenham, Havering, Newham, Redbridge and Waltham Forest became just five of the 32 new London Boroughs. Essex was not the only county to be truncated. The new GLC took territory from Kent, Surrey and Hertfordshire. Middlesex, much of it abutting the River Lea, and which had existed for 1000 years, ceased to exist as a county.

The GLC had a relatively short life and was abolished by the government of the day in 1986. In turn, the existing boroughs including those in *Metropolitan Essex* were given greater responsibilities especially in the field of education. Fourteen years later in the year 2000, London-wide government was re-established with the creation of a new Greater London Authority (The GLA) based in a new city hall in Queens Walk close to Tower Bridge. The change also brought about the introduction of London's first directly elected Mayor and a new London wide assembly. The boundaries and responsibilities of the London boroughs though remained largely unchanged.

Evidence of the Essex legacy is still much in evidence throughout the municipal buildings of *Metropolitan Essex*. The illustration to the left shows an

The Essex County Shield in Dagenham

Essex County shield which can clearly be seen on Henry Green Primary School in Dagenham. The school was originally opened in 1923 and has undergone several modifications and upgrades since, which have always included ensuring that the Essex shield is fully and lovingly maintained.

Despite the five new boroughs having been part of London for two generations, it is still the case that, for much of Dagenham, Romford, Hornchurch, Ilford, Chingford and Woodford, the local inhabitants and much of the media still consider these areas to be, at least geographically, part of Essex today.

Just after 5.30am on 16th May 1968, Ivy Hodge went into her kitchen to put the kettle on. She lived in flat no 90, on the 18th floor of the just completed 22 storey tower block in Silvertown called Ronan Point. Ivy struck a match. There was a sudden explosion and she was blown right across the kitchen. Ivy miraculously survived but remembered nothing of the incident.

A few seconds later there was a second explosion which blew out the upper pre-cast concrete panels which formed the side of the building. The south east corner of the building then collapsed just like a pack of cards. Four occupants were killed and seventeen injured. The death toll could have been far higher but, as Ronan Point was virtually brand new, not all of the accommodation was fully let. Four flats above the seat of the explosion were empty.

In 1968 local councils were hard at work replacing Victorian housing, perceived as slums, or bomb damaged from World War II. Ronan Point was one of nine tower blocks built on the Freemasons Estate. Tower blocks like Ronan Point were system built and assembled from pre-fabricated concrete panels that were bolted together on site.

In the twelve months before Ronan Point collapsed a record number of housing units had been built in the UK in an endeavour to fulfil promises made by successive Governments. Tower blocks were very much the fashion. Their concept was originally based on the Swiss/French architect Le Corbusier's philosophy of urban living; central to this were high rise blocks making better use of inner city space.

As an added incentive, the 1956 Housing Act gave government subsidies to local councils for every extra floor that was added to a construction of over five floors in height. Unfortunately, in the great rush to build as many tower blocks as possible quality suffered; there were design faults and perfectly good housing was demolished to make way for them. It didn't take very long for the often described 'brutalist' tower blocks to be associated with anti-social behaviour and urban decay – the very problems they were supposed to eradicate.

A three man tribunal was set up to investigate the collapse at Ronan Point. It was chaired by Hugh Griffiths QC. Very quickly it was established that the explosion was caused by gas. In all 150 witnesses were called. Ivy Hodge was brought from hospital to give evidence. She said she had a keen sense of smell and at no time during the previous evening had she smelt gas. The offending gas cooker was even wheeled into the hearing as a prime exhibit. The fitter who installed the cooker was then requested to give a detailed explanation of how it was put in.

The enquiry concluded that it was careless building work and lack of quality control that had caused the disaster although there were also severe flaws in the design. A local architect stated that he had examined joints within the structure and found them filled with newspapers rather than concrete. When called, the spokesman for the builders testified that Ronan Point met existing bylaws and regulations. He then added that the walls of the flat were not designed to withstand an explosion of the magnitude that had occurred.

The disaster at Ronan Point sent seismic shock waves through the world of modern architecture. It spelled the end of high-rise tower blocks as a viable solution to long term housing problems. The press had a field day; feverishly speculating about possible cosy connections between local and national politicians and building contractors.

Ronan Point was rebuilt and new tenants moved in, yet there were continuing doubts. In 1986 all the tower blocks on the Freemasons Estate, including Ronan Point, were demolished and replaced by the two storey terraced housing that exists today.

The campaign to stop the building of tower blocks, as a 'one size fits all' solution to solve the housing problem was a victory fought in the main by tenants who found the strength to stand up to experts and their jargon and demand answers in plain English to the serious questions over tower blocks.

After recovering Ivy Hodge was given a new home. She even, allegedly, took with her the same cooker that she had owned in Ronan Point.

The Beckton Alps

Along the Newham Way (A13) between Canning Town and London's North Circular Road and falling within the old Essex Becontree Hundred is a very odd road junction sign. The A13's intersection with the A117 Woolwich Manor Way is oddly called the 'Beckton Alps'.

Although there is an Alpine Way and an Alpine Business Centre close by, there are no alpine chalets to be seen or any evidence of a winter sports paradise. However, abutting the south east corner of the junction is the highest point in Newham. This feature was not created millions of years ago but by Victorian industrialists. The 'Alps' were originally the toxic spoil heaps from the former Beckton Gas Works. After the gas works closed the 'Alps' were cleaned up, landscaped and reduced in size.

Much of east Beckton, from Creekmouth in the east, along the north bank of the River Thames was low-lying marshland. In 1867, the Gas Light and Coke Company applied for Parliamentary Authority to erect a huge new gas works. A year later 550 acres of marsh had been drained and on the 25th November 1870 the first gas was manufactured on the site. Apart from gas, the plant produced coke from coal and supplied numerous by-products such as coal tar. In due course it made and supplied gas for most of London north of the Thames. In its day it was described as the largest gas works in Europe and sometimes even as the largest such plant in the world. The name Beckton was given to the plant and the surrounding area in honour of the company's governor, Simon Adams Beck.

The principal reason why the site was selected, apart from its proximity to the capital, was that it gave direct access to the River Thames. The construction of deep water piers facilitated the unloading of ships bringing coal from Durham directly into the site. The plant had a storage capacity of 250,000 tons. In its heyday the Gas Light and Coke Company owned a fleet of seventeen coastal colliers. These delivered, on average, a million tons of coal annually. Nearly as much again was transhipped onto barges and sent to other gas works. Transport within the Beckton site was accomplished by an extensive internal railway system, with more than 40 miles of track which in turn was linked to the national rail network.

On 1st of May 1949 the Beckton Gas Works was nationalised, under the 1948 Gas Act, and became part of the North Thames Gas Board. However, with the discovery of natural gas in the North Sea, the manufacture of gas from coal became increasingly uncompetitive. After nearly 100 years of continuous operation the works closed in 1970.

The freight rail line closed a year later in February 1971. Much of the defunct works lay within the London Docklands area and nearly all of the old works have been demolished. The internal railway lines have been demolished with one exception. Part of the rail route has since been used for the Docklands Light Railway between Beckton station and Royal Docks Road. Many new roads have been built through the area. The original gasworks site has since been developed for housing or industrial and retail parks leaving only the 'Alps' as a landmark legacy.

No one knows who coined the term Beckton Alps. It seems to have come into use during the mid 1980s and began appearing on street atlases around about that time. Transport for London (TfL) added 'Beckton Alps' to road signage in 2006, following upgrades on the A13, to give the area an easy to remember point for local traffic reports.

However, the Beckton Alps did live up to its name when, on the 8th November 1986, a dry ski slope was opened by Councillor Jimmy Newstead, the Deputy Mayor of Newham and Mel Hague, the Director of Operations of the London Docklands Development Corporation. Two years later, on December 7th 1988, there was a second official opening by the late Princess Diana, Princess of Wales. Beckton Alps then boasted a village including a chalet containing changing facilities, a shop and a restaurant. A ski-lift had also been installed and the slope upgraded.

Alas skiing in Beckton was short lived and the ski slope has since closed.

All the facilities have been dismantled and removed. Ambitious plans to reopen the ski slope have come to nothing.

The 'Alps' are now classed as a site of Metropolitan importance for Nature Conservation in the London Borough of Newham. If the reader can manage the hike to the summit, whilst it is unlikely any snow will be encountered, a clear day will reveal excellent views of Canary Wharf and a great panorama of central London.

Real snow on the Beckton Alps in 1991

173

Ten Steel Guardians

The Thames Barrier at Silvertown is nearly a mile up stream from the Woolwich Ferry. Government approval for the barrier's construction was given in 1972. Ten years later it became operational and after a further two

years it was officially opened by Queen Elizabeth II on May 8th 1984.

The Barrier consists of 10 steel gates each weighing 3,300 tonnes. These, when raised into position across the River Thames, form protection for central London against flooding caused by abnormal tidal surges.

The River Thames and its tributaries such as the Rivers Lea, Roding and Beam have been prone to flooding over the centuries. Inundations on the lands of Barking Abbey occurred frequently during the middle ages which resulted in the Abbess pleading with the King of the day for help. The Dagenham Breach in 1707 has already been mentioned on page 66 and severe flooding was recorded in Barking and Dagenham in 1928. The solution to the problem had always been to plug the breaches and build higher and higher embankments.

However the events of the Great Surge of 1953 changed all that. On Saturday January 31st a huge depression formed near Iceland and moved south around Scotland into the North Sea. As air pressure fell, the sea level rose and the waters were pushed south by winds approaching hurricane force. With a record spring tide adding to the surge, an ever-growing wall of water was being forced down the narrowing funnel of the North Sea that separates England from the continental land mass, to its narrowest point at the Dover straits.

The first of what was to become a catalogue of disasters struck in the morning of the 31st January when the Stranraer to Larne car ferry, *Princess Victoria,* was overwhelmed by mountainous waves in the Irish Sea resulting in the loss of 130 passengers and crew. News of the catastrophe was slow to filter through. Although the sinking was the top story on the radio, details were sketchy. The 24-hour breaking news we know today did not exist. Those who heard about the disaster, whilst shocked and saddened, carried on as normal.

No-one connected weather patterns in the Irish Sea with the events about to unfold further south, along the Essex Coast and River Thames. In mid-winter severe weather was not unusual and the storm force winds and rough seas did not seem out of the ordinary. However, all along England's East Coast, from Yorkshire to Norfolk, waves relentlessly battered the coast. One by one sea defences began to unravel as the tidal surge moved south.

The first signs of the deadly potential of the climatic fury were felt on the Lincolnshire coast at Skegness. Yet coastal communities in Suffolk, Essex and along the Thames remained oblivious to the impending disaster. There was no coordinated sea defence warning system. While people were being drowned in their homes further north, cinemagoers in Harwich patiently queued in the cold and wind for the next performance at the Electric Cinema, just yards from the seafront. At Southend-on-Sea, a dance was taking place on the pier head with the water rising all around, lapping right up to the boards.

Late Saturday evening the great surge hit Harwich. The audience leaving the Electric Cinema just after 10pm were greeted by the first breaches in the sea wall. By midnight virtually the whole town centre was underwater. Jaywick, just south of Clacton, was next to succumb, followed by Maldon. In the Thames Estuary, Canvey Island suffered at least 40 breaches to its sea defences. At both Jaywick and Canvey most residents were in bed when the water broke through. They were woken by the tremendous noise of the crashing water and within minutes were literally fighting for their lives in the pitch dark.

The surge raced relentlessly on up the River Thames flooding industrial areas and severing telephone and power lines as it went. On the Kent coast either side of the River Medway, the Naval Dockyard at Sheerness and the Isle of Grain Oil Refinery were overwhelmed. Tilbury was flooded and further up stream the Rivers Roding and Lea burst their banks. Water cascaded into the tidal basin by Bow Creek at the mouth of the River Lea after a 300ft section of embankment collapsed and water flooded into Canning Town. Silvertown and North Woolwich suffered a similar fate with overflows from the Royal Docks.

For a while it was complete chaos. The BBC midnight news bulletin carried a message that an exceptionally high tide was expected in the Rivers Thames and Medway at 3.00am and ended tersely with 'It will be cold'. Then, without a hint of the chaos that was already raging, as normal the BBC closed down for the night. Being the weekend, several key emergency personnel and civic leaders were absent and unreachable. What communications there were suffered further disruption when floodwater poured down manholes into underground telephone and electricity chambers.

175

By the middle of the night virtually all of West Ham's Fire Brigade telephones had failed. Power failure also disabled the riverside pumping stations that were operating. As the water poured into residential and industrial areas an enormous amount of debris, some of it toxic, was swept upstream, not only creating a hazard in itself but compounding the difficulties by clogging up drainage outlets. With waters rising all around, the fire engines at Silvertown Fire Station had to be hastily moved as they were in imminent danger of being stranded.

A resident of Mary Street, Canning Town, Mrs Annie Shepherd, waded through freezing cold waters in the pitch dark to warn her neighbours. Mrs Shepherd described her traumatic experience as being worse than the blitz. She said "I went through all the air raids but this was worse than any of it – we didn't have a minute's warning, there was no time to do anything before the ground floor rooms were flooded".

As the floodwater retreated it left behind a devastating trail of death and destruction. People were left marooned and traumatised. Precious amounts of food stored in homes were ruined and the water was undrinkable. There were enormous amounts of material damage. Farm animals died in their thousands and the soil had been ruined. In built-up areas giant rats emerged from flooded sewers.

In the United Kingdom over three hundred people died as a direct result of the surge. Fifty-eight people had died on Canvey Island and more than 30 at Jaywick. Canning Town, Silvertown and North Woolwich only recorded one death in the tidal basin, but more than 1000 houses were flooded and nearly 200 people had to be temporarily re-housed. One family who had been evacuated from Canvey planned to stay with relatives in Canning Town, arrived only to find that they too had been evacuated.

Over the next few days residents returned and the immense task of clearing up sprang into action. The Salvation Army, the Red Cross and the WVS gave sterling assistance along with hundreds of volunteers. The mayor of West Ham started a flood relief fund. Among the donations were food parcels from the USA, dried fruit from Greece and even coffee from the Emperor of Ethiopia.

Despite the scale of the disaster on the east coast and the Metropolitan Essex stretch of the River Thames, central London had had a lucky escape. The record high tide had brought water to the top of the embankments from Westminster to Chelsea but no further. The consequences of unexpected large scale flooding in London would have been horrendous, not only in terms of potential loss of life and property damage but also in economic and social terms.

Within the flood risk area were more than 30 underground stations, eight power stations, 16 hospitals and 400 schools. In all more than half a million properties would have been subject to flooding. Parliament, Downing Street, Westminster Abbey, the Supreme Court, City Hall, Lambeth Palace, the Royal Festival Hall and the Intelligence services building, Thames House, at Vauxhall were all in the threatened zone. During the flood of 1928, 14 people were drowned in the vicinity of Thames House.

The flood defences today are much better since the construction of the Thames Barrier, plus a further barrier on the River Roding at Barking Creek (right) and continued strengthening of protective embankments. Even so, much of central London remains under threat.

The risk factor is likely to increase in the future as a result of climate change, rising sea levels, population increase and construction in the Thames Gateway allowing for the building of 120,000 homes below sea level. To illustrate the risks the Department of Environment has released figures which show the increase in Thames Barrier closures through the decades. It was closed four times in the 1980s, 35 times in the 1990s, and 80 times in the decade that ended in 2010.

One of the more unusual consequences of the flood risk at Dagenham was that, in January 2010, the Ministry of Justice scrapped proposals to build a 'giant' prison for 1,500 inmates on a 45-acre site which was once part of the Ford estate. A spokesman said the Ministry had "carefully considered the planning risks and in particular the potential cost of mitigating flood risk".

In the view of the Environment Agency one of the biggest problems in minimizing the damage caused by flooding is lack of knowledge. The agency estimates that over half the people living and working in flood risk areas are unaware of the potential threat and of those that are aware perhaps only 10% take any action to reduce the threat. One simple course of action the Agency recommends to reduce the impact of flooding is to ensure that run offs and drainage channels are kept clear of debris at all times.

The name Chobham Manor would initially indicate a large stately home somewhere in the stockbroker belt of Surrey. There is a Chobham near Woking and the town may well have its fair share of stately homes, but Chobham Manor in *Metropolitan Essex* is the designated name for a new neighbourhood to be built in Stratford on the eastern part of the Olympic Park site as part of the legacy of the 2012 London Games.

Within Stratford there has been a Chobham Road for 150 years. It runs west from the Leytonstone Road towards what was once Chobham Farm. The farm disappeared during the late 19th century with the industrialisation of the River Lea valley and the expansion of Great Eastern Railway's works at Temple Mills (see page 190/1). By the 1960s, Chobham Farm was just a quaint place name for an industrial estate where storage and distribution were the main businesses.

In July 1972, Midland Cold Storage Ltd, a company based at Chobham Farm became the centre of an industrial dispute of epic proportions. The dispute unfolded against the backdrop of the ongoing clash between the trade union movement and newly the elected Conservative Government of Edward Heath. Britain was experiencing the first national miners' strike since 1926 and widespread mass picketing by builders, dockers and transport workers.

Midland Cold Storage Ltd although not located in the docks was supposed to employ registered dockworkers to pack and unload containers. A complex union agreement obliged employers to use dockers for such work within five miles of any dock. At the time London Docks, were rapidly losing business mainly due to their inability to accommodate the ever increasing size of cargo ships. Also, containerisation had resulted in freight being unloaded straight from ships onto trucks or railway wagons. This meant considerable job losses in the docks as the containers could be packed or unpacked away from the docks by almost anyone.

Midland Cold Storage Ltd, only two miles from the Royal Docks, chose not to employ dockers. As a consequence they were targeted by mass pickets in an attempt to stop them trading. After eight weeks of picketing the company had had enough and its directors applied to the newly formed National Industrial Relations Court (NIRC) for an injunction to halt the pickets. The injunction was duly issued, nevertheless the picketing continued.

Private investigators working for the cold storage company identified five shop stewards from the Transport and General Workers Union as pickets. The five were charged with contempt of court and warrants were issued by the court for their arrest.

On 21ˢᵗ July 1972, Bernie Steer, Vic Turner, Derek Watkins, Cornelius Clancy and Anthony Merrick were apprehended and taken to Pentonville Prison – hence the name *The Pentonville Five*.

The arrests and imprisonment lead to outrage in union circles. Thousands of striking workers marched through North London to Pentonville Prison. There was a series of rolling strikes and work stoppages that turned into a general strike in all but name. The Trades Union Congress (TUC) then called for an official national strike on 31ˢᵗ July and demanded the release of the five shop stewards.

Stalemate ensued. The government seemed powerless to act. Then, to everyone's surprise, salvation came when the previously unheard of Official Solicitor, Norman Turner, stepped in. An obscure figure from the ancient machinery of English justice, he successfully applied to the Court of Appeal for the release of the five. The arrest warrants were overturned. The Appeal Court ruled that there were insufficient grounds to deprive the men of their liberty since the evidence garnered by the private investigators was flawed. A week later the five were released and a constitutional crisis in the making had

WARNING THIS DEPOT IS DOCK WORK KEEP OUT

Picketing outside Midland Cold Storage Ltd

been averted, for the time being. The then leader of the opposition, Harold Wilson, commented "the government had been saved by a fairy godmother". Yet despite all the protests and the perceived success of the *five*, the dock labour force inexorably declined. All the London docks closed as major cargo handling centres within ten years. Containerisation was an irreversible fact of cargo movement world wide.

After years of industrial strife, power cuts and the infamous three day week the Prime Minister Edward Heath called an election in February 1974, and was defeated. The incoming Labour Government immediately abolished the National Industrial Relations Court (NIRC). The *Pentonville Five* went their separate ways, although each retained their strong union links.

One of the five, Victor Turner returned to work at the Royal Docks but later transferred to Tilbury docks. In 1994 he was elected to Newham Borough Council for the Bermersyde ward. During 1997/8 he had the honour of being chosen as Mayor of Newham. During this period he was also presented with the Transport and General Workers Union Gold Medal for his union work. Vic Turner retired from the council in 2006.

179

In 1850, Parliament passed an act enabling the construction of a new dock on the Plaistow marshes where the River Thames loops south from Gallions Reach before curving back to Bow Creek. The proposal to build the dock was the brainchild of George Bidder, described as the 'Maker of modern West Ham'. Excavations began three years later and in 1855 the Victoria Dock was officially opened by Prince Albert the Queen's Royal consort. Within remarkable foresight and against much opposition Bidder had recommended that a much larger area of land than the dock required, nearly 100 acres in total, be purchased.

Business at Victoria Dock soon exceeded all expectations and in 1874, immediately to the east of it the London & St Katharine Docks Company began construction of the Royal Albert Dock. This was opened in June 1880 by Prince Arthur the Duke of Connaught, Queen Victoria's third son.

In 1911 the design of a third dock, to run parallel to the Royal Albert on its southern flank, was agreed. Construction began in August the following year but halted in 1914 on the outbreak of the First World War, when most of

the workmen left to join the military. Eventually completed in 1921, King George V officially opened the dock bearing his name on 8th July that year. Collectively three docks became known as the 'Royal Docks'. Their construction required the removal of millions of cubic yards of earth, then a lining of concrete and bricks. At times over 3,000 men were employed.

The Royal Victoria Dock was the first dock to be designed for steamships and incorporated hydraulic machinery to handle their cargo.

The Royal Albert Dock when it opened also had a number of firsts; it was London's first dock to have electric lighting, electric power and then refrigeration. For this reason it soon became a sought after destination for offloading and storing meat, fruit and vegetables. The Royal Albert Dock could accommodate the largest vessels afloat in 1880, but could still handle sailing vessels. It was also used as a terminus by passenger vessels.

The Great Eastern railway ran a 'ship to rail' service from Fenchurch Street to Gallions, close to today's Gallions Reach DLR station, where it built the Gallions Hotel for first-class passengers staying overnight.

The King George V Dock was built to facilitate the ever growing trade passing though the Victoria and Albert Docks. Although smaller than the other two Royal docks it was well equipped with electric cranes and mechanical devices to aid the dock workers in achieving fast turn around.

For a time the Royal Docks became the worlds greatest dock complex. They created a wealth of jobs for the local community as many new industries set up or moved into West Ham which in turn spurred the expansion of the local railway and road networks.

During the 1920s and 30s the entrance locks were continually being enlarged for the ever larger cargo ships and passenger liners being built, and in 1939 the 35000 ton liner *Mauretania* was successfully berthed. The *Mauretania* was over four times the size of the first ships to enter the Royal Docks. The Port of London boasted it had the biggest maritime cargo handling business in the world with a workforce of nearly 100,000.

With the advent of the Second World War the Docks were one of the first targets to be attacked by enemy bombers in 1940 and suffered extensive damage. The end of the war saw ships getting bigger and bigger and the Royal Docks could no longer cope. The average modern container ship had become over twice the size of *Mauretania* and navigating up the River Thames was increasingly challenging. The construction of the Thames Barrier made passage even more difficult. Gradually trade in the docks diminished; a process which was hastened by continuous labour disputes throughout the 1960s and 1970s.

The new bigger ships moved away to offload their cargoes at Tilbury or Felixstowe and the Royal Docks closed in 1981. A year later a planning application for an airport was filed.

Take off at London City Airport

181

The projected runway was to be located on the disused quays between the King George V and the Royal Albert Docks. The idea for the airport had been mooted jointly by Reg Ward of the London Docklands Development Corporation that now owned and managed the Royal Docks and Sir Philip Beck the chairman of the construction firm John Mowlem.

A public planning enquiry was begun in June 1983, which lasted 63 days and in 1984 the proposals were approved. Three years later the on the 5th November, Queen Elizabeth II officially opened London City Airport. Fifteen Thousand passengers had used the airport by the end of the first year. In 1988 this had risen to 133, 000 and within ten years, the figure had reached one million with over 30,000 flights coming and going anually.

Other major developments have included the construction of a new university campus (for the University of East London), the ExCeL Exhibition Centre and new offices for Newham Borough Council. Thousands of new homes and apartment complexes have been built and the Docklands Light Railway (DLR) has been extended to the airport and beyond. Another addition to the rail infrastructure will be London's *Crossrail* that will link the south eastern and eastern parts of the rail network to the west through central London in a series of tunnels.

Crossrail had been on the drawing board since 1943 but parliamentary approval and funding was not put in place until 2005. The cross London link should be operational by 2018. A branch of the *Crossrail* line will pass beneath the Royal Docks, between Canning Town and Woolwich, and serve Custom House station (with future provision for another at Silvertown). The route re-uses the southern part of the former North London Line that originally terminated in North Woolwich by the Ferry. Intriguingly one of the giant

Tunnel Boring Machines (TBMs) shown on left that will be used to carve the tunnels out for *Crossrail* will be called Victoria.

Although the Royal docks are closed for commercial shipping, most are still navigable. Little of the original infrastructure remains though some historic warehouses and cranes (see page 180) have been preserved.

A Tunnel boring Machine

The Home of John Bull

At the entrance to Romford's 'Brewery Shopping Complex' stands a copper brewing tun. It was unveiled on April 26th 2001 by the Leader of Havering Council, Cllr. Ray Harris, to mark the opening of the new complex. This had been built on the site of the former Ind-Coope Ltd., Romford Brewery which ceased production in 1993. The complex retains one of the brewery's original 160 foot chimneys and this along with the brewing tun are visual reminders of the town's nearly 300 years of beer making.

The original brewery stood on the banks of the River Rom. It was founded in 1708 as an addition to the Star Inn in the High Street which was then the main road to London. In 1799 the brewery was purchased by Edward Ind and it grew in importance becoming, at times, Romford's main industry. From 1845, when he was joined by Octavius and George Coope, it became known as Ind-Coope Ltd. A year later a second brewery was opened in Burton-on-Trent.

The Romford brewery continued to prosper and with the coming of the railways a direct link was built from the brewery to Romford station. By 1908, it had its own railway sidings and was employing 450 workers. In 1934 Ind-Coope merged with Samuel Allsopp & Sons to become Ind-Coope & Allsopp. Then in 1961, together with Ansells and Tetley Walker, they formed Allied Breweries. This merger meant the group became one of the largest brewers in the world.

At its peak in 1970 there were over 1000 workers employed. Twenty years later however Ind-Coope decided to concentrate its business in Burton-on-Trent and the Romford site was sold.

The copper brewing tun shown on the right was preserved when the brewery closed and was donated by Havering Council

The Romford Brewery was the home of *John Bull* bitter one of Ind-Coope's most popular beers. *John Bull's* caricature first appeared in 1712, three years after the brewery opened. Drawn as a bluff, bull-headed farmer wearing a squat top hat and a waistcoat decked out with the Union Jack he purported to show a typical Englishman.

Survivor

At 11.40pm on the 14th April 1912, the White Star liner *Titanic* on her maiden voyage, en route to New York, struck an iceberg. Within three hours, at just after 2.00am, the liner had disappeared beneath the surface of the Atlantic Ocean. One thousand five hundred people perished, almost two-thirds of the people on board. At 46,000 tons and with a top speed of 23 knots, the *Titanic* was the largest and fastest passenger liner afloat. Her owners, the White Star line, had declared the ship unsinkable.

On board was seven-year-old Ilford born Eva Miriam Hart who was travelling with her parents Benjamin and Esther Hart as second class passengers. The Harts had boarded the *Titanic* on 10th April in Southampton. They were emigrating to Canada where Benjamin Hart, a builder who had sold his business, had plans to make a new start in Winnipeg, Manitoba.

Esther Hart was uneasy about the crossing and particularly sceptical of the owner's extravagant claims that the ship was unsinkable. Fearing the worst she would only sleep during the day and at night insisted on staying awake in the cabin, fully clothed.

When the ship struck the iceberg Eva was sleeping. Her father rushed into her cabin to alert Eva and her mother. The little girl was wrapped in a blanket and carried to the boat deck. Luckily for them the standing orders of 'women and children first' were observed and mother and daughter were allocated places in lifeboat No. 14. Eva was instructed by her father to 'hold Mummy's hand and be a good girl'. It was the last thing her father ever said to her and the last time she ever saw him. Eva and her mother were rescued by RMS *Carpathia* and taken to New York, arriving three days after the disaster. If her father's body was recovered, it was never identified.

With the loss of her husband Esther Hart abandoned their plans to move to Canada and sailed back to England with Eva on the following 25th April. They settled in Chadwell Heath, where Esther rented a house in Whalebone Lane. They were two of only 700 *Titanic* passengers who survived the disaster. Despite her age, Eva never forgot what she had seen and heard that night; she was plagued with nightmares for years afterwards.

Esther died in 1928. At 23 years old Eva was alone. She received an invitation to live in Australia with her uncle. Though the thought of a long sea voyage terrified her, she decided to confront her fears and booked a passage via Singapore. On sailing she locked herself in her cabin for two days and nights feeling terrified and seasick. Eventually, when she emerged to find daylight and the ship still afloat, the nightmares went away. She did not settle in Australia though and returned to Chadwell Heath.

For years Eva never spoke about the *Titanic*. She held several jobs, including periods as a professional singer and working as a magistrate. In 1982 she returned to the United States for a 'Titanic Historical Society' convention joining several other survivors to commemorate the 70th anniversary of the sinking. On 1st September 1985, the oceanographer, Dr. Robert Ballard, discovered the wreck of the *Titanic* at a depth of 13,000 feet, some 500 nautical miles east of the North American coast. The discovery made world headline news and prompted Eva Hart, still living in Chadwell Heath, to become one of the most outspoken survivors.

In interviews Eva vividly describes her trip on the boat train to Southampton and her excitement at the prospect of the journey. Recalling

with anguish how she clung to her mother in the lifeboat. She said "I saw that ship sink, I never closed my eyes. I didn't sleep at all. I saw it, I heard it, and nobody could possibly forget it - the worst things I can remember are the screams".

Criticizing the White Star Line for providing insufficient lifeboats and boasting of the *Titanic's* invincibility, Eva also spoke out against the 1987 salvage efforts, saying the *Titanic* is a gravesite and should be treated as such and kept free of "fortune hunters, vultures, pirates, and grave robbers".

Eva Hart died on 14th February 1996 aged 91. In 1997, James Cameron's epic disaster movie *Titanic* was released. A year later the pub chain J.D. Wetherspoon opened the 'Eva Hart' pub in the High Road Chadwell Heath. The building was formerly Chadwell Heath's police station.

Stratford's Mills
and Film Studios

Stratford's 'Three Mills' is surrounded by water. It stands on the confluence of the River Lea and Channelsea River and is bounded on the east by the Prescott Channel. Today only two mills remain on the island sharing it with the location of the twenty acre site of, arguably, London's biggest film studio. Since the late 1990s, Three Mills Studios have produced many film and television programmes and have been the home to several fashion shoots. Throughout 2011 and 2012 their facilities were used continuously for the auditioning and rehearsals of thousands of performers who took part in the 2012 Olympic Games opening and closing ceremonies.

At the time of the Domesday Book there may have been as many as nine working mills on this part of the River Lea and its Bow Back Rivers tributaries. Some of them were tidal which the area was well suited to.

Collectively they laid the foundations of an industry that survived into

House Mill and Clock Mill at low tide

our times. Sometime after its establishment in 1135, Stratford Langthorne Abbey (see page 32) acquired three of the mills that became known as 'Three Mills'. Under the Monks of the Abbey the mills prospered, providing flour for the bakers of Stratford. After the dissolution, while the Abbey was left a ruin, the mills continued to thrive, though in the late 16th century the three mills were reduced to two.

During the next century the milling took another direction. Grain ground for use in the distillation of alcohol became big business. It could be said that the mills played a part in fuelling the enormous rise in London's gin consumption. The two surviving mills are known as the House Mill and the Clock Mill and date from 1776 and 1815 respectively. They have had many owners, the most prominent of them being the Nicholson gin distilling company of Clerkenwell. They took over in 1872 with their 'Lamplighter Gin', gradually moving their total business to 'Three Mills' and continuing gin production until 1941. House Mill ceased operation a year earlier when rationing, due to the Second World War, curtailed the use of grain for distilling. The Clock Mill continued working until 1952 and up until the 1970s the distillery was used as a bottling facility by the brewers, Bass Charrington.

Today the River Lea Tidal Mill Trust Ltd. owns House Mill and the Miller's House buildings. With the help of Heritage Lottery funding the mill is being restored. The plan is for the two eastern wheels to operate the milling process and a sack hoist and the two western wheels to be used for electricity generation. House Mill is one of Newham's grade 1 listed buildings and is still the largest tidal mill in the world. It is open to visitors on Sundays during summer months.

The Clock Mill is used as offices by the Three Mills Studios. Most of the machinery has been removed and there are no plans for restoration although it still carries a Grade II listing.

Filming is not new to Metropolitan Essex. Further upstream on the River Lea, Walthamstow emerged as one of the first centres of the British Film industry. The Victorian film making pioneer (and former hairdresser), Edward George Turner, was co-founder of the first film company in Britain, which was first called *Walturdaw*. It was later renamed the Walthamstow Film Company. Turner claimed to have shown the first 'cinema broadcast' film at the former Victoria Hall in Hoe Street in 1896. Later the Walthamstow Company became the first in the UK to rent films out. The area began to attract prospective film makers and in 1910 the first purpose built film studio was set up by the Precision Film Company in Whipps Cross.

In 1913, the British and Colonial Kinematograph Company, specializing in travel films, created another film studio at the junction of Grove Road and Hoe Street. The 'Dark Stage Studio' was then set up on Lea Bridge Road by the I. B. Davidson company. This was followed, in October 1914, by Cunard Film Co. Ltd., building a new studio in Wood Street, Walthamstow. With the studios came processing laboratories, carpentry workshops, set decorators and costume makers. For a time it appeared Walthamstow had stolen the march on Hollywood.

Allegedly Walthamstow had been chosen as a desired location because of its proximity to London's West End which meant a steady supply of actors was always available between theatre performances. The borough also had cleaner air, it was generally free of fog, and locations such as Epping Forest provided excellent scenery for anything from a cowboy film, to a jungle adventure, or a historic battle scene. There were also a number of buildings nearby that could double as stately mansions.

One of the legends of cinema, Alfred Joseph Hitchcock, was born at 517, High Road, Leytonstone. He was the third child of William and Emma Hitchcock. His father was a poultry dealer and fruit-importer and the family home above the shop survived until it was demolished in the 1960s to make way for a filling station.

Hitchcock began his early film career as a title card designer at the Gainsborough (or Islington) Studios in Hackney. He went on to become famous as the master of the suspense film. Locally he is commemorated at Leytonstone tube station in a series of mosaic tiled panels sited along the underground entrance walkway. They were created by the Greenwich Mural Workshop and are collectively known as the Hitchcock gallery. One panel shows the young Alfred sitting on a horse outside his father's shop. More

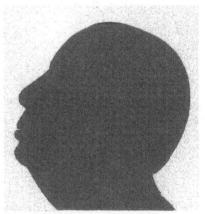

Hitchcock Master of Suspense

chillingly, at the centre of the walkway, and perhaps tellingly at its deepest point, another illustrates the terror of the shower scene in the classic film *Psycho* (see page 106). Hitchcock is also remembered close by in Whipps Cross Road where the *Sir Alfred Hitchcock Hotel*, constructed from a series of town houses, stands. Its lobby walls display Hitchcock memorabilia and stills from many of his films. The filling station in Leytonstone High Road carries a heritage blue plaque noting Hitchcock's birth.

Filmmaking was short lived in Walthamstow and by 1926 all the diverse companies and studios had either closed down or moved away. The famous personalities went on to find fame and fortune elsewhere. In 1929 Alfred Hitchcock directed *Blackmail* the first British 'talkie' which was made at Elstree Studios, Borehamwood. Ten years later Hitchcock moved to Hollywood. His first Hollywood release, *Rebecca* earned the director an academy award.

Windmills on My Mind

Windmills have been around for more than 600 years. Generally used for pumping water or grinding flour, they reached their greatest numbers in the 1830s. However, within 30 years, many mills were struggling to survive against coal and steam then oil fired engines and finally electricity.

Many were demolished, others just abandoned and left derelict. By 1950, nearly all had ceased to be used commercially. Most of the windmills we see today owe their existence to their status as heritage attractions maintained by dedicated bands of volunteers.

Coal as a primary fuel was superseded by the cheaper and more efficient oil. This accelerated the demise of the windmill. However, following the 1973 Arab–Israeli conflict the cost of oil soared. Together with concerns over security of supply and environmental worries over increasing CO_2 emissions, a determined search for alternative energy sources began. The outcome of this search meant the wheel had turned full circle. 'Windmills', in the form of wind powered turbines were seen as one of the solutions for electricity generation.

Henry Ford (see page 136) was keen on recycling when he used London rubbish as fuel in his Dagenham power station in the 1930s. So it is no surprise that one of the pioneers of wind generated power for industrial use was the Ford Motor Company. In April 2004 two turbines, each 120 metres tall, the same height as the London Eye, were erected at Dagenham. The power generated from these satisfies the needs of the Ford Diesel Assembly Hall. During August 2011, a third more powerful turbine was installed.

Yet not all wind turbine proposals have met with approval. The 2012 Olympic Delivery Authority (ODA) considered building a turbine at Eton Manor, adjacent to the Olympic Park, to provide sustainable power. Billed as a green beacon and nicknamed the *Angel of Leyton* it was hoped the turbine could deliver 20% of the Olympic Park's energy needs. However, in June 2010, the ODA announced that the plans had been scrapped as the project was considered "no longer feasible".

Wind turbine projects attract support and hostility in equal measure. Construction and operation still requires public subsidy or tariff support and, with the best will in the world, wind is fickle and cannot be relied on to provide essential energy requirements when needed. On the plus side, as Ford would seem to have demonstrated, it works and provides surplus power at times, which is then sold to the national grid.

If the wheel really has turned full circle for wind power, then windmills may well be here for another 600 years. Whether turbines will be commercially viable then or just heritage landmarks from a bygone age is another matter.

Robert and Friends

Robert had been sadly neglected, but in 2008 he was sent away to Colchester for a complete makeover at the East Anglian Railway Museum, courtesy of the Olympic Delivery Authority. In 2012 *Robert* returned to Stratford in a new shiny crimson and black livery and has pride of place on a prominent location on the forecourt between the train and bus stations.

Robert, the saddle tank steam locomotive, began life in 1933 at the Avonside Engine Company of Bristol where he was known simply as number 2068. He began his working life at Staveley Coal and Iron Ltd. in Northampton with a new identity; Lamport No. 3.

In 1969, Lamport No. 3 was 'retired' and later moved to the Quainton Railway Centre in Buckinghamshire. There he acquired the name *Robert*. In 1993 *Robert* was purchased by the Dockland Development Corporation

and sent to Kew Bridge Steam Museum. He was refurbished and painted in Red and Black to look like a locomotive that had once worked in the Beckton Gasworks. On completion *Robert* was given his own plinth at the entrance to the former works.

In 1999, the Docklands Development Corporation was wound up and Newham Borough Council obtained custody of *Robert.* He was again moved, this time to his present location in Stratford.

In Stratford, on the other side of the Olympic Park from where *Robert* stands, is Temple Mills. This was once an enormous complex of rail marshalling yards, sidings and workshops that stretched north by the side of Eton Manor to Lea Bridge Road. The area used to be agricultural and was originally owned by the Knights Templars, who installed mills on the River Lea to grind corn, hence the name Temple Mills. As London expanded eastwards across the River Lea, the farming lands were gradually taken over for industrial manufacturing and the mills were put to other uses including the manufacture of gunpowder. As the railways developed in the mid 19th century, the mills were demolished.

Temple Mills became the hub of the Eastern Counties Railway's and then later, the Great Eastern Railway Company, works. Some tank locomotives, (Roberts' predecessors maybe), were built there in the 1850s. Following many reorganisations, takeovers and buyouts, locomotive manufacturing was moved elsewhere. The works at Temple Mills remained active but only for major overhauls and repairs to engines and rolling stock.

Following the 'Beeching Cuts' the railway works were closed in 1963. During the next 30 years many of the tracks and sidings were torn up and large areas of former railway land were disposed of for retail and commercial development. One of the consequences was that much of the freight that formerly flowed through this yard had to be switched from rail to road.

Eurostar locomotive no. 3101 awaiting attention at Temple Mills

In the 1970's, Temple Mills was given new life when a workshop was opened for diesel repairs. Two years later this closed and again most of the site became derelict. However, Temple Mills railway heritage was not lost and it received a tremendous boost in the 21st century.In October 2007, the Parliamentary under Secretary of State for transport, Tom Harris MP, and Eurostar's Chief Executive Officer, Richard Brown, opened the £400 million Eurostar Engineering Centre at Temple Mills. The state of the art facility is equipped for the different power requirements of the British, French and Belgian rail networks and has made it possible to bring all the Eurostar and High Speed (HS) train maintenance under one roof.

So it seems *Robert* is in good company. As a fitting monument to the area's railway heritage he is destined to be an attraction in Stratford for the foreseeable future.

Beyond Reasonable Doubt

On Friday 17th January 1992, just after 9.00am, when the office had opened its doors for the day's business, Peter Gibson arrived at the Reliance Mutual Insurance Society in Eastern Avenue, Ilford. Gibson confirmed a previous discussion that he wanted to invest some cash. To the astonishment of the manager and his assistant he proceeded to empty from a carrier bag £100,000 in bundles of £50.00 and £20.00 notes. A week later a Michael Nairn turned up at the same offices to make an investment this time of £30,000 which was also in cash emptied from a carrier bag.

As a matter of routine, large cash deposits are notified to the police and in due course these cases were looked at by the Drug Intelligence Unit, the CID and the Fraud squad. Neither Gibson nor Nairn were known to the police but preliminary enquiries established that Peter Gibson seemed to have no regular income and paid little tax or national insurance. However, he owned a number of top range cars and, together with his wife, enjoyed expensive holidays in the Far East, the Caribbean, and Hawaii. It was noted that Peter Gibson's wife Christine worked at the Bank of England's bank note printing plant in Debden. The police grew more curious when it came to light that Michael Nairn also worked for the Bank of England at Debden. Further probing uncovered that not only did Michael Nairn and Mrs Gibson work for the Bank of England, but both, by amazing co-incidence, worked in the bank's note 'returns' unit. This unit was responsible for shredding or incinerating worn or damaged notes not fit to go back into circulation or be loaded into cash machines.

Growing ever more suspicious, the police now felt they had a prima facie case to mount a thorough investigation. This resulted in the arrest of nine people, six of whom worked in the bank's returns unit. Although the police had taken action at this stage there had been no complaint from the Bank of England that anything was wrong or any money was missing!

All those arrested were interviewed at length. The course of enquiries revealed that the Gibsons, the Nairns and another couple, Kenneth and Janet Longman (Kenneth Longman worked in the returns unit) enjoyed life styles far beyond their apparent income. Searches of their homes revealed large unexplained bundles of cash, none of which was in pristine condition. When the police suggested they had stolen the money all three couples vehemently denied the insinuation claiming that security was so tight in Debden such a thing was impossible. And anyway, they asserted, the bank had never complained or even hinted that anything was out of order.

Two of those arrested were women supervisors in the returns unit. Also arrested was Kevin Winwright. The two supervisors, when interrogated, soon admitted to being part of an elaborate scheme to steal used banknotes rather than sending them off for destruction. Mrs Gibson was identified as the mastermind behind the scheme.

Kevin Winwright confessed to taking at least £170,000 in league with Nairn, Longman and Mrs Gibson. The two women supervisors admitted to receiving smaller amounts of money for interfering with the locks on the cages where the banknotes due for destruction were stored. Kevin Winwright received an 18 month prison sentence for his part and most of his share of £170,000 was recovered. The bank also took a charge on his house. The supervisors escaped prosecution in return for giving evidence against the Gibsons, Nairns and Longmans.

No way out?

The Bank of England was left in a quandary. It still didn't know it had been 'robbed' or by how much. The bank was also unable to confirm how the money had been smuggled out of Debden. Colourful stories from the perpetrators who confessed indicated that Mrs Gibson had removed the cash concealed in her underwear, but this could not be corroborated - and the principal movers in the affair still continued to flatly deny all knowledge of any theft.

The possibility of bringing a criminal case was now complicated because the substantive evidence against Messrs Longman and Nairn and Mrs Gibson came from three self confessed criminals. At a trial, defence lawyers could reasonably argue the witnesses had been coerced into confessing in return for receiving lenient treatment.

Subsequently the Bank of England abandoned a criminal trial and opted for the Civil Courts. It sued for the return of the money with interest, and sought damages for breach of trust.

The case came before the Queens Bench of the High Court on 12th April 1994 in front of his Honour Judge Norman Rudd.

During the two week hearing the lifestyles and finances of the Gibsons, Nairns and Longmans were forensically examined. On 26th April the Judge found for the Bank of England. In a lengthy judgment he rejected all the defense claims as to how the cash had been acquired. He said the arguments put forward by the defence were wholly incredible and unbelievable in that such amounts could be accumulated without a single supporting document. He was scathing too of Michael Nairn's statement that he had found £30,000 in cash in his deceased father's house whilst at the same time failing to tell his sister and two brothers about the miraculous find.

The Gibsons were ordered to repay £250,000, the Longmans £150,000 and the Nairns £110,000. In the Judge's view it was beyond reasonable doubt that large scale thefts had taken place and the spouses who didn't work at the bank couldn't fail be fully aware of the nefarious activities of their partners. The spouses were willing participants and quite happy to spend their ill-gotten gains. To this date is not known how much money was actually removed from Debden.

Throughout all police interviews and the subsequent trial both Peter Gibson and Michael Nairn insisted they believed cash was king and they didn't trust or believe in the banking system or financial institutions. At the High Court trial, one defence witness after another was called forward on their behalf to say much the same. So it is perhaps ironic that the two men's undoing, if that is right word, was due to their attempts to invest money in a financial institution in Ilford.

The first banknotes came off the presses at Debden in October 1956. Prior to that, notes were printed in St Luke's Printing Works in Old Street London. This building, when acquired by the Bank of England, was originally 'St Luke's Hospital for Poor Lunatics'. The move from Old Street to Debden was supervised by an Essex man, Valentine George Crittall, 1st Baron of Braintree and a director of the Bank of England.

In 2003, the Bank of England sold its banknote printing operations, which now numbered some 150 States around the world as clients, to De La Rue PLC. The Bank still retains ownership of the Debden site.

An important part of the De La Rue operation is still the disposal of notes that have become too dirty or damaged. These are withdrawn from circulation by commercial bank branches and returned to Debden where, as far as is known, they are all accounted for before being shredded.

Eton Manor transformed out all recognition for the Paralympic Tennis

During the summer of 2012 The Games of the XXX Olympiad and the Fourteenth Paralympic Games came to *Metropolitan Essex*. The Olympic Park at Stratford was home to the great majority of the sporting events, as well as containing the athletes' village and a giant media centre (see page 128 and 152). The main Olympic stadium was also the scene of the spectacular opening and closing ceremonies for both games. When London was chosen to host the Games of the XXX Olympiad, in July 2005, planning had been under way since 1997.

Despite some initial misgivings in respect of the cost and worries about security, the games were a tremendous success and judged to have been one of the best organised summer Olympics on record.

For six weeks, from the start of the Olympic Games on Friday, 27th July until Sunday, 9th September, when the Paralympic Games ended, the greatest show on earth had come to Stratford. The National Olympic committees of more than 200 nations had sent over 10,000 of their best athletes to compete for the honour of becoming an Olympic champion.

The games were a triumph of organisation for the host nation. The hundreds of thousands of visitors that descended daily on the newly revitalised Stratford came into a magnificent sporting complex. The physical transformation was matched, perhaps even eclipsed, by the fantastic achievements of the home teams in the competitions. Success in the Olympics accumulated *Team GB* a huge haul of medals, 65 in total, including 29 gold. Overall, the UK came third in the medal table, after the USA and China. Similarly, in the Paralympics, *Team GB* were third after China and Russia with 120 medals, including 34 gold.

The Queen Elizabeth Park is set to be a lasting legacy of the games. Many of the sporting venues will remain, though somewhat modified. However, one of the more unusual features, not actually a sporting venue, is the huge steel sculpture; the *ArcelorMittal Orbit,* a 115 metres (377 ft) high observation tower located between the main stadium and the aquatics centre. It is claimed to be Britain's largest piece of public art.

The title *Orbit,* given by the designers Anish Kapoor and Cecil Balmond, was chosen to reflect the "extraordinary physical and emotional effort" required by Olympic athletes. In their view the world was full of banal meaningless objects and the *Orbit* would reinvent the tower and in the process transform the London skyline.

Orbit was the winner of a competition held once London had been chosen to host the games. From over 50 competition entries *Orbit* was the unanimous choice of a panel of nine people, appointed by the Mayor of London and the Culture Secretary.

Approximately 1,400 tons of steel were used to construct the sculpture which consists of a series of continuous looping lattices of tubular steel. In the words of the designers the *Orbit* combines sculpture with structural engineering. Its appearance of instability belies the strength of its structure.

Visitors enter via 'the dark sinister entrance canopy', which was manufactured in Holland, then take a lift to the two viewing platforms. Each of these platforms give 150 visitors panoramic views over the Park.

On the viewing platform the visitors would be met with an 'explosion of light' and 'visual mayhem' created by the huge steel mirrors, that were made in San Francisco. Presumably they might also enjoy an excellent view across London before taking the option of walking down the spiralling staircase.

By way of comparison, the *Orbit* is taller than London's Big Ben or New York's Statue of Liberty. Controversy has raged over the structure since its completion. It has been praised and criticised in equal measure. On one hand it has been praised for bold design and innovation yet on the other its legacy value as an iconic landmark has been questioned as well as its 'lack' of artistic merit.

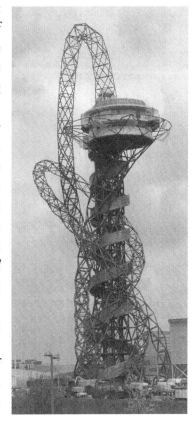

On the *Orbit's* cost of £22m, against an original estimate of £10m, the Mayor of London was quoted as saying, "Of course some people will say we are nuts – in the depths of a recession – to be building Britain's biggest ever piece of public art". He also conceded that the *Orbit* may become known by something other than its official name. "Hubble Bubble" or "The Supersized Mutant Trombone" being two of the more colourful alternatives bandied about. Nearly three quarters of the cost was provided by Britain's richest man, Lakshmi Mittal, the chairman of the *ArcelorMittal* steel company. He was quoted as saying 'I am very proud to show what steel can do and the *Orbit* has provided an excellent showcase as to how steel can be used'.

The *Orbit* may become a beacon of Stratford's regeneration and a positive legacy. Alternatively it could be just a rich man's vanity project and a monumental folly. Only time will tell, but as always with 'art', beauty is in the eye of the beholder.

The Olympic park is due to re-open for public use in stages from July 2013 onwards.

NATIONAL / INTERNATIONAL TIMELINE 1900-

DATE   **EVENT**

DATE	EVENT
1901	*Death of Queen Victoria, Edward VII becomes King*
1909	*Louis Bleriot first to fly the English Channel*
1912	*Titanic sinks on maiden voyage*
1916	*Battle of the Somme*
1919	*Michael Collins forms the Irish Republican Army*
1921	*British Legion holds its first 'Poppy Day'*
1922	*Stalin becomes Soviet Leader*
1925	*John Logie Baird creates first TV transmitter*
1928	*Alexander Fleming discovers Penicillin*
1929	*First Telephone Boxes appear in London*
1930	*Amy Johnson first woman to fly solo England to Australia*
1931	*National Government formed in UK*
1933	*Hitler appointed German Chancellor*
1935	*Alcoholics Anonymous formed in NY*
1939	*Start of World War II*
1940	*Winston Churchill becomes PM*
1943	*The 'Dambusters' raid takes place*
1944	*'D Day' Landings in Normandy*
1945	*World War II Ends*
1948	*Britain Hosts Olympic Games*
1951	*Festival of Britain*
1953	*Coronation of Elizabeth II - Hilary and Tensing climb Mt Everest*
1963	*The Great Train Robbery*
1964	*BBC2 starts broadcasting*
1964	*Harold Wilson becomes PM*
1966	*England Wins Football World Cup*
1971	*Decimal currency introduced in UK*
1972	*Bloody Sunday in Northern Ireland*
1976	*First Concorde passenger flight*
1982	*Falklands war begins*
1991	*Iraq invading Kuwait triggers first Gulf War*
1992	*'Black Wednesday' UK leaves ERM*
1992	*English FA Premier League formed*
1994	*The Channel Tunnel is opened*
1999	*Welsh Assembly opens in Cardiff*
2002	*EURO notes and coins introduced.*
2003	*Second Iraq War begins; A million march in protest in London*
2005	*Parliament banns Fox Hunting with Dogs in England*
2007	*Smoking Ban introduced in England*
2012	*England hosts the Olympic Games*

Select Bibliography

Abels, Richard, *Alfred the Great,* Addison Wesley Longman, 1998.

Beckham, Ted, *David Beckham My Son,* Pan, 2005.

Belton, Brian, *When West Ham went to the Dogs,* Tempus, 2002.

Bevan, Bryan, *King Richard II,* Rubicon Press, 1996.

Bigg H. O, Frost P. T, Herington C, O'Leary J. G and Strickland F. C, *Danger over Dagenham,* Borough of Dagenham, 1947.

Birtles, Philip, J. *Mosquito the Illustrated History,* Sutton Publishing, 1998.

Bloch, Howard, *Newham Dockland,* Chalford, 1995.

Burgess-Wise, David, *Ford at Dagenham,* Breedon Books, 2007.

Chisenhale-Marsh, T.C. (Trans.), *Domesday Book relating to Essex.* W.D. Burrell, 1864.

Collingridge, Vanessa, *Boudica,* Ebury Press, 2005.

Connor, J.E. *Branch Lines around North Woolwich,* Middleton Press, 2001.

Connor, J.E. *Stepney's Own Railway - A History of the London & Blackwall System,* Connor & Butler, 1987.

Dovey, Zillah, *An Elizabethan Progress,* Sutton Publishing Ltd, 1996.

Dudley, Donald.R, *The Rebellion of Boudicca,* Routledge and Kegan Paul, 1962.

Fletcher, Winston, *Keeping the Vision Alive, The Story of Barnardo's,* Barnardo's 2005.

Fraser, Antonia, *The Warrior Queens, Boadicea's Chariot,* Phoenix Press, 1988.

Given-Wilson, Chris, *Chronicles of the Revolution, 1397-1400: The Reign of Richard II,* Manchester University Press, 1993.

Green, Georgina, *The Story of Hainault Forest,* London Borough of Redbridge, *2002.*

Goodman, Anthony, *The Loyal Conspiracy,* Routledge & Kegan Paul, 1971.

Halliday, Stephen, *The Great Stink of London,* Sutton Publishing, 2001.

Hart, Eva, Denney, Ronald,C. *Shadow of the Titanic,* Greenwich University Press, 1994.

Hilton, R.H, & Aston, *The English Rising of 1381,* Cambridge University Press, 1984.

Haynes, H, Alfred, *The Dagenham Girl Pipers,* Faber & Faber Ltd, 1957.

Home, Dr. Robert, *'A Township Complete in Itself', Becontree/Dagenham Estate,* London Borough of Barking and Dagenham, 1997.

Hunt, Richard, *Queen Boudica's Battle of Britain,* Spellmount, 2003.

Jackson, Robert, *de Havilland Mosquito,* Airlife Publishing, 2003.

Kendrick, T.D, *The Vikings A History of,* Dover Publications Inc., 2004.

Lewis, Jim, *From Eton Manor to the Olympics,* Libri Publishing, 2010.

Lewis, Jim, *From Gunpowder to Guns, Middlesex University Press,* 2009.

Lewis, Jim, *Waste and Water*, Middlesex University Press, 2009.

Lewis, Jim, *East Ham & West Ham Past*, Historical Publications, 2004.

Lewis, Jim, *Battleships, Buses and Bombers*, Middlesex University Press, 2009.

Lewis, Jim, *London's Lea Valley: Britain's best kept secret*, Phillimore, 1999.

Liddell, W.H, & Wood, R.G, Wood, *Essex and the Great Revolt of 1381*, Essex Record Office, 1982.

Lindsay, Philip & Groves, Reg, *The Peasants' Revolt 1381*, Hutchinson, 1950.

Luckin, W, *The final catastrophe-- cholera in London, 1866*. The Wellcome Trust Centre for the History of Medicine at UCL, 1977.

Mack, Charlie, *Lesney's Matchbox Toys, Edition 2*, Schiffer Publishing, 2000.

Martin, John, *Beyond Belief. The Real Life of Daniel Defoe*, Accent Press, 2006.

Morris, Richard, *The Harveys of Rolls Park Chigwell Essex*, Loughton and District Historical Society, 2005.

O'Leary, J.G, *The Book of Dagenham*, Borough of Dagenham, 1964.

Oram, Sir Charles, *The Great Revolt of 1381*, Greenhill Books, 1906.

Neale, Kenneth, *Discovering Essex in London*, Essex Countryside, 1971.

Powell, W. R, *History of the County of Essex: Volume 5*, Oxford University Press, 1966.

Powell, W.R, *History of the County of Essex: Volume 6*, Oxford University Press, 1973.

Poos, L. R, *A Rural Society after the Black Death*, Cambridge University Press, 1991.

Pugh, R.B, *Essex - A History Volume V*, Oxford University Press, 1973.

Ray, Barbara, *Chingford Past*, Historical Publications, 2003.

Rhodes, Linda, Shelden, Lee, Abnett, Kathryn, *The Dagenham Murder*, The London Borough of Barking and Dagenham, 2005.

Rose, June, *Elizabeth Fry*, Quaker Books, 1994.

Savage, Anne, *The Anglo Saxon Chronicles*, Tiger Books, 1995.

Seddon, Jeffrey, *Queen Elizabeth's Hunting Lodge - A Brief History*, Corporation of London, 2003.

Sharpe, James, *Dick Turpin The Myth of the English Highwayman*, Profile Books, 2005.

Smith, Graham, *Essex And Its Race For The Skies*, Countryside Books, 2007.

Smith, Harold, *Havering-Atte-Bower, A History*, Bentham & Co. Ltd, 1925.

Starkey, David, *Six Wives, The Queens of Henry VIII*, Vintage, 2004.

Sugar, Alan, *What You See Is What You Get*, Macmillan, 2010.

Times UK, *The Times Atlas of London*, Times Books, 2011.

Williams, A.E., *Barnardo of Stepney*, George Allen and Unwin Ltd, 1943.

Williams, Benjamin, *Chronique de La Traison Et Mort de Richart Deux Roy Dengleterre (1846)* reprinted by Kessinger Publishing, 2010.

Magazine, Newspapers.
"Buffalo Bill at Ilford" *The Ilford Guardian, June 24th 1904.*
"Community Play Worth Waiting For" *Ilford Recorder,* July 27th 1989.

Internet sources
Judgement - Bank of England v. Gibson http://www.ucc.ie/law/restitution/ archive/englcases/boe.htm

Climate Impacts Programme (UKCIP) April 2002 http://www.ukcip.org.uk/

Taylor, Kathy, The Great Floods of 1953
http://www.docklandsmemories.org.uk/Floods1953.pdf

The Thames Barrier open but ready to protect the City from the unthinkable.

Index of some of the People, Places, Events

Essex Hundred Publications

The Essex Hundred
The history of the county of Essex described in 100 poems and supported with historical notes and illustrations.
A unique book written by Essex poets covering 2000 years of county history.
ISBN: 9780955229503 £7.99

Essex Hundred Histories
From the sacking of Roman Colchester to Ford's modern day wind turbines, each chapter reflects the diversity of the county as well as showing the role Essex has played in the nation's development.
ISBN: 9780955229510 £8.99

The Essex Hundred Children's Colouring and Activity Book
The Colouring and Activity Book is another title from the Essex Hundred family aimed at children and part written by children. The book includes pictures to colour in, word searches and other puzzles and questions.
ISBN: 9780955229534 £4.99

ON THIS DAY in ESSEX
ON THIS DAY in Essex follows on from the Essex Hundred and the Essex Hundred Histories. It builds a comprehensive day by day record of events in the county's history.
ISBN 9780955229541 £9.99

Aeolus Ruler of the Winds
Aeolus Ruler of the Winds is a whimsical story of sailing adventures around the Essex and Suffolk coast. From Leigh-on-Sea, in the Thames Estuary, to Aldeburgh, on the east coast, it contains a magical collection of eclectic stories and poems inspired by many years of exploration of the diverse rivers and creeks that are characteristic of this coastline by the author Shirley Baker.
Aeolus Ruler of the Winds
ISBN: 9780955229589 £7.99

Essex Hundred Publications. Books written, designed and printed in Essex. Available from bookshops nearby, book wholesalers, direct from the publisher or online.
www.essex100.com